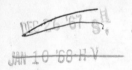

G O L D

and World Monetary Problems

G O L D

and

World

Monetary Problems

National Industrial Conference Board
Convocation, Tarrytown, New York
October 6 – 10, 1965

The Macmillan Company, New York
Collier-Macmillan Ltd., London

The Macmillan Company, New York

Collier-Macmillan Canada Ltd., Toronto, Ontario

Contents

Participants

JULES BACKMAN
Research Professor of Economics,
School of Commerce, Accounts & Finance
New York University
New York, New York

EDWARD M. BERNSTEIN
President, EMB (Ltd.)
Washington, D. C.

WILLIAM BUSSCHAU
Chairman, Goldfields of South Africa Inc.
Johannesburg, South Africa

WILLIAM F. BUTLER
Vice President, The Chase Manhattan Bank
New York, New York

RICHARD P. CHAPMAN
Chairman, New England Merchants National Bank
Boston, Massachusetts

ANGUS C. COLLIE
Johannesburg, South Africa

JOHN B. CONDLIFFE
Stanford Research Institute, Menlo Park, California

PHILIP CORTNEY
Geneva, Switzerland

EMILE DESPRES
Research Center in Economic Growth, Stanford University
Stanford, California

HON. C. DOUGLAS DILLON
New York, New York

OTMAR EMMINGER
Member, Board of Governors, German Federal Bank
Frankfurt/Main, Germany

JOHN EXTER
Senior Vice President, First National City Bank
New York, New York

SOLOMON FABRICANT
National Bureau of Economic Research
New York, New York

MARTIN R. GAINSBRUGH
Senior Vice President & Chief Economist,
    National Industrial Conference Board
New York, New York

MILTON GILBERT
Economic Adviser, Bank for International Settlements
Basle, Switzerland

GOTTFRIED HABERLER
Economist, Harvard University
Cambridge, Massachusetts

SIR ROY HARROD
Economist, Christ Church
Oxford, England

EDWARD C. HARWOOD
  Director, American Institute for Economic Research
  Great Barrington, Massachusetts

MICHAEL A. HEILPERIN
  Professor of Economics, Institut des Hautes Etudes Internationales
  Geneva, Switzerland

GEORGE P. HITCHINGS
  Vice President—Economic Research and Financial Relations,
    American Airlines, Inc.
  New York, New York

WALTER E. HOADLEY
  Vice President & Treasurer, Armstrong Cork Company
  Lancaster, Pennsylvania

LELAND HOWARD
  Director, Office of Domestic Gold and Silver Operations,
    U.S. Treasury Department
  Washington, D. C.

ADRIAN M. MASSIE
  Member of the Trust Committee, Chemical Bank
    New York Trust Company
  New York, New York

DONALD H. McLAUGHLIN
  Chairman of the Board, Homestake Mining Company
  San Francisco, California

ALLAN H. MELTZER
  Graduate School of Industrial Administration,
    Carnegie Institute of Technology
  Pittsburgh, Pennsylvania

LEIF H. OLSEN
  Vice President, First National City Bank
  New York, New York

H. BRUCE PALMER
  President, National Industrial Conference Board
  New York, New York

HERBERT V. PROCHNOW
  President, The First National Bank of Chicago
  Chicago, Illinois

ROY L. REIERSON
  Senior Vice President & Chief Economist,
    Bankers Trust Company
  New York, New York

DAVID ROCKEFELLER
  President, The Chase Manhattan Bank
  New York, New York

ALEXANDER SACHS
  Economic Adviser & Industrial Consultant
  New York, New York

MICHAEL SPIELER
  Economist, Union Corporation Ltd.
  London, England

ALLAN SPROUL
  Kentfield, California

JESSE W. TAPP
  Director, Bank of America National Trust & Savings Association
  Los Angeles, California

ROBERT TRIFFIN
  Professor of Economics, Yale University
  New Haven, Connecticut

JACOB VINER
  Economist, Princeton, New Jersey

HENRY C. WALLICH
  Professor of Economics, Yale University
  New Haven, Connecticut

HANS A. WIDENMANN
  Partner, Carl L. Loeb, Rhoades & Company
  New York, New York

RALPH A. YOUNG
  Adviser to the Board & Director, Division of International
    Finance, Federal Reserve System
  Washington, D. C.

Foreword

OVER THE PAST TWO DECADES the National Industrial Conference Board has repeatedly found it necessary to bring together under its auspices leading experts at home and abroad for a discussion of the changing role of gold in the world's evolving monetary mechanism. Throughout this entire period the question of the function of gold in the international financial system has been heatedly debated—and remains unresolved. Knowing the Board's deep and continuing interest in this field, the Transvaal and Orange Free State Chamber of Mines provided funds that enabled the Board to convene a special enlarged conference on "Gold and World Monetary Problems" at Tarrytown, New York, during the weekend of October 6–10, 1965. This document sets forth the verbatim proceedings of that meeting, but rephrased in a few instances to give greater clarity to the published version.

The Conference Board was particularly fortunate in having present at this special conference a number of authorities whose names are now associated with proposed solutions for the world's gold and monetary problems. The diverse backgrounds of the participants, drawn as they were from business, finance, government and academia, and their broad geographic distribution yielded a unique cross section of current thinking and touched off a thoughtful and provocative discussion and fruitful interchange of views.

In the months intervening, the debate has continued, but no substantive international action has taken place to limit the importance, or even the topical flavor, of the Tarrytown exchange. Indeed, national concern about the problem has now been intensified by what appears to be an increase in the 1966 U.S. balance-of-payments deficit and the gold outflow. The Group of Ten's continuing study of the problem and the recent *Annual*

Report of the Bank for International Settlements reinforce the view that the question of *Gold and World Monetary Problems* has yet to approach the threshold of a solution.

In this report, as in others, the experts disagree on how well the current monetary system works or is likely to work in the future. Difficulties in diagnosis are compounded because of the large balance-of-payments deficits incurred by the United States during the past eight years. If the United States should bring its international payments into balance, would there then be adequate means for increasing future liquidity to meet the world's growing trade and investment needs? What was not seriously questioned at the conference was that the amount of gold currently being mined and not siphoned off for industrial demand or hoarding before it reaches official reserves, is inadequate to provide, by itself, sufficient liquidity to meet future world requirements.

The Conference Board is deeply indebted not only to the Chamber of Mines for its generous support in meeting the operating and publication costs of the conference but also to each of the participants, many of whom came from great distances and all of whom responded readily to the Board's invitation on the shortest of notice. This conference was organized by Martin R. Gainsbrugh, the Board's Chief Economist, who also edited the initial transcript. Other staff members who aided in this undertaking were John G. Worssam and Joseph L. Naar who handled arrangements and operations at Tarrytown, and Lawrence A. Veit who edited the final manuscript prior to publication.

H. BRUCE PALMER
President

GOLD

and World Monetary Problems

Chapter I

Perspective on Gold and World Monetary Problems

H. BRUCE PALMER
MARTIN R. GAINSBRUGH
Chairman: ROY L. REIERSON
Background Paper: RALPH A. YOUNG

MR. PALMER: On behalf of The Conference Board, I welcome this assembly of experts from all parts of the free world to this historic meeting on "Gold and World Monetary Problems." As you know, gold has been a favorite topic of discussion by the Conference Board's annual Economic Forum for well over the past decade. With each passing month, the world's monetary problems now seem to grow more acute, so that your deliberations on this occasion will find an eager and receptive audience, both domestically and internationally.

Indeed, the interest of the entire free world is so centered upon world monetary problems currently that we have selected this theme as the first for a series of World Convocations The Conference Board proposes to conduct throughout the next twelve months by way of celebrating its semi-centennial anniversary. We are particularly fortunate that our interest in this problem area coincided with that of the world's leading gold producers. Learning of our desire to explore this field anew, an offer to provide funds for this purpose was generously forthcoming from a group of Board Associates including the major gold producers of the world. We are particularly indebted to the Transvaal and Orange Free State Chamber of Mines with whose assistance we were able to bring the several leading monetary experts from abroad to this meeting.

I am especially pleased to acknowledge the constructive assistance we had in planning this meeting from Donald H. McLaughlin, Chairman of the Board, Homestake Mining Company and from Philip Cortney, Vice Chairman of the Monetary Committee of the International Chamber of Commerce. Without the help of these two long-standing friends of The Conference Board we could not have assembled so broad a cross-section of viewpoints as is here represented, particularly in the light of the limited time available to us for convening this Forum.

During the past year whenever The Conference Board has assembled its Associates for regional, national or international meetings, one immediate and continuing topic of discussion has been this nation's difficulties with its international balance of payments and the accompanying drain on its gold stock. The Board's renewed interest in the entire area of public affairs is still another reason why we consider ourselves most fortunate to be able to provide our associates with this free, frank and uninhibited examination, lasting over a period of days, of a problem that has become a matter of growing concern to every informed citizen. The drastic alterations in the United States' balance-of-payments position have already led us to break part of the link between gold and this nation's monetary system. How much further can we or should we pursue this policy? And in the proposals so frequently voiced for some new international monetary body that would assume responsibility for the direction of the world's monetary problems, what loss of economic sovereignty would we, in the United States, experience? These and many related questions are much in the minds of all of us who read the news of the latest proposals for world monetary reform and ponder their impact not only upon our businesses but upon our very way of life.

MR. GAINSBRUGH: May I, too, welcome you all here and express our gratification and relief that you are here. We had all too short a period in which to plan this meeting and we are much in your debt for accepting our invitation to participate on so short a notice.

It is understood, of course, that each of you speaks as an authority in his own right and that the views you express do not necessarily reflect the views of the organization with which you are associated. We start tonight with a session chaired by Roy L. Reierson. He will function not only as chairman but as reactor. In other words, he will open the discussion in offering his own comments on the views of the first speaker. We do want a free, frank and uninhibited discussion at this forum meeting, in keeping with the precedent that has always prevailed at the meetings of The Conference Board Economic Forum during the past twenty years of its existence.

Our first speaker tonight, Ralph Young, is a Board alumnus. We feel ourselves particularly fortunate for having prevailed upon him to participate in our Fiftieth Anniversary and setting the stage for us through his initial presentation.

CHAIRMAN REIERSON: It would be presumptuous of me to introduce Ralph Young. He is an alumnus of The Conference Board and also of the National Bureau of Economic Research. Before becoming Economic Adviser to the Federal Reserve Board, he was head of its Division of Research Statistics. In addition to his duties as Economic Adviser, he is head of the International Finance Section of the Board and is a frequent traveler to foreign parts, especially to Europe. It would be difficult to find anyone on the American scene better qualified to open this discussion and to provide the essential background on what has been happening to the world's monetary systems in general and to that of the United States in particular.

MR. YOUNG: I undertook this assignment with some misgivings. When Martin Gainsbrugh asked me to undertake it, I felt some reluctance because there are so many others here who are better qualified to perform this introductory role.

I also said that I had some misgivings about putting myself in the position of being a target for all the questions that might be asked after my remarks. He assured me that my function was to set the stage and that the discussion would pretty much take care of itself.

I am going to take gold for granted to begin with. It is an essential part of our present monetary arrangement, domestically and internationally. It is not my province to trace how it got there. It is there. I am not concerned with whether it should remain there or whether it should be demonetized or any similar proposals.

Our preoccupation with the world monetary problem seems to me to arise out of the existence and need for solution of United States and United Kingdom balance-of-payments problems. Let's start then with the existence of the deficits and the prospects for their correction.

U.S. and U.K. Balance-of-Payments Deficits

The United States has had its deficit much too long. It is now launched on a course of correction and it is my judgment that this imbalance will be corrected. Certainly it has been made clear by the government and most recently by the President that it is the government's determination to bring this imbalance to a prompt termination.

In the same period that we have had our imbalance, the U.K. has suffered recurring deficits. These deficits, because they have been large when they have come, have brought very sharp doubt about the pound exchange rate. They have impaired the function of sterling as a medium of international payments and a secondary reserve currency. They have handicapped London's functioning as an international, and especially as a European, capital market.

At the present time, at long last, the U.K. has rounded out a program which has promise of re-establishing equilibrium and enabling that country to sustain it. Of course, there is a long way for it to go and there is some distance to go for us. But it is the problem of these two currencies that raises the big problem of monetary arrangements internationally.

With gold supplies available to the monetary authorities increasing only slowly and with the prospect of equilibrium coming for the reserve currencies, the world as a whole confronts a creeping limitation on international reserve availability. This also means, over the longer run, a cumulating deflationary pressure from inadequate growth in monetary reserves.

This prospect is aggravated by the propensity of those major trading countries, which have enjoyed payments surpluses as the counterpart of U.S. and U.K. payments deficits, to pursue policies calculated to maintain their payments surpluses. In other words, these countries appear to be retaining an unduly high demand propensity for monetary reserves.

International Liquidity and the
Adjustment Process

The whole outlook raises the problem of what steps can be and should be taken by the community of nations to assure a growth of international reserves consistent with international needs and to avert potential deflationary dangers. The magnitude of future liquidity needs obviously depends upon the effectiveness of the adjustment process for translating money flows internationally into real goods flows. The more effective this adjustment process, the less the need for international liquidity. But the converse is also true. The greater the availability of liquidity, the less intense the incentive to adjust and the slower the process of adjustment is likely to be.

But balance-of-payments adjustment is only one objective of economic policy. It cannot be pursued in disregard of other objectives relating to growth, employment, price stability and freedom of international transactions. In recent years payments adjustment has no doubt been too slow on the part of both deficit and surplus countries. This problem is being studied by Working Party 3 of the Economic Policy Committee of the Organization for Economic Cooperation and Development, under instruction of the Ministers of Finance and Central Bank Governors of the Group of Ten[1] with a view to reaching some general agreement or understanding as to the standards of national policy that could facilitate the adjustment process.

Two observations appear appropriate here. One is that not all members of the Group of Ten can be in, or even move toward, over-all payments surplus at the same time. If they try it, the world faces a deflationary catastrophe. On the other hand, all of them might experience an increase in reserves at the same time, if the proper kind of international monetary arrangements could be agreed upon.

We live in a world that is trying to have and to maintain for purposes of facilitating international commerce fixed exchange rates between the major countries and prices that are more or less inflexible downward. Deflation and inflation are both ruled out as acceptable solutions to balance-of-payments problems. The adjustment process under these conditions, even if it is strengthened, even if the various governments can agree on policies and programs that would help to accelerate adjustment, still is likely to be very time-consuming. Hence the need that individual countries feel for liquidity and the need of the system over-all for liquidity is probably greater than in a more flexible economic universe.

Another of the key issues in this knotty problem is that of rules versus authority. Some well-intentioned observers call for automatic policy reactions to payments imbalances. Others, who are no less anxious to strengthen the adjustment process, reject automatic rules, both domestically and internationally. Instead

[1] United States, Canada, Japan, United Kingdom, Belgium, Holland, France, Germany, Italy, and Sweden.

they look to a growing international consensus on appropriate discretionary policies, consistent with respect for other economic objectives, to correct imbalances as they possibly come.

The Need for Liquidity

Up to this point I have tried to give a little background that would pave the way for understanding the function and definition of international liquidity. Its function, I think we would all agree, is, as the residual element in the adjustment process, to provide financing of the net balance, whether surplus or deficit, which the monetary authority is called upon to finance. It is not concerned wtih financing trade. That is for another part of the mechanism.

For each country this need for reserves shows up in the process by which the monetary authority maintains its exchange rate at parity. In today's monetary mechanism, incidentally, because of the key currency role of the dollar, deficits and surpluses most commonly show up as need for or accession of dollars by foreign central banks, regardless of bilateral payments positions with the United States.

As regards definition, the function of liquidity makes it clear that both credit facilities available to monetary authorities and reserves constitute liquidity. These credit facilities are in the process of being increased; this year we are having an increase in the International Monetary Fund quotas. In addition, very short-term credit facilities have come into being between the central banks in the form of swapped facilities and between treasuries by way of exchanges of short-term obligations. These facilities have established their worth and they are slowly being further developed and expanded.

In most cases the use of these facilities by deficit countries increases reserve assets in the form of credit, so when they are being used there is as a counterpart to their use an increase in international reserves for the time being.

The Position of Gold

Let's look next at gold. To what extent can it be counted on to fill the world's need for growing reserves? In the past decade free world gold production has averaged about 1.2 billion dollars per year. Over the next few years it is hard to imagine more than, say, 1.6 billion dollars. We read every year about the forecast from South Africa that this is just about the ceiling. But each year it continues to go up. This is understandable because each year there is new progress in extraction of gold from existing deposits and new gold discoveries are made in South Africa and elsewhere. We know little of Russian resources, but there is reason to believe that Russia is developing new reserves and output of gold that will sooner or later become available to the western world, at least in part.

In the past decade industrial use has taken an average of about 300 million dollars per year. This too is growing. Over the next few years it could average 600 hundred million dollars or more.

Most variable and uncertain has been hoarding demand. Our rough estimates put this at over 500 million dollars per year over the past decade, leaving, on average, 400 million dollars for absorption by monetary reserves from free world production.

The supply of newly produced gold available for additions to monetary reserves has been supplemented by Soviet sales of gold to the West. These sales have averaged 350 million dollars in the past five years and have, along with western production not absorbed by industrial uses or hoarding, permitted free world monetary gold reserves to rise by about 600 million dollars per year.

It is possible to imagine a set of conditions in which hoarding demand virtually disappeared and Soviet sales continued. Consequently, Western gold reserves might conceivably increase at a rate between 1 and 1.5 billion dollars per year.

One can go further and imagine a process of rehoarding.

Let's take the period from 1950 to date. Subtract what gold has gone into industrial uses and the amount that has come into monetary reserve. The residual amounts to 7.5 billion dollars. The gold market people tell us that gold absorption in the Middle East and Southeast Asia and the Far East has probably run around 300 million dollars a year or 4.5 billion dollars since 1950. If true, that would still leave the sum of around 3 billion dollars which ought to have been available for monetary reserves, but for hoarding. If, with restored confidence, it should become available in the future, the western world could begin to experience a period in which its gold reserves would rise at close to a satisfactory rate. Such a period would represent a final realization by hoarders that over the years they have been barking up the wrong tree in anticipating, with whatever probability they assigned to it, an increase in the dollar price of gold. In these circumstances gold availability would provide a substantial part of needed growth in international reserve assets. I think it must be some feeling such as this that causes the words "contingent planning"[2] to be inserted into the action of the Group of Ten which provides for further study of the problem of liquidity, or potential liquidity shortage, and how best to meet the problem.

As another matter of speculation, if there could be an annual availability of gold of close to 1 billion dollars for monetary reserves over the next decade, and there could be an annual accumulation of non-gold reserve assets of, say, three-quarters of a billion to one and a quarter billion dollars, it would be possible to predict a negligible deficiency in total liquidity growth during this period.

These possibilities cannot be ruled out. But we should by now have learned that in monetary affairs, if not in life generally, it is unwise to project today's problems indefinitely into the future. It is also clear, however, that these possibilities—growth and availability of gold production from South Africa, sales by

[2] *Ministerial Statement of the Group of Ten and Annex Prepared by Deputies*, August 10, 1964.

the Soviet Union, and disappearance or reversal of hoarding demand—cannot be counted on. The world must be prepared to
meet the need for international reserves in other ways.

Alternative Solutions to the Payments Problem

The foregoing may suggest to some of you that there may
need to be an increase in the price of gold at some point in the
future. First let me remind you that our government's policy
with regard to the 35 dollar price per ounce of gold is firmly
held. Next, let me add that such a step would contribute not
one whit to solving the payments deficit problems of the U.S.
and the U.K.; and that, by breaking faith with creditors, it would
strike a death blow at the dollar and the pound as reserve currencies. Finally, it would be most inappropriate from a reasonable monetary management standpoint in a period of substantial
monetary growth—and for many countries which have inflationary problems. As among nations, it would be a most inequitable
way of trying to solve a prospective inadequate international
liquidity problem.

But how, if we are going to have equilibrium on the part of
the reserve currencies, can we provide the western world an
adequate availability of international liquidity? We have the gold
and super gold tranche claims on the International Monetary
Fund. Generally, these are the primary claims that countries are
willing to regard as unconditional or owned reserves along with
gold and reserve currencies. Such claims grow at an average of,
say, 200 million dollars annually—in the past year they have
increased by about 500 million dollars. But still that doesn't look
like much of a supplement to gold and reserve currencies as
owned reserve assets. So we must carry on a search for still other
means.

In addition to these reasons for looking for other means by
which world liquidity can be increased, there are other good
reasons. Many scholars and a good number of financial observers

feel that we should have internationally a more deliberate and systematic approach to the creation of reserve assets. It is true that money doesn't manage itself, nor do international reserves. Perhaps there is a case to be made after the world's long experience with monetary arrangements, including crises, near breakdowns and actual breakdowns, for trying to develop some international understanding as to how best to go about creating additional liquidity.

A related reason is what some in Europe regard as an asymmetry in the present international monetary system with its reliance on the dollar. Many Europeans think that their countries are limited in ability to incur payments deficits while the United States creates international reserves in the form of dollar balances as it runs deficits. The freedom of action of the U.S. is limited only by the willingness of other monetary authorities to hold these balances.

These arguments cannot be dismissed as unduly biased. But those who use them do overlook somewhat the counterburden that a reserve currency function imposes. For instance, the interest price paid by the United States in performing this function currently runs about three-quarters of a billion dollars. In addition, our reserve currency responsibilities oblige us to come to the help of nations in distressed situations and also to keep our capital markets as open as we can for use by foreign borrowers in accordance with their needs.

Creating a New Reserve Asset

Now, if we are going to try to create a new reserve asset via international cooperation and agreement, what are the problems that will have to be met? In answering this question account must be taken of national differences of attitude, background, approach, and understanding of what the problem is. It is pretty clear that those who are approaching this matter with responsibility are no longer coming forward with the thought that perhaps we ought to take the quite radical step of supplanting the reserve currencies. They are rather looking at what might be done to supplement gold and dollar balances as reserve assets.

The other issues that arise are no less important even though more technical. They are highlighted in the Ossola Report,[3] which many of you have read. Briefly they are these:

How closely should a new reserve asset be linked with gold —or should it be linked with gold at all—in its distribution and in its use?

How broad a group of countries should participate in and manage reserve creation and how open or closed should the group be?

What role should the International Monetary Fund play in this process?

What rules should govern decision-making?

These are all questions that we ourselves will be discussing in the next day and a half and it isn't necessary to go much further than just mentioning them here.

In concluding my remarks I'd like to cite some paragraphs from Chairman Martin's address at the University of Rutgers in late June.[4] His comments are particularly relevant to our discussion. He observed:

> The international monetary system must be flexible rather than rigid. It must be adaptable to the differing and, over time, changing needs for the various countries. It would be a great mistake to act as if all countries were alike in their size, structures, policies, and values.
>
> Any change in the monetary system must recognize the great diversity that exists among countries, even among the major industrial countries. And any change must be an evolutionary one, preserving and building upon the valuable elements of the existing system.
>
> In particular, any change in the international payments system must respect the monetary sovereignty of individual countries.
>
> I have stressed that monetary policy in the United States cannot

---

[3] *Report of the Study Group on the Creation of Reserve Assets to the Deputies of the Group of Ten,* May 31, 1965.

[4] Address presented on June 25, 1965.

be formulated in isolation from the world beyond our borders. We must reconcile domestic and balance of payments objectives in pursuing the art of central banking. But as long as nations remain as independent entities, with separate power of decision over economic policies, monetary policy too must remain in national hands. And, within the context of international financial cooperation, the right of each country to make bilateral arrangements should be preserved. It is notable, in all these connections, that membership in the International Monetary Fund and participation in supplying and using the Fund's resources are quite consistent with the retention of monetary powers.

The central role that the International Monetary Fund now fills makes it a natural repository for any new monetary functions that may merit consideration. Gold tranche positions in the Fund, which are usable virtually on demand by countries in deficit, are already widely regarded as reserve assets. If and when the need is felt for additional reserve assets, there is much to be said for adapting the Fund mechanism to this purpose and building upon its tested and respected institutional framework. To rely on such an evolution of the International Monetary Fund, rather than to establish a rival center in the international monetary field, would help to assure that any innovations undertaken would contribute to world prosperity without disturbing market processes, violating national sovereignty, or disrupting international cooperation.

CHAIRMAN REIERSON: I was informed that I am supposed to be a reactor as well as chairman at this session. As a reactor, I would observe that Ralph Young's statement provides an excellent basis for our ensuing discussion. I do hope that we shall be giving concrete attention to some of the problems that have been troubling me and perhaps others as well. It is rare to have in one room at one time so many people from so many different countries and who are so highly competent in the area of monetary economics.

Let me list some of the questions that I think are pertinent and which I hope will be covered in our discussion.

The first observation relates to the nature of the present monetary problem. I would submit that the current problem is not one of a shortage of liquidity but rather one of confidence, especially in the reserve currencies, i.e., the American dollar and the pound sterling. Underlying the question of confidence is the problem of adjustment, i.e., avoiding large and persistent deficits (or surpluses) in balance-of-payments positions. The biggest risk of a shortage of international liquidity is a loss of confidence in sterling or the dollar. Ralph Young alluded to the role that adjustment plays in the international monetary mechanism. He gave us his judgment that both the U.K. and the United States are on the road to balance-of-payments equilibrium. In this regard I would propose two questions: Is there agreement as to this judgment? And, supposing this judgment is wrong this time, as it has been in the past, then what?

As to the present and future adequacy of international liquidity I have two questions: What should be included in international monetary reserves—should a distinction be made between liquidity "to hold" and liquidity "to spend"? And, how should the requirements for international liquidity be determined or measured? This is not an academic question; it is basic in any discussion of international liquidity. I submit that if we are going to embark on a plan for the creation of new reserve assets we must develop some criteria by which to determine what amounts are necessary or desirable under the circumstances.

On the adjustment process I have two questions that I think are pertinent. First, how can the real or alleged conflict between domestic expansionary objectives and policies be reconciled with the need for international monetary stability? A second troublesome question is, what are the responsibilities of the surplus and deficit countries versus other countries? No useful purpose is served by finger pointing on the part of either surplus or deficit countries. This is a very difficult problem which has to be resolved if we are to make much progress in improving the international monetary system.

Mr. Young mentioned one of the alternatives to the creation of new reserve assets. He made a reference to gold. I have a feeling that his position may not be shared by all the people at this meeting. I suspect before we are through that we shall hear some differing opinions as to the role of gold in the monetary system of today and tomorrow.

I question Mr. Young's dismissal of fluctuating exchange rates with the observation that we live in the world of experience. You and I both know many academicians who want to change the world. Flexible exchange rates are of considerable interest, especially in the academic area, and perhaps deserve some attention in our discussions.

On the question of the reserve currencies I believe that until the United States and the United Kingdom get their balances of payments into sustainable equilibrium, and this means for more than one or two quarters, the chances of real progress in the pending international monetary negotiations are modest.

The problem of the new reserve assets was alluded to by Ralph Young. One cannot expect a person in an official position to give his views as to how the various conflicts of interest involved in the creation of new reserve assets can be resolved, but I think there are those around the table whose views would be of interest and I hope they will express their views.

The final point made by Mr. Young was the problem of the creation of the new reserve assets in the International Monetary Fund. We need to explore various techniques because there are many different ways by which this may be done and there are many troublesome questions to be answered. A basic question, of course, is whether such a system for creating new reserve assets is to be part of the International Monetary Fund, a separate entity, or a separate activity in the IMF. If the last, is there a conflict between the conventional credit function of the International Monetary Fund and the function envisioned here of creating additions to the supply of reserve assets?

MR. HARWOOD: If I recall correctly, for the first time in my lifetime, after some forty-two years of writing and studying in the field, the gold reserves of the leading nations of the world have decreased in the past few months. This, of course, has been noted by the Federal Reserve System and it would be very interesting to me to know what explanation is believed to account for it, and what possible significance it may have.

MR. TRIFFIN: The gold reserves have indeed decreased by 200 million dollars, or even more in the first few months of this year, but I regard as far more ominous the liquidation of more than 2 billion dollars of foreign exchange holdings previously accumulated by central banks.

MR. YOUNG: Where the gold has gone is difficult for anybody to know; there has been an increase in unaccounted for purchases. Our statistics are not good enough to tell us what precisely has happened in the first six months of this year. They do indicate a decrease in the monetary gold stocks of about 65 million dollars whereas in the postwar period from one quarter to another there has been an increase.

I can only report to you what I have picked up from the gold market. There have been a lot of buyers in the gold market representing smaller countries; these have been partly central banks and partly other government institutions. Most of the buying in the gold market other than the usual amount for hoarding —and this is an untraceable demand—apparently went to foreign governments and in due course will reappear in monetary gold stocks.

Whether that will happen or not I don't know. That is just a report from people who deal in the gold market in London. But it does not at all come as a surprise to me, considering the duration of the recent international monetary crisis and the extent of the shock to the confidence that the world has experienced. It is a slow process correcting a confidence crisis. It can't be accomplished overnight. It requires the proper steps, not necessarily dramatic steps, but persevering steps by major governments to put their economies in order, and this does take time. I expressed as my opinion earlier that the U.K. was taking steps in the proper direction. They may not have taken all the steps that they may need, but they have taken important and far-reaching ones.

CHAIRMAN REIERSON: The first question has two parts, one on

gold and one on reserve credit. Would you care to answer the reserve credit question?

MR. YOUNG: All I know about the reserve currency figures is that they went down. They went down in part because of the British crisis. They went down in part because of the reshifting of holdings as between the central banks of the monetary authorities.

MR. EMMINGER: I want to speak on two points. The first point concerns the reasons for the fall—or lack of increase—in visible gold reserves. In the first half of 1965 all the gold coming to the world's markets was absorbed by non-official buyers. Private gold buying was persistently large for well known reasons: uncertainties about the future gold policies, uncertainty about the pound sterling, Chinese conversions of sterling reserves into gold, etc.

Much more important is the second development which was mentioned here—namely, the decrease in the reserve holdings. Mr. Young mentioned one explanation. As everybody knows, during the first half of 1965 the French alone have converted about 800 million dollars of their holdings of U.S. currency into gold. The reasons behind this French move go, of course, beyond a mere temporary crisis of confidence and represent a definite and permanent shift in the attitude toward reserve composition of a big country. As to the rest of the conversions of foreign exchange into gold, I think they are mostly related to this change in the reserve policy of the French; at least some of the countries that have converted currency holdings into gold have been imitating the French policy. And to that extent I think it would be wise not to underestimate the shift in the attitude of the monetary institutions concerned.

MR. CORTNEY: Chairman Reierson has raised the question as to a real or alleged conflict between domestic expansionary objectives and the need for international monetary stability. Can they be reconciled? I submit that there is no conflict between two objectives provided fundamental economic laws are not violated as for example by labor-union abuses or other interferences with the market-price mechanism. Quite to the contrary. We can have sound expansion of economic activity and of international trade only in a system characterized by international monetary stability, by which I mean stable exchange rates and a relatively stable level of world prices.

Mr. Ralph Young said that a rise in the price of gold would not solve the problem of the balance of payments of the United States. Can Mr. Young tell us who is the advocate of a rise in the price of gold as a solution of the problem of the balance-of-payments deficits of the United States? I have never heard any responsible authority or person maintain that a rise in the price of gold would, among other things, also solve the balance-of-payments problem of the United States.

MR. YOUNG: I think I can find sources for that. I might have to do a little research. But I am not upset if you don't agree with me.

SIR ROY HARROD: My question relates to Mr. Young's statement that the problems of adjustment are very serious. He didn't say whether these problems have been assigned to the delegates of the Group of Ten by the ministers or by whom. I would assume by the ministers. I would then ask by what right the ministers of the Group of Ten assigned this important question to them? Surely this should be decided by the recognized international agency.

The United States of America has a constitution and so has the United Kingdom. I believe that the problems we are discussing here have been snarled up and solutions unduly delayed by the whole constitutional situation. In the United States there is a definite procedure for amending the constitution. In the United Kingdom the constitution can be amended by the House of Commons and the House of Lords. But there is nothing in the Articles of Agreement of the International Monetary Fund to provide for the amendment of its constitution. I feel that this lack of constitutional procedure is serious. It may be said that in these delicate questions we will proceed by good will and not by constitutional arrangements. I suggest that we now have the position that is known as *liberum veto,* as in eighteenth-century Poland. I believe that we need greater constitutional clarity. The members of the Group of Ten are going outside their proper function. The world monetary system, if this goes on, will suffer. It is up to the top people to give greater definition to the constitutional position as to how the existing system can be altered.

CHAIRMAN REIERSON: Has the point of view been expressed in Britain, Sir Roy, that an increase in the price of gold would contribute to the alleviation of balance-of-payments problems of the United Kingdom?

SIR ROY HARROD: I am in favor of it. The increase in the price of gold I think would help the United States and the United Kingdom. But I don't think myself that a rise in the price of gold would itself produce equilibrium.

MR. BERNSTEIN: I just want to add to the statement made by Sir Roy Harrod. At some earlier occasion, in 1952, the International Monetary Fund asked Sir Roy to make a study of the factors that caused so much difficulty for the United Kingdom and other countries in keeping their payments in order in the early postwar period. Sir Roy made his study and in his opinion one of the great difficulties was the failure of gold to buy as much commodities from the United States as it did in other times. And he recommended a rise in the price of gold. I pointed out then to Sir Roy that the sterling area probably lost more exchange earnings from the development of synthetic rubber than from the failure to raise the price of gold.

I believe that both the analysis in Sir Roy's study for the International Monetary Fund and his specific recommendation to raise the price of gold are indications that he believed that the balance-of-payments problem of the United Kingdom specifically and of the world as a whole could be largely solved by a higher price for gold. I don't see why Ralph Young cannot call on this statement as evidence that some people have advocated a change in the price of gold as a solution to balance-of-payments problems.

MR. TRIFFIN: Let me first offer my sincerest congratulations to our Chairman for his brilliant and incisive questionnaire. In any investigation such as this, asking the right questions is as difficult as getting the right answers; and it certainly would not do us much good to get even right answers to wrong, or muddled, questions.

Chairman Reierson was certainly right to ask, for instance, whether the main problem raised by our present international monetary system is that of a liquidity shortage, and whether the major task of international monetary reform is, therefore, to increase that liquidity.

This, as many of you know, has never been my view. I have long stressed as the main defects of the system its haphazardness and built-in vulnerability, or instability. I agree basically with the point made at the Vienna meeting of the International Monetary Fund, in 1961, by Governor Holtrop of the Nederlandsche Bank: the present system can be inflationary as well as deflationary, depending on a host of factors—among which are speculative attitudes toward the future price of gold and gold sales by the Russians in western markets—but primarily, since the last war, on the size and persistence of U.S. balance-of-payments deficits, and on central banks' confidence in the dollar.

My judgment as to the present position coincides, I think, with that of our Chairman. In recent years, our large and persistent deficits, together with the willingness of central banks to finance half of them, or more, by the accumulation of dollar IOU's in their monetary reserves, have probably created too much, rather than too little, liquidity, although in the highly vulnerable form of dollar balances, theoretically exposed at any time, to sudden, massive, highly disruptive and potentially deflationary conversions into gold metal.

Creating more liquidity, right now, would certainly be the wrong answer to the problem. Our most urgent task is not to increase present liquidity levels, but to protect them against the threat of collapse. The reality of this threat has been amply demonstrated, to my mind, by two facts: (1) the fact that it

had to be warded off, ever since 1960, by the continuous negotiations of our Under Secretary of the Treasury, Dr. Roosa; and
(2) the massive liquidation of more than 2 billion dollars of
foreign exchange reserves by central banks in the first six months
of this year.

The second, less urgent but nonetheless essential, task is to
substitute a more rational process of future liquidity creation,
adjusting it to non-inflationary requirements of a growing world
economy rather than to the unrelated hazards of gold production, speculators' whims, Russian policies, and U.S. balance-of-
payments deficits. Everybody now agrees that this is most likely
to require, at some point, a mechanism for concerted liquidity
expansion, to be put into operation after we have recovered equilibrium in our balance of payments.

A strong consensus was evident, on both points, among many
of the spokesmen for the Group of Ten at the IMF meeting last
month. Priority was given to the first problem, but agreement
was also reached on the need for so-called "contingency planning" on the second. I have myself argued in favor of a brief
moratorium, at least, on the discussion of the highly complex and
divisive issues raised by the adoption of a new machinery for
contingent future liquidity expansion, in order to accelerate negotiations—and, let us hope, agreement—regarding the consoli-
dation of present liquidity levels.

Our European creditors are particularly concerned at the
moment with the need to preserve, or rather restore, necessary
balance-of-payments pressures on the countries in deficit. Certainly, no new machinery for liquidity creation can be devised
and adopted that would relieve individual countries from responsibility to maintain, over the years, proper equilibrium in
their international transactions. I stressed that very point in the
first pages of my first presentation of this problem to Congress, as
long ago as October, 1959 (see pp. 3–8 of my *Gold and the Dollar
Crisis*). We, on the other hand, are more concerned about forc-
ing the creditor countries to assume their proper share of the

burden of adjustment, and not to leave it all to the deficit countries, particularly if and when deflationary pressures prevail over
inflationary ones in the world economy.

Another obstacle to be overcome is our reluctance to accept
reasonable limitations on the use of the dollar as a *reserve currency* by central banks. This is basically due, I think, to a feeling
that any such limitations would undermine the role of the dollar
as a *key currency* in private trade and investment transactions
or, to use Dr. Roosa's words, as a "vehicle currency." The truth
is exactly the opposite: by refusing to negotiate adequate protection against wanton conversions into gold metal of the large
short-term IOU's handed by us to central banks over the last
fifty years, and by trying to defend our gold instead through increasing controls over bank lending and other capital movements,
we are running far greater risks of driving private investors out
of the dollar and of weakening the position of New York as the
major monetary and financial market in the world today.

The instability of the foreign exchange component of international reserves could be shown indeed to be the major, if not
the sole, cause of our residual balance-of-payments deficits today.
But I shall not try to develop this point today.

Finally, as to what should be the proper pace of future liquidity increases, I feel myself just as unable to answer that
question in advance as every central banker is to decide what
should be the proper rate of domestic money supply increase
over the course of future years. Only Professor Milton Friedman,
of Chicago, feels able to give an extraordinary simple and un-
varying answer to this problem, irrespective of the inherent un-
predictability of future economic developments. I might be able
to agree with him if the 4 or 5 per cent rate of increase which
he advocates were to be put forward as a presumptive guess,
to apply only over an average of years, and subject even then
to revision in the light of changing circumstances.

But I prefer the answer of Professor Machlup who compared
the thirst of central bankers for reserves to the desire of his wife
for dresses. Does she *really* need four, twelve, fifty-two, or three

hundred and sixty-five to feel sufficiently comfortable not to nag her husband for more? And would she be satisfied with the advice of borrowing dresses from friends or from a rental agency, instead of buying more? The answer to these questions may not be very different from those of a central banker questioned as to whether he would aim at some magic ratio of 20 per cent, 30 per cent, 50 per cent, or any other x per cent between, on the one hand, reserves, and on the other, imports, sight liabilities, money supply, etc., and to the substitutability of so-called "conditional reserves" to be borrowed from the IMF, for "unconditional owned" reserves? The answer, within a very wide range at least, will depend on traditions and psychology rather than economics. But certainly both Mrs. Machlup and the central bankers are likely to be far more worried by declines—even from comfortable levels—than by increases in their wardrobe or monetary reserves.

MR. SPIELER: Let me ask what constitutes an adequacy of reserve? What do people regard as a reserve? Someone has challenged the fact that a reserve can immediately command purchasing power. The danger that I see is not here at the moment but is lurking in the background.

MR. YOUNG: There is certainly a law operating in this. Any new reserve asset must be governed as to supply or it will drive out of reserves established reserve assets. However, it isn't clear yet that a new reserve asset can be invented. But if one could be, it would have to be limited in supply or you would not long retain gold in your system at all. I assume that, in part, any international monetary arrangement must make use of gold and the conversion of other moneys into gold. We would have a very difficult problem were we to try to get away from gold and it is better not to attempt it. There are more important problems than demonetizing gold and if we are going to develop a better system we had better work it out in some other way than by supplanting gold altogether.

MR. VINER: That the United States dollar is the strongest currency in the world is a statement that is frequently made. In the rubber-dollar period of 1933–34, I used to comment that that isn't saying much. There is a sort of inevitable rigidity in any standard terminology, and that is true of the terms like "equilibrium" and "liquidity" that we are obliged to use at present. There may be insecurity in anything that we do. There may be potential liquidity in any item in a balance-of-payments statement and lack of it in the items which we label as "liquid." Some of this has been brought out here, but it would perhaps be worth someone's while to examine how much the appropriateness of the labels used in balance-of-payments accounting depends on the circumstances of the moment and on the objectives which a country is pursuing.

I have a feeling of unease about specific recommendations for structural changes or particular actions unaccompanied by a fairly clear statement of the range of objectives intended to be served by the international monetary system that is being recommended. In this connection, Mr. Chairman, your questions and your introduction dig deeper than anything else I have heard this evening. I hope as we move on that some attempt will be made to answer your searching questions.

MR. EMMINGER: Can we find some generally accepted criteria for the creation of international reserves? That is the most important problem and the criteria must be acceptable to everybody. I would come back to Mr. Triffin's analogy about dresses. It is a fact of life that a wife in the beginning of a marriage may be quite happy with a certain number of dresses. But after ten or fifteen years of this standard of living she may not be happy with that number of dresses. And there were a number of central banks that were quite happy with relatively modest reserves, but after five years of having been spoiled with much more they are very unhappy now.

Finally, just one remark on Ralph Young's reference to "contingency planning." I would here disagree with the explanation given by him when he said that in using the word the Group of Ten had in mind that the gold supply may, for some time, be quite sufficient. I don't think this is what they had in mind. What they had in mind is much more the explanation given by Professor Triffin. According to the present feeling there is not any impending shortage of international liquidity. There is no deflation around in the world. Many people have the feeling that there is even too much international liquidity, and that some part of it has to be absorbed. Some people may have been uncertain whether the United States and the United Kingdom are going to continue their deficits, and thus to export reserves to the rest of the world in the old way. In view of all these uncertainties, planning for additional reserves can only be a planning for a future contingency.

MR. SACHS: While as professionals and specialists we are habituated to treat the problems that have engaged us in this conference within an assumed self-contained and sufficient order of financial determinants, the origin of these predicaments, and also the prospects and methods of solution, require us to take into account other dimensions and domains of national and international life. In our preoccupation with the immediacies of these problems we become like surf skiers over the flux of oncoming situations and fail to take the deeper soundings for the proper understanding and for the potentially promising solutions. May I, therefore, submit that what has made this year 1965 into a crisis year is that the evolved new monetary order of this postwar has been subjected to attacks and threats of disintegration, starting not only with the propaganda of President de Gaulle's press conference at the beginning of the year, but his claimed return to a rigid gold standard of prior to World War I that, in fact, differed from the functioning gold standard.

In deliberately sharp and bold strokes, that classical gold standard, which in completed form covered the half century prior to World War I, involved not only the first dimension of marginal gold settlement for international trading accounts, but had the supplementary and interacting three dimensions of an operative system centered in London for the financing of the then annual trading in agricultural commodities, the long-term investment in development projects in the newer countries of the American continent and of the British Empire in Asia and Africa, and finally, the transnational flows of credit and of savings by individuals and institutions through the diversified banking and capital markets of the European creditor countries.

The decade of reconstruction following World War I failed to re-establish that complex multidimensional gold exchange standard and monetary and capital order, and the Great Depression at the end of the Twenties, having been followed by attacks on the political settlements after the war, brought in train continuous undermining of the system—the enormous time stretch from 1914 to the end of World War II was the equivalent of a Thirty Years War of unsettlement. The sequel to that long unsettlement started out with the overture to a new monetary order with the establishment of the International Monetary Fund and the World Bank, and only by the end of 1958 did our world enter on its new gold standard and new international monetary order. In consequence, we have had in the last near dozen years a consistent and cumulative prosperity and volume of trade without precedent and parallel even in the presumed golden age of the gold standard prior to World War I.

It is in that perspective that we should be considering the problems and the predicaments of this period since the challenges to our evolved more elaborate and more subtle monetary order. Mindful of the admonition of the Danish thinker Kierkegaard that "We live forward and think backward," it is urgent for us not only to link up the problems of the American imbalance in international payments to those challenges but to take immediate stock of the fact that aggression on the new monetary order has failed, and that the member nations of the renascent and reconstructed Common Market, along with the United States, have resisted the attack and are devising solutions.

The U.S. program for restoring balance in its international payments has entailed restraints on the previous pattern of external direct investment and utilization of capital resources and markets outside of the United States. Whereas in the immediate wake of the so-called voluntary program there was a spreading chorus of anxieties and forecasts of an exported deflation and recession throughout Europe, by now, in this closing quarter of 1965, we can record that both the European economic system and the American have continued in prosperity and avoided reversal of the prolonged prosperity into economic depression—and what is more, are looking forward to the continuance of this prosperity in the coming year. Concurrently, the fears of sterling devaluation and its repercussions have failed of fulfillment, not just because of a wrong forecast, but because of the constructive statesmanship of the strong and thoughtful cooperative new central banking of our free world. As an ironic commentary on that initial attack in January and beyond on our new monetary order, we have now the spectacle that a French oil company, in which the French Government has a 35 per cent interest, has announced that it will float a huge bond issue in the very denomination of the American dollar.

Moreover, in addition to this intra-free world monetary ideological disputation and struggle, this year has witnessed the monetary consequences stemming from international political disturbances. The outbreak of the Pakistan-India war was followed by an attempt by Communist China to enter it on the side of Pakistan; and in the expectation of enlarging the sweep and intensifying the nature of that war, China liquidated into gold a presumed 100 million pounds of sterling holdings. That liquidation aggravated the strains on sterling and thus reinforced the expectations throughout the free world that the seasonal strains of the autumn would bring about the speculators' hope of a break up of the monetary system with its stable exchanges. The prompt and resourceful intervention by the United States through stoppage of foreign aid and the attendant diplomatic intervention brought about a cease-fire on the Pakistan-India fronts and nullified the plans and stratagems of Communist China to unleash an Asian war.

Thus the outstanding historical facts about the year 1965, as thus far lived through, are the overcoming of grave threats to the economic-monetary order and also the international-political order, and the continuing manifestation of the vitality and productivity in monetary and political statesmanship of the cooperant free world economies.

MR. GILBERT: I am going to answer the first question raised as to why the gold reserve went down in the first half of the year. The answer is quite simple and can be traced to two events. First, President de Gaulle gave a press conference and he told the world to go back on the gold standard. It is just as simple as that. The next day there was a run on the gold market.

The second event was arranged by our good friend Martin Gainsbrugh. He and the Board invited Mr. Rueff to come to the United States. Mr. Rueff with considerable publicity advocated up-pricing gold and he did it in circumstances which sounded, to some official gold buyers, as though he had the backing of the President of the French Republic. Now, it is no mystery as to why people then started to buy a little gold. The idea that this was not the policy of the French Government was not denied by France until the speech before the French Bankers' Association in June, which said France was against raising the price of gold.

That is all it is, a feeling that something is going to happen to gold. We will just have to wait until it quiets down. I think we have seen some evidence in the past month that it is quieting down.

CHAIRMAN REIERSON: Mr. Spieler, from your vantage point, how much gold did the Chinese take? Isn't the figure about 400 million dollars?

MR. SPIELER: From the information I have from the London gold market I think the figure was around 100 tons, equivalent to approximately 100 million dollars' worth. There may be a danger of exaggerating the significance of the Chinese move. China has hitherto held its reserves in gold, sterling and other currencies (but for obvious reasons not dollars). Really, when you think of the doubts overhanging the value of sterling, if any one of us were in charge of the Chinese People's Republic's Central Bank we might have decided to take the precaution of converting some of the sterling into gold. The London gold market is in effect the only market in which China can acquire gold at around the official price to meet its requirements.

MR. TRIFFIN: The Chinese may be even far more fearful of a straight blocking of their London accounts than of sterling devaluation.

MR. BACKMAN: It seems to me that the cause-and-effect relationship between the balance of payments and liquidity is getting mixed up in this discussion. Adding to international liquidity isn't going to solve the balance of international payments deficits of either the U.K. or the U.S. It is true that if we do balance our payments in both countries we may—and understand, I said *may*—solve the liquidity problem. But in our concentration upon problems like liquidity and the international problems of the balance of payments we should not ignore the fact that in the past, when the world has had ample liquidity, there still have been many problems in international trade and international relationship. It has often set up a very explosive possibility in the form of inflation.

Both inflation and deflation have been urged as a solution for some of these problems. One speaker suggested that various countries must set their houses straight if they are to solve these problems. Now, when you set your house straight, in many instances you get involved in problems of inflation or, more importantly, deflation. While we may pay lip service to eliminating inflation and deflation as a solution, the fact remains that inflation or deflation takes place regardless of whether governments think they would like to rule them out. Government often seeks to bail itself out by inflation. It takes a tremendous amount of pressure before some countries are willing to take even mild measures of deflation. That does not change the fact that basic international forces must be respected.

I don't have to remind this group as to what the history of the world has been in this area. There have been periods of deflation but unfortunately the emphasis has been in the other direction. Even though we try to exclude inflation or deflation, most European countries have had quite a quickening in the rate of increases in prices, thus indicating inflation is still a very important force.

CHAIRMAN REIERSON: I have a hard taskmaster on my right who would now like to speak under the two-minute rule.

MR. GAINSBRUGH: I would like to propose a question to our opening speaker so that he may have the last word.

Mr. Young, during your opening comments I listened with considerable pleasure to the emphasis that you were placing upon the prospect of emerging from the difficulties surrounding the two key currencies. Our Chairman picked up that particular point, too, and posed some additional questions to you about the approach toward equilibrium.

You made a point, however, in your discussion about the confidence crisis. Are the two developments concurrent, or is the crisis of confidence in your judgment behind us while the approach to equilibrium is now before us?

MR. YOUNG: The crisis of confidence is something that no one can say is behind us. We hope it is largely behind us and some of us are optimistic enough to think that perhaps it is. But this is something no one knows. It is a matter of human behavior. Much can happen that could bring responses that may be rational or irrational, depending on one's point of view.

Certainly the problem of equilibrium is ahead of us. It is not easy to attain but we are making progress. The British, too, are making progress. At least we have some programs and they have some programs and with a reasonable amount of luck it may be possible to attain a satisfactory equilibrium. There is uncertainty and the fact that there is uncertainty contributes to the explosiveness of public psychology. There is just no telling what might happen.

Chapter II

The Role
and
Price of Gold

Chairman: DONALD H. McLAUGHLIN
Position Paper: PHILIP CORTNEY

CHAIRMAN MCLAUGHLIN: It gives me great pleasure to introduce my old friend Philip Cortney. Mr. Cortney can be introduced not only as an economist and a man of affairs, but also as an engineer, and engineers I find are more apt to be concerned about stable units of measurements than my friends in the social sciences. Consequently, I think he appreciates the importance of gold as the basic unit in monetary systems.

Mr. Cortney comes to us as a former member of this organization, The National Industrial Conference Board. He was Chairman of the United States Council of the International Chamber of Commerce. He was a National Director of the National Association of Manufacturers. He is a Commander of the Legion of Honor. Mr. Cortney has been a fighter most of his life in the field of economics and one of the first battles, and a battle which I think he won with brilliance, was in fighting the Havana Charter.

MR. CORTNEY: Before I begin my prepared speech I wish to make a statement. Some of you who will hear my speech, or others who may later read it, will observe that I am repeating many things which I have said in the last ten years or more. Do not take this fact as an argument against me. My purpose was to warn the powers-to-be that we were on a dangerous path and that if we persevere in the mismanagement of our monetary affairs a bitter day of reckoning will ensue. I am afraid that we are not far from a perilous situation. If someone had told me nine or ten years ago that the United States would conduct its affairs in such a manner, that in 1965 we would owe nearly 30 billion dollars short-term funds to the rest of the world, I would certainly have thought the person was not quite of sound mind. But here we are in 1965, saddled with a difficult monetary problem while many economists, particularly of the younger generation, proclaim that we live in a wonderful world with manifold economic miracles. I wish I could be convinced of this in time.

Many people assert that a rise in the price of gold is unobtainable because of the opposition of the United States. It is my contention that a rise in the price of gold is unavoidable if we are to restore monetary order and maintain a free economy and a free society. I share the view that after the money and price inflation accompanying a big war, any monetary system based on gold (like the IMF system instituted in 1946) is in great danger of collapsing unless the price of gold is rightly priced to take into account the distortion and new circumstances brought about by the war. The price of 35 dollars an ounce may have been the right price in 1933 when the price was decided, but it is not the right price today, as I shall attempt to prove.

The Monetary System Today

What kind of monetary system have we today? It is not the "classic" gold standard. But Per Jacobsson, Edward Bernstein, and even Jacques Rueff hold that we are on an international gold standard "in a modern form" because the monetary unit of each country is kept at the value of a fixed weight of gold. Jacques Rueff considers that the accidental adoption of the dollar-exchange standard in the last ten years constitutes only a perversion or aberration (albeit dangerous) of the gold standard as instituted by the IMF.

The International Monetary Fund has three objectives: 1) to request its members to maintain stable exchange-rates; 2) to assure the interconvertibility of currencies and gold; and 3) to pool resources in order to assist countries in overcoming temporary difficulties due primarily to wrong domestic policies.

Hence the global monetary gold reserves must be adequate to enable gold to perform the first two objectives of the Fund. Besides, the annual production of gold has to meet the growing need of the world economy for monetary reserves.

The accidental adoption of the dollar-exchange standard has, in the last ten years, helped the work of the IMF and particularly the growing need for new monetary reserves (called currency reserves). The majority of monetary experts agree that the U.S. must put an end to its external payment deficits, which means an end to the creation of "dollar-reserves." This implies that, with the elimination of the U.S. balance-of-payments deficits, the growth of monetary reserves will depend almost entirely on the newly-mined gold available for monetary purposes. At the present price for gold, the Central Banks were able to put their hands on, for the last seven years, only about 600 million dollars per annum, an amount completely inadequate. The balance is absorbed by industry and primarily by hoarders who, distrusting paper money, believe that gold is the cheapest and safest "store of value." The increment of 600 million dollars per annum of gold reserves is inadequate for the needs of an expanding economy because it represents barely 1.2 per cent of the global gold reserves while production and trade are increasing at the rate of 3.5 to 4 per cent per annum.

If we admit that an end will be put to the U.S. balance-of-payments deficits, then the only alternative to a rise in the price of gold is the "creation" of synthetic money reserves, acceptable in international settlements, according to Mr. Bernstein's plan or that of Mr. Valery Giscard d'Estaing (not yet approved by the French Government). I believe that these plans will not be adopted essentially for two reasons: first, the creation of artificial monetary reserves would have to be small to inspire any confidence, and, therefore, will prove inadequate for the needs. Second, even at its best, the synthetic reserve will be discriminated against in favor of gold. Other plans have been recommended for the needed monetary reform, the best known being that of Mr. Triffin (in fact, an international central bank). The world is not ripe, either politically or psychologically, to accept this kind of idea. One should be convinced of the simple truth that no monetary system can function or be stable, if it does not inspire confidence to the users of money—a commonplace which is too often forgotten.

Gold and Domestic Monetary Policy

Many persons, instructed or not, are surprised that so much importance is attached to the annual production of gold presumably needed to sustain economic expansion and prices when the global gold monetary stock, and above all the monetary circulation (bank notes and demand deposits), appear to be out of proportion with the amount representing the annual production of gold. I wish to point out in this connection that those who have to explain the influence of gold, usually give as an example of how gold movement from one country to another helps to restore a disturbed monetary equilibrium, the restrictive effect on the credit policy in the market losing gold and the opposite effect in the market gaining gold. Yet the amounts of gold involved in the movements necessary to re-establish balance of payments are not large.

The distinction between the factors which govern the general price level and those which influence the trend of prices, up or down, can also help us understand the importance of an adequate annual production of gold. The general price level is governed by the volume of purchasing power directed to the buying of the current output relative to the volume of this output. On the other hand, the trend of prices, all other things being equal, is influenced by the trend of the ratio of the increment of money supply (hence by the production of gold) to the increment of the volume of production.

In reading the considerations which follow one should keep constantly in mind that in our present international monetary system, national currencies have to be interconvertible and *convertible into gold* (even though limited to external claims presented for conversion by central banks) at fixed exchange rates.

However loose the connection may be between the money supply and gold, it is no less true that this connection exists in a monetary system based on gold. In other words, if the money supply is to expand, the quantity of gold will also have to increase more or less commensurately.

Many people seem to forget that gold has been chosen as an international currency and as a standard because it is a commodity. Now for this commodity, as indeed for every other, there is a production cost. Gold is produced in larger or smaller quantities depending on its cost relative to the costs of other commodities. If commodity prices are pushed up substantially as a result of the injection in the economy of inconvertible paper money (as happens during a major war) and the price of gold is held down at an arbitrary level fixed before prices rose, it is obvious that gold production will decline relative to the production of other commodities. If the monetary system returns to the gold standard following the war at the prewar price of gold, gold production will be inadequate to provide the necessary increment of purchasing power for the expansion of production and trade at the high prices prevailing due to the war and inflation.

Assuming an end has been put to the dollar-exchange standard, every country should manage its economic, monetary and fiscal affairs so that its monetary gold stock is adequate to 1) provide a cushion to meet deficits in the balance of payments, and 2) to assure the convertibility of its currency into other currencies and/or into gold, either through the dollar or through the International Monetary Fund. In attempting to evaluate "adequate" gold reserves we should keep in mind that in a world of convertible currencies there may be considerable movements of short-term funds as a result of changes in the timing of foreign payments and receipts—so-called "leads and lags"—and also as a result of differences in the level of interest rates in the various countries.

There is no clear cut or hard and fast answer to the question of how large the monetary gold stock of a country should be in order to be "adequate" to the work it has to perform. For that matter, it is not possible to say exactly how much liquidity is required by national commercial banks. However, experience and common sense offer us a certain amount of guidance. A French economist, Mr. Maurice Allais, has estimated that in 1913 the proportion of world monetary gold reserves in relation to the total amount of money in circulation (bank notes plus demand deposits) was about 32 per cent (a high figure because of the gold coins in circulation); the corresponding figures were 15.7 per cent in 1928 and 11.9 per cent in 1964. In the United States the figure is now about 8.5 per cent, and only 3.5 per cent if we take into account the time deposits.

What is extremely serious is that the gold held by the United States is "mortgaged" by foreign claims of over 25 billion dollars (14 billion dollars held by foreign central banks). It is therefore neither an exaggeration nor incorrect to state that the gold liquidity of the monetary system of the United States is not only nil, but that the United States has a gold debt vis-à-vis other countries. This situation makes the gold value of the dollar unstable and vulnerable. The same is true of Great Britain's gold reserves. In the light of past experience, Mr. Maurice Allais considers that the total amount of gold in relation to the amount of money in circulation should be between 20 and 25 per cent to ensure the stability of the international monetary system. Yet the actual figure for the free world at the end of 1965 is only about 10.5 per cent.

It should be realized that the interconvertibility of currencies and gold has to be guaranteed by a minimum gold coverage in the same way as it is assumed that bank deposits are guaranteed by the ability of banks to supply banknotes in exchange for such deposits. Inasmuch as the amount of money in circulation tends to increase as production rises and trade expands, it is necessary that gold production should increase appropriately.

Mr. William Busschau has, in two books, *The Measure of Gold* and *Gold and International Liquidity*, dealt in an original and thorough way with the subject of the gold liquidity necessary to ensure the gold convertibility of the international debts of various countries.

Per Jacobsson used to devote special attention to the role played by money in the exchange of goods, and thus to the fact that when production increases with a rising population there must be an actual increase in the new means of payment.

In a famous paper presented at the Twenty-fifth Anniversary meeting of the National Bureau of Economic Research (June 6, 1946), Per Jacobsson showed how a wrong price for gold in the 1920's (after the monetary and price inflation due to World War I) had resulted in an inadequate growth of the gold stock necessary to sustain monetary purchasing power in the different countries.

Gold and Real Output

The average annual increase in monetary gold stocks representing newly produced gold available for monetary purposes was at the rate of 250 million dollars in 1913 and 230 million dollars in 1929. The money increase in national income was 2.7 million dollars in 1913 and 8.6 million dollars in 1929. Hence the relation between the amount of gold available for monetary purposes and the increase in national income was as one to eleven in 1913 while it was as one to thirty in 1929. I evaluate this same relation as one to eighty or ninety in 1965! In dollar value the national income was 95 billion dollars in 1913 and 200 billion dollars in 1929; of the increase, about 30 per cent was due to real growth and the rest to a rise in prices.

From these figures Jacobsson draws the conclusion that the

current gold production contributed less to sustaining prices in
1929 than in 1913. The level of costs and prices in 1929 was,
on a gold basis, some 50 per cent higher than in 1913–1914, but
the annual gold production was lower than before 1914 because
of the increased cost of production, and thus insufficient to provide a proper impulse to an expansion in liquidity in relation to
the general level of money incomes.

At first, Jacobsson explained, the 1929 depression could be
regarded as the downward turn of an orderly business cycle,
intensified by coincidence with an agricultural depression. However, as soon as the recession set in (1929, after the stock market
crash) the fall in prices became steep. The fall in prices was the
root trouble from which most of the other difficulties arose, being
chiefly responsible for the monetary convulsions from 1931 onward and the paralysis of so much of the international credit
system.

Many economists, particularly in Great Britain, attributed
this state of affairs to the "gold shortage" which had been a cause
of continuing concern since the end of the war. I share the
views of Charles Rist, Jacobsson, Schumpeter and Hicks that such
an interpretation was wrong. The great mistake made after the
1914–1918 war was to maintain the dollar and the pound sterling
at their prewar gold value, while sustaining economic activity and
thereby the level of prices in terms of gold (50 per cent higher
compared with 1914) by adopting the gold exchange standard
accompanied by an abnormal expansion of credit in the United
States. World War I, as a result of the issuance of paper money
to finance the war, had sent all prices rocketing to levels that
were inconsistent with normal conditions for the production of
goods, since the dollar and the pound were maintained at their
prewar gold value (in other words the price of gold in dollars
and pounds remained unchanged as compared with its prewar
price).

If knowledge of monetary phenomena had been more advanced at the time, the experts would have probably recommended a devaluation of the dollar and of the pound in 1925

when Great Britain decided to revert to the gold standard. As Charles Rist once wrote, at that time the world did not have the good fortune to have "a madman of genius" who could make such a recommendation.

The lesson which Per Jacobsson drew from the events in the 1920's was formulated by him at the end of the address given June 6, 1946: "We must watch carefully the signs of the times to ensure that we do not again commit the mistake of trying to stabilize [prices] in gold at an unsuitable level."

I submit and I dare assert that if Per Jacobsson had had a free choice, by which I mean without antagonizing the United States at the time he was General Manager of the IMF, he would have recommended a rise in the price of gold, in preference to any alternative plan, to meet the problem of inadequate gold liquidity.

There is a passage in J. R. Hicks's excellent book, *A Contribution to the Theory of the Trade Cycle,* which was often quoted by Jacobsson as representing his own views:

> Really catastrophic depression is likely to occur when there is profound monetary instability—when the rot in the monetary system goes very deep. . . . My interpretation of the Great Depression is that the slump was an exceptional one because it impinged upon a monetary situation which was quite exceptionally unstable. . . . The monetary system of the world had never adjusted itself at all fully to the change in the level of money incomes which took place during and after the war of 1914–1918; it was trying to manage with a gold supply, which was in terms of wage units extremely inadequate.

The Historical Perspective

The lesson we can learn from the economic and monetary events, covering the period from 1870 (when practically all Europe adopted the gold standard) to 1933 seems clear:

In normal times (by which I mean essentially the absence of a big war) when there is a link, even non-rigid, between the global quantity of monetary gold reserves and the global monetary circulation, with gold fixed at a certain price, there arises a state of quite stable equilibrium between the monetary circulation, the level of commodity prices and the production of gold (while the production of goods is increasing with rare interruptions).

If and when this equilibrium is disturbed by a big war, and the concomitant inflation of money and prices, and we reinstate the link, however loose, between the gold monetary reserves and the monetary circulation (like in 1925 and in 1946), it is essential to set the price of gold at the right value in order to obtain an adequate global monetary gold stock and an adequate annual increase in the quantity of gold produced.

After the money and price inflation accompanying a big war any monetary system based on gold (like the IMF system instituted in 1946) is in great danger of collapsing unless the new price of gold has been correctly decided upon.

The present monetary system has so far resisted the pressure resulting from its fundamental instability, due to a wrong price for gold, for five main reasons: 1) the U.S. came out of World War II with a huge stock of gold; 2) the U.S. has helped the world get on its feet again by adopting the Marshall Plan and various kinds of aid—military and economic—following the Marshall Plan; 3) inflation in the U.S. has given rise to chronic balance-of-payments deficits which have become alarmingly large since 1958, thus feeding the rest of the world with currency monetary reserves but undermining confidence in the dollar; 4) the good luck of discovery of new gold mines in South Africa, and also the sales of gold by Russia in order to purchase badly needed commodities; and 5) for the last two to three years the gold mechanism that re-equilibrates balances of payment in disequilibrium has been "blocked" with the consent of all nations (except France since early 1965). The present unstable, precarious and dangerous situation is being artificially maintained by the common fear of all governments involved not to "upset the applecart." Everyone understands, however, that we are at the end of "clever" manipulations to sustain a sick situation. Besides, the United States has had recourse in the last two years to administrative measures aiming at eradicating the external deficits. These measures control investment abroad, the movements of capital (short and long) which smack of the unsavory taste of exchange controls.

The Price of Gold

The question arises, of course, whether and how we can decide upon the "right" price for gold. I share the opinion that it can be determined *approximately* by appropriate calculations, and in any case better than by any other known method. It is my opinion that the price of gold would have to be raised to a minimum of 70 dollars an ounce, if we are to put the international monetary system on a sound and stable basis.

The foregoing remarks should make us realize the absurdity of the position of a few economists—some of international repute! —who are recommending that the United should lower the price of gold to 20 dollars or even 10 dollars an ounce, as if it were within the power and discretion of the U.S. Government to fix the price of gold!

The present price of gold is kept arbitrarily by the U.S. Government at 35 dollars an ounce, thus maintaining an unstable international monetary situation in danger of collapse. The 35 dollar price was chosen after the upheaval of World War I and the Great Depression of 1929–1933, in the light of circumstances —prices, debts, costs, etc.—prevailing at that time. It is completely unrealistic in 1966!

In his speech "Does Monetary History Repeat Itself?"[1] Mr. Martin, Chairman of the Federal Reserve Board, makes the following comments:

> In 1931 and 1933 an increase in the price of gold was recommended in order to raise commodity prices. Today, a gold price increase is recommended as a means to provide the monetary sup-

[1] Delivered June 1, 1965.

port for world price stability. In 1931 and 1933 an increase in the price of gold was recommended in order to combat deflation; today it is recommended in effect as a means to combat inflation. . . . Can there be worse confusion?

I submit respectfully and with all my warm feelings for him that his analysis of the situation in 1931–1933 and in 1965 is unsatisfactory. As I see it, *gold was not rightly priced in 1929–1931 and it is not now.* In 1929–1933 we had no choice but to correct the situation after the outbreak of the Great Depression. This time, having learned our lesson, we should be wise enough to set the price of gold at the right price (and restore monetary order) before it is too late to prevent a new calamity.

Mr. Martin himself, like other American monetary experts such as Mr. Bernstein, former Chief Economist of the IMF, seems to admit that the economic and monetary disaster which occurred in 1931–1933 made it necessary to raise the price of gold to help offset the effects of the abrupt drop in prices and the indebtedness which existed at that time.

The situation in 1965 is in many respects similar to that in 1928–1929. Today, as at that time, war-induced inflation and the postwar boom have created a number of imbalances and distortions. Two of these distortions are obvious: first, the relationship between monetary circulation, international debt and world gold stock is inadequate; and, second, at the price of 35 dollars an ounce there is an unsatisfactory relationship between the global monetary circulation, the price level of commodities and the production of gold. The result is that the amount of gold being produced at 35 dollars an ounce, as compared to the production of commodities at present prices, is inadequate to provide the free world with the gold-basis necessary for the sound monetary expansion which should accompany the growth of production and trade.

If we continue to maintain the price of gold at its present artificial level, we shall be running the risk of a worldwide depression of the same kind as in 1929–1933. (I have in mind the risk of a monetary war, a contraction of credit and deflation of prices.) However, I share the view that the free world will no longer tolerate a crisis which would bring about widespread and prolonged unemployment as in the years after 1929. What are the implications of this view?

When the present situation turns sour, as I am afraid it will if nothing is done to correct it, our and other governments frightened by the prospect of a new depression of the 1929–1933 type would certainly turn to inflation on a massive scale, using paper money to finance the public expenditure that would be considered necessary to combat unemployment. This paper money inflation would be of such magnitude that nationalist and socialist economies, strictly planned and controlled, would have to be established everywhere.

MR. WALLICH: I don't know why I have such difficulties with the excellent talk of Mr. Cortney. I agree with his objectives. Inflation is very bad and so is our payments deficit. We want to get rid of both. It is a question of means and here I do see very great difficulties.

Inflation in this country is not, by and large, considered a great evil. Hence Mr. Cortney and I don't have much company in opposing it. But I think inflation did not even begin to be taken seriously, at least by a majority of my academic colleagues, until we experienced a large balance of payments deficit. Before that the rise in the price level was simply a statistic. Most of my economic colleagues might have said that we are concerned with real variables, such as production and employment. The price level is a monetary variable, they might say, which makes no difference. Given this attitude toward inflation, I am not certain that the pressure on our balance of payments and our shortage of reserves isn't a useful antidote to inflationary propensities. Let us not give up that defense too easily.

Now, as to the role of gold in this framework, there is one historic fact that is indisputable. It is that the role of gold in the monetary system has diminished for one hundred fifty years or so. At first, gold was displaced by paper domestically. Now it is being displaced gradually internationally. I don't see any advan-

tage in going the other way, toward enhancing the role of gold.
If I thought that price stability could be achieved that way it
would be worth considering. But sole reliance on gold would
mean price deflation. This is very undesirable. What would come
out in the end would be devaluation and disorder. That is not the
road to travel.

We must ask ourselves what are the ways of minimizing the
role of gold internationally, continuing on the road on which we
have been traveling for such a long time.

The first step is, of course, to minimize international imbalances and get rid of long drawn-out large payments deficits.
Without this we will not have a stable world monetary system.

Another possible step, assuming better balance to be reached,
is to reduce the use of gold by funding some of the existing key
currencies. I would have no objection to funding provided it
comes cheap and imposes no harsh conditions on the debtor
countries. I don't believe, however, that such conditions are available. I suspect that any kind of funding of dollar liabilities and
sterling liabilities would resemble what in private business we
call the procedure under Section 10-B or 11-B of the Bankruptcy
Act, a procedure that no debtor will undergo who has any chance
of meeting his obligations in some other way.

Alternatively, the next step might be something of the kind
proposed by Mr. Blessing of the Bundesbank who suggested fixed
proportions of currencies and gold in international payments.
Or we might consider separating out that part of reserve gains
that results from capital movements. We might try to reach an
understanding, perhaps unwritten, that a country that increases
its reserves through an inflow of short-term funds would not
convert these reserves into gold. In that case we would have
sterilized to some extent the effects upon gold holdings of short-
term capital flows and of speculation.

As a final step, and following what seems the standard view
now, I would suggest creating an additional reserve unit to round
out the role of gold and the key currencies. Here I am concerned
that the present proposals may give us a unit that is rather weak,

and far from "as good as gold." Failure of any one of the participants in the scheme as now envisaged could cause the unit to lose value. I am not impressed by the fact that when value of a country's currency goes to zero, the country can make up for it by increasing the amount of currency in the pool to infinity.

Hence I would like to see a unit backed by substantial reserves to make up for possible defaults of participants, or a unit based upon the IMF. The Fund, as a going concern, could absorb some of the losses that might occur.

MR. CORTNEY: Professor Wallich said that sole reliance on gold would mean price deflation. At the present price of gold his position seems to me correct.

Then Professor Wallich wants to minimize the role of gold on grounds which are not very clear to me. Neither can I visualize realistically the means to reach his goal. We have to put an end to further national monetizing of foreign currencies or assets. To create man-made reserves like the proposed CRU[2] requires a degree of international confidence which does not exist in the present conditions of the world.

I would like to understand why those who advocate minimizing the role of gold do not propose an international monetary system without gold. With the present system based on gold (IMF) currencies are to be freely convertible and interconvertible into gold. Besides, the exchange rates are to be maintained stable.

A system which would not be essentially based on gold means a different system. Let the antigold advocates propose such a system. If they do, they will also have to provide a substitute mechanism to the gold mechanism for the re-equilibration of balance-of-payments deficits or surpluses, without which we shall not obtain monetary order.

CHAIRMAN MC LAUGHLIN: I quite agree, though I must confess I do have a special love for gold. However, one can make a much more logical argument for doing away with gold entirely than for a monetary system such as our present one, under which

[2] Composite Reserve Unit.

dollars held by foreign central banks are convertible into gold but dollars in domestic hands can not be redeemed in gold. We endeavor to keep the dollar abroad as good as gold—even at a rate established prior to World War I—and at the same time "enjoy" the stimulation of deficits and inflation at home where the citizen is denied the right to protect himself by claiming and owning gold. It seems to me that such a system can last only as long as our stock of monetary gold remains above some critical level—or critical mass, if I may borrow a term from the atomic physicists—or that we conduct both our international and domestic fiscal and financial affairs as though we were on the gold standard.

MR. HARWOOD: In connection with Ralph Young's paper there was some talk about France taking out gold and others following suit. It is interesting to note that from the 1961 total of nearly 3.6 billion dollars the German dollar holding had been reduced to 1.9 billion dollars by the end of February of this year. Now they are down to 1.3 billion dollars. I think France was in the position of being left holding the bag if she didn't wake up.

I was much interested to note Philip Cortney's reference to the causes of our present situation. There is so much talk about what to do. And it seems to me there is a wholly inadequate consideration of how we got where we are.

My personal belief is that an ideal solution of the problem would be as follows:

Revision of United States banking laws to restore the principles of sound commercial banking first established (to a degree) in the United States by the initiation of the Federal Reserve System, but so soon abandoned and now nearly forgotten. Involved would be

(1) Separation of the commercial banking function from the investment functions (short-term installment loans, term loans, and longer-term investments) of our commercial banks. This need not require splitting each bank, but appropriate accounting and examination procedures.

(2) A requirement that all commercial banks work toward and reach, say in ten or fifteen years, a condition such that investment type assets are balanced by savings and capital type liabilities, and

therefore necessarily that all purchasing media (currency and checking accounts) represented either gold or goods being offered in the markets.

(3) Require the United States Treasury to use all the "profit" on a devaluation of the dollar to retire United States securities held by the Federal Reserve Banks; then require the Federal Reserve Banks to sell within ten to fifteen years all government securities except an amount equal to their capital liabilities less real estate.

(4) Reduce the gold weight of the dollar to roughly the inverse of 160 divided by 100, or, say, 60 per cent. of 1/35 of an ounce of pure gold. This would make the new dollar about or a little less than 1/60th of an ounce. For all practical purposes and having in mind the probable undervaluation of the commodity price index attributable to quality changes in manufactured products, a so-called "price" of 60 dollars per ounce of gold would appear to be about as reasonable a figure as could be justified by any scientifically useful procedures.

(5) Announce that during the ten- to fifteen-year period ahead additions of gold to the United States monetary stock would be used to retire United States securities held by the Federal Reserve Banks and that losses of gold would be reflected in curtailment of credit extensions in order to avoid any resumption of the creation of inflationary purchasing media.

By following the procedure outlined above, with certain added safeguards I shall not describe in detail, I presently believe that the United States could unilaterally lead the way toward the establishment of sound money-credit systems for the leading industrial nations of the world. Those who chose to follow that lead would benefit; those who did not would continue to suffer the consequences of depreciating currencies.[3]

What I expect will happen is an altogether different matter. Note that I have given first place to the restoration of sound commercial banking principles. Until that is accomplished devaluation will not only stamp the seal of approval of temporary success on past unsound policies but also will inevitably encourage their continuation. Witness the monetary history of the world.

[3] Paraphrased from the statement of E. C. Harwood to the Chairman of the Joint Economic Committee which may be found in U.S. Congress, Subcommittee on Economic Progress of the Joint Economic Committee, *The Federal Reserve Portfolio: Statements by Individual Economists*, 89th Cong., 2d Sess., 1966, pp. 37–40.

I don't pretend to know how long we shall continue on the present course of economic disaster. After all, the French remained on that course for more than four decades until their monetary unit lost 99.6 per cent of its gold value. However, my guess is that we shall encounter trouble much earlier, perhaps in the next few months or years. I know that the American banking situation is about twice as unsound today as it was in 1929. Witness the facts reflected in our index of inflation. When trouble comes I have little hope that the United States Government will act wisely. I expect a repetition of the mistakes of the 1920's, including attempts to reflate and devaluation.

That gold will win as always is, I believe, inevitable, but just when or after how much folly or whether we then shall have anything recognizable as a Constitution of the United States I have grave doubts.

SIR ROY HARROD: I am one of those who regards himself as a friend of gold. I want to see its price raised. Now a few days after the Treaty of Munich was signed, I was named as chairman of a committee supporting Mr. Lindsay, who ran on a non-party ticket, opposing the government candidate at our Oxford by-election, and we had to decide whether also to have the Communists on our platform. Well, they seemed to have very sound views about Hitler, and we decided to have them, and they proved quite effective on the platform. And so some of my Conservative friends of gold here have got to make a decision whether to have me on their side or not.

Just two points, one internal and one external. I don't look to a sound restoration of the position of gold to counter the domestic inflation. I don't believe that domestic inflation recently has been caused by too easy money but by the new situation as regards full or high employment.

So far as the domestic scene is concerned we have almost gone onto a "wages standard" of value. When you have full or high employment it is difficult to resist wage increases, demanded and granted. I therefore believe—I personally am a great enemy of inflation—that we shall only succeed in preventing it by something in the nature of "guideposts." Well, that is a new thing, but it is due to the new position that the government is in as regards maintaining high employment and growth.

As the full employment policy now takes priority, in the minds of people, over price stability—and rightly so I think—if we want price stability we have got to have a new method. I don't think it would help to have something more like a semi-automatic gold standard. In any case, we shall need a guide-posts policy if we are to combat the domestic price inflation.

Secondly, the internal situation. I want a change in the price of gold for the opposite reason to that which has been expounded in this room. I want to see more latitude about countries getting deficits ironed out and settled promptly. I think the idea that it is needful to get deficits paid promptly is doing harm. I want to see more international liquidity.

Now it is true that the United States deficit has been going on for rather a long time and in rather large amount, but we oughtn't to have to take it nearly so seriously as some have recently been doing. If you take the U.S. deficit in ratio to services as well as merchandise, it is not more than 10 per cent of its recurrent annual liabilities. It doesn't seem to me to be such a terrible thing. I personally would not in the least mind if the U.S. deficits went on forever. They kill two birds with one stone, enabling the United States to continue a domestic expansionist policy and giving the rest of the world about the amount each year of additional international liquidity that we want—say 2 or 3 billion dollars. To have a world dollar standard, based on U.S. deficits, would be quite a good way of solving the problem.

As a British subject I might have just a tiny, little bit of jealousy because of the old position of sterling in the world. But I would waive that. The trouble with the solution isn't that there is anything extremely wicked about the United States having a deficit, but that, whether President Johnson takes action or not, that deficit is probably going to come to an end, so that that solution of the world monetary problem wouldn't last very long.

I want to see more liquidity internationally so as to delay the need for very prompt adjustments. I think that people here and in the rest of the world have sometimes been under the illusion that, because the United States has had a deficit for so long, other countries can also run deficits for a long time. Certainly we British, who have had a number of years in which we have had deficits, have had, because of our weaker position, to snap out of those deficits very promptly. You will find that each time that a deficit has occurred we have succeeded in snapping out of it very quickly, but to the detriment of our domestic policy. So I want gold to play a larger part.

You say, why gold? Why not those other means of reserve that are being discussed around this table and around the world? Simply because I fear that you won't get any adequate increase of liquidity by those other means. I think the gold miners and silver miners of the world, in California and Nevada, and in South Africa, by producing gold and silver, have sustained the great world expansion of trade in the last century or two. I don't believe that we shall get so generous an increase of reserves out of the central bankers. I am sorry to say this, since there are many here. It is simply my judgment of what is probable.

MR. BACKMAN: Some of our friends here believe that there is a pretty close relationship between gold and prices. That is a statement I don't understand. I gather from Mr. Cortney's statement—"We must prevent a sharp economic setback and a steep decline in prices during this troublesome transition"—that we must increase the price of gold so that the price of gold will be in line with existing price levels.

To me this is an exaggerated, if not unrealistic, emphasis upon the role that gold plays in determining the general price level. The key determinant of what happens to world prices is what happens right here to the price level in the United States. The probability of any significant deflation in prices in the United States is practically nil. I am not talking about periodic declines of 2 or 3 per cent. I am talking, if anything, of the dimensions of deflation that have followed previous wars.

I know that there are those who will agree with Mr. Cortney

regarding the dangers of a major price decline. I must say that since the end of World War II I have had the unwavering position that a repetition of past experience was impossible in this country. We have built up under our price structure higher wages and other labor costs. In addition, there has been an inflation built into our money supply and this cannot be reversed unless we have large budgetary surpluses. The emphasis upon full employment should also be noted.

I am not saying that you cannot have declines of significant nature in certain prices, for example, raw material prices, as we have seen periodically. But a significant decline, or decline even worth talking about, in the general level of finished goods prices is just not in the cards, whether we have the present monetary system, whether we hold gold at 35 dollars an ounce, or whether we change the price of gold.

I don't think that what happens to the price level is going to be influenced very much by what happens to gold. It has no relationship of any importance.

CHAIRMAN MC LAUGHLIN: Mr. Cortney, may we have your final comment?

MR. CORTNEY: I realize that the subject of the relationship between gold and prices in the present international monetary system is not easy to understand. My feeling is that this is due primarily to the large stock of gold which the United States possessed at the end of the war and, secondly, to the creation of international currency reserves (dollar reserves) by the national monetizing of the dollar reserves acquired by many foreign countries, particularly since 1958, as a result of the balance-of-payments deficits in the United States.

My good friend Jules Backman is certainly aware that our present international monetary system (the International Monetary Fund) is based on gold. This means that all currencies are interconvertible and into gold (at stable exchange rates). With the expansion of production, trade and population, we need an appropriate growth in monetary reserves, because we need an appropriate expansion of the world monetary supply, which, I repeat, is interconvertible and into gold. In fact, he has certainly heard Mr. Ralph Young last night, and Mr. Wallich today, express fears as to the adequacy of the growth of international reserves (at the present price of gold) consistent with international needs in order to avert potential deflationary dangers.

Paul Samuelson, after having explained why prices rise swiftly in major wars, has made the following significant comment:

> As an omen for the future, note one *terribly significant fact.* After World War II there was no decline in prices at all comparable with what followed previous wars. Wages and prices seem to have become sticky as far as downward movements are concerned; also government has become quick to act to stem any depression that begins to get under way. If prices rise in good times and do not fall much in bad times, what is the long-term direction of prices?[4]

Now, if the long-term trend of prices is to be constantly upward or even stable at the present levels, it will require a considerable expansion of the world money supply interconvertible into gold. Where is the gold to come from at the present price of gold?

[4] Paul A. Samuelson, *Economics* (6th edition), New York: McGraw-Hill, pp. 267–68.

Chapter III

Alternatives to Gold— Proposals for the Creation of a New Reserve Asset

Chairman: WALTER E. HOADLEY
Position Paper: EDWARD M. BERNSTEIN

CHAIRMAN HOADLEY: Edward M. Bernstein is well known to everyone here. A product of the University of Chicago and Harvard, he certainly has won for himself an excellent reputation as an outstanding authority in international monetary affairs. Distinguished economist, teacher and writer, he has also been an exemplary civil servant in his extensive service with the United States Treasury. A pioneer in international economic research at the International Monetary Fund, he has established himself as a valued consultant to the financial leaders of the free world. It was my pleasure to serve with Mr. Bernstein on the White House Review Committee for Balance-of-Payments Statistics during the past two years. I found him to be an effective, tireless, thought-provoking, restless, and cigar chain-smoking chairman. Like you, I await with keen interest his paper.

MR. BERNSTEIN: The gold standard as we know it today is the product of historical evolution. No one planned an international monetary system based on gold. Far back in the dawn of history gold (and even more important, silver) became money because it was a commodity that merchants were willing to accept and hold. When coinage was invented, the temples sometimes took over the function of minting—in Rome, it was the temple of Juno Moneta, from which comes our generic term *money*. The sacred origin of money may originally have been an assurance of the quality of the coinage. But it is the economic, not the mystical, aspect of gold that has ultimately determined its role in the national and international monetary system.

The fact that the supply of gold entails the employment of real resources is at once the strength and the weakness of gold as money. The commodity nature of metallic money has not always prevented the debasement of money. As Adam Smith pointed out: "In every country of the world, I believe, the avarice and injustice of princes and sovereign states, abusing the confidence of their subjects, have by degrees diminished the real quantity of metal which has been originally contained in their coins." Nevertheless, even princes and sovereign states found it more difficult to inflate the money supply when it consisted principally of gold and silver than when new forms of money came into common use.

Against this advantage of gold as money must be set the great disadvantage that arises from the limitation it places on the growth of the money supply. After the price revolution caused by the enormous inflow of precious metals from the New World had reached a peak in the middle of the seventeenth century, there was a period of about one hundred years when the growth in the supply of gold and silver was inadequate for a world in which economic activity had begun to quicken. It is no accident that from about 1640 to 1700 goldsmiths extended their operations from dealing in precious metals to private banking based on goldsmiths' notes. Nor is it an accident that in this period banks were formed in Europe with the authority to issue notes.

Once bank notes and the deposits were in wide use, it became important to maintain the equivalence of credit money with gold. In general, there were two distinct ways in which this was done. The first was the requirement that all other forms of money be convertible into gold which alone had unlimited legal tender power. The second was the limitation of other types of money by reference to a gold reserve. The limitation of the money supply on the basis of the gold reserve was a precaution against the excessive increase in other forms of money and thus an indirect means of assuring the gold equivalence of all forms of money.

The concept that the stock of monetary gold within a country provides an objective measure of the proper supply of money was severely shaken during World War I and completely abandoned during the Great Depression. Gold coins were withdrawn from circulation in all belligerent countries from 1914 to 1918. Furthermore, no belligerent would or could restrict the expansion of its money supply during the war by reference to its gold reserve. While the gold standard came back into fashion in the 1920's, the uneven inflation and the overvalued currencies generated during the war gave birth to centers of deflation after the war. This gradually undermined the world economy and ultimately destroyed the old-fashioned gold standard.

The devaluation of sterling in 1931 and of the dollar in 1933, and the subsequent devaluation of the currencies of the European gold bloc in 1936, marks the end of an era. No country could accept the principle that the primary aim of economic policy is to maintain the gold value of the currency in the face of massive unemployment. The money supply continued to be linked to gold reserves, but the relationship was no longer unalterable. This is exemplified by the experience of the United States. In 1941 this country had an enormous gold reserve, 75 per cent of the world total. Yet such is the expansive power of modern wars that by 1945 the Treasury regarded it as prudent to reduce the gold reserve requirements from 40 per cent on Federal Reserve notes and 35 per cent on Federal Reserve deposits to 25 per cent on both note and deposit liabilities of the Federal Reserve Banks. And more recently, as the gold reserves were depleted by the prolonged payments deficit, the 25 per cent gold reserve requirement was eliminated on Federal Reserve deposits and now applies only to Federal Reserve notes. Nobody believes that the money supply of the United States can any longer be determined by the gold reserve, although monetary policy will continue to be very much affected by the balance of payments.

The policy of the United States on gold is defined in the Gold Reserve Act of 1934. By Presidential proclamation, the gold content of the dollar was fixed at 13 5/7 grains, equivalent to 35 dollars an ounce. The coinage of gold was terminated and private holding of gold was forbidden. The gold reserve was concentrated in the Treasury, with the Federal Reserve Banks given gold certificates to be used for the note backing. Under the authority of the Gold Reserve Act of 1934, the Secretary of the Treasury buys and sells gold for the settlement of international transactions. In brief, the United States established an international gold bullion standard, with the dollar defined in terms of gold, and dollars convertible into gold only for foreign monetary authorities. Every monetary development since then has been designed to emphasize the international aspect of the gold standard while the national aspect of the gold standard was allowed to fade away gradually.

Gold and the International Monetary Fund

The Tripartite Agreement of 1936 of the United States, the United Kingdom, and France brought international acceptance of the U.S. gold policy. With the adherence of the Netherlands, Belgium and Switzerland, the principle of fixed exchange rates based on gold and supported by the purchase and sale of gold for international settlements was accepted by all of the great industrial countries except the Axis Powers. The Bretton Woods Agreement adopted the international gold standard and extended it to all members of the Fund. The provisions of the Fund Agreement on gold may be summarized as follows:

1) The par values of the currencies of members must be defined in gold or in the U.S. dollar of the weight and fineness of 1944, which is to say, in gold.

2) The par value of a currency can be changed when this is necessary restore the balance of payments of a country, but the change can be made only after consultation with the Fund and generally requires its concurrence.

3) No member may buy or sell gold at a price above or below par value plus or minus the margin prescribed by the Fund, now 1 per cent.

4) Members of the Fund must take measures to maintain exchange rates within 1 per cent of parity. "A member whose monetary authorities, for the settlement of international transactions, in fact freely buy and sell gold . . . shall be deemed to be fulfilling this undertaking."

5) The Fund may make uniform proportionate changes in par values (a rise in the price of gold in all currencies) by a vote including its largest members, but no country need accept a change in the price of gold in its own currency.

6) The gold value of the Fund's assets must be maintained notwithstanding changes in the par value or the foreign exchange value of a currency. This is done by having the member pay the Fund an amount of its currency equal to the reduction in the gold value of the Fund's holdings of its currency.

7) Original subscriptions to the Fund were paid in gold to the extent of 25 per cent of the quota or 10 per cent of a country's net official holdings of gold and U.S. dollars. For subsequent increases in quotas, 25 per cent must be paid in gold. The balance of quota subscriptions is paid in the currencies of members.

8) The Fund is authorized to sell any member's currency in exchange for gold or for the currency of the member desiring to make the purchase (drawing).

9) "Any member desiring to obtain, directly or indirectly, the currency of another member for gold shall, provided that it can do so with equal advantage, acquire it by the sale of gold to the Fund." This does not, however, preclude any member from selling its own newly-mined gold in any market (e.g., the London gold market).

10) To assure the revolving character of the Fund's resources, members must repurchase their own currencies from the Fund when they have an increase in their reserves or, in any case, within three to five years. Repurchases may be made in gold or in any currency of which the Fund holds less than 75 per cent of the quota.

11) A member may repurchase from the Fund for gold any part of the Fund's holdings of its currency in excess of its quota.

12) Charges for transactions (½ per cent of the drawing) and interest charges on net reserve credit extended by the Fund (i.e., holdings of a currency in excess of a member's quota) are payable in gold.

13) The Fund may require a member to sell its currency to the Fund for gold whenever this is necessary to replenish its holdings of that currency.

14) Each member is required to convert balances of its currency held by the monetary authorities of other members either in the currency of the member making the request or in gold.

These provisions of the Fund Agreement are designed to establish an international monetary system based on gold and to enable the Fund to function effectively as the center of such a system. They have three objectives. First, to establish the international gold standard by defining the parities of currencies in terms of gold and by requiring members to maintain stable exchange rates based on these parities. Second, to assure the interconvertibility of gold and currencies by letting a member sell gold to the Fund for any currencies it may need and by requiring all members to convert their currencies held by a foreign monetary authority either in gold or in that currency. Third, to maintain the liquidity of the Fund in the currencies required for its operations by the steady acquisition of gold through subscriptions, repurchases and charges and by the obligation of members to sell their currencies to the Fund for gold.

It is worth noting that in the negotiations prior to Bretton Woods there were objections to some of the gold provisions of the Fund Agreement. All countries accepted the principle that the parity of currencies should be defined in terms of gold and that changes in parity should be made, when necessary, after consultation with the Fund and with its approval. The objections were largely directed to the requirement of paying part of the subscription in gold and to the obligation of converting currencies for other monetary authorities in gold, particularly when a country could no longer draw on the Fund. The attitude of the United States was that an international gold standard required the Fund to hold gold and to accept gold, and that convertibility of currencies in gold, as well as through the Fund, was essential to provide an assured use for gold reserves in the international monetary system.

Gold in International Monetary Reserves

During the past twenty-five years, the proportionate role of gold in international monetary reserves has declined steadily. In part, this was by accident; in part, it was by design. At the end of 1938, gold constituted 93 per cent of the total reserves (gold and foreign exchange) of all countries outside the Communist bloc. At the end of 1949, gold constituted 74 per cent of total reserves (gold, foreign exchange and Fund gold tranche positions) of all countries. At the end of 1957, gold constituted 66 per cent of total reserves and at the end of 1964, only 59 per cent of total reserves. These ratios do not allow for the gold holdings of the international financial institutions—the International Monetary Fund, the Bank for International Settlements, and the European Fund or its predecessor the European Payments Union—although the omission does not affect the analysis.

The accidental cause of the rise in foreign exchange reserves relative to gold was the enormous increase of sterling and dollars in monetary reserves from 1939 to 1964. During World War II, the United Kingdom financed a large part of its military expenditures in the Far East, the Middle East, in Europe and in

Latin America by payment in sterling. These sterling balances became part of the monetary reserves of other countries. It should be noted that there has been no increase in official holdings of sterling as reserves since 1950. Just at this time, the U.S. balance of payments changed to a deficit and the deficits became particularly large from 1958 to 1964. A considerable part of these deficits was financed by the increase in the dollar reserves of other countries. Through most of this period the U.S. deficit performed the positive function of replenishing the gold and dollar reserves of other countries, particularly in continental Europe, that had had a serious deficiency of reserves.

The establishment of the International Monetary Fund in 1946 also resulted in a reduction of the gold component of the reserves of its members. In small part this came about from the holding of gold by the Fund (about 2.2 billion dollars at the end of 1964 and 1.8 billion dollars at mid-1965). Mainly it came about through the operations of the Fund which increased the reserves of its members in the form of the gold tranche (about 4.2 billion dollars at the end of 1964 and 5.3 billion dollars at mid-1965).

In recent years, there has also been a very considerable increase in reserve credit facilities. The most important of these credit facilities are the quota rights of members of the Fund. Since 1959, and including the recent adjustment, the quotas of members of the Fund have been increased by nearly 100 per cent. Beyond that, the Group of Ten, Austria, Switzerland and the Bank for International Settlements have reciprocal-currency arrangements with the United States (and to some extent with each other) under which this country can swap up to a total of 2.8 billion dollars in their currencies for U.S. dollars. This does not take account of the ad hoc credits that have been made available from time to time in a period of crisis.

Strangely, this haphazard growth of monetary reserves has not resulted in an excessive level of reserves. From 1958 to 1964, the gross reserves of all countries increased at an average annual rate of only 2.8 per cent, although the reserves of the Common

Market countries increased at an average annual rate of 13 per cent—much too rapidly for their needs. The world economy cannot depend upon U.S. deficits for the growth of monetary reserves, even if the increment were better distributed. From the point of view of the European surplus countries, the financing of the U.S. deficit in large part with dollars acquired by foreign monetary authorities removes a major incentive for the prompt correction of the U.S. balance of payments. From the point of view of the United States, the continued growth of the dollar reserves of foreign monetary authorities poses the threat of large-scale conversions into gold at a time of economic or political crisis.

The United States is determined to eliminate its payments deficit and to maintain a surplus until the outflow of gold has been brought to a halt. This necessary policy creates a serious dilemma for the world economy. With the elimination of the U.S. payments deficit, the growth of monetary reserves will depend almost entirely on that part of newly-mined gold and gold sales of the Soviet Union which is not absorbed by industrial uses and in private hoards. From 1958 to 1964, the stock of monetary gold (including the gold holdings of international financial institutions) increased by an average of 600 million dollars a year. This is equivalent to an average annual increase of 1.5 per cent in monetary gold and 1 per cent in total monetary reserves. Clearly, a growing world economy will require a larger increment of reserves than can be provided by gold alone.

Strengthening the Reserve Base

The reserve problem has many facets. First, the world cannot rely on newly-mined gold and gold sales of the Soviet Union for an adequate growth of monetary reserves. Second, it is necessary to strengthen the narrowing gold base of monetary reserves, as gold alone is now the ultimate reserve asset into which all other reserve claims must be convertible. Third, unless a new reserve asset is created, some of the largest countries will be unable to replenish their reserves except through a reduction in the reserves of other countries and a contraction of aggregate monetary reserves. Fourth, the less-developed countries are chronically short of reserves and, as they cannot afford to invest real resources in reserves, some other means must be provided to enable them to meet their reserve needs.

It is not my purpose to discuss all of these questions in this paper. We are concerned today with the one question of the appropriate role of gold in the international monetary system. We must start with the premise that gold can no longer meet the growing need of the world economy for monetary reserves. Thirty years ago, when I wrote a book entitled *Money and the Economic System*, I defined a proper balance of payments as follows (p. 503): "In gold standard countries, the balance that results in sufficient import (or export) of gold to provide for industrial and monetary needs." I question whether we can have a well-balanced pattern of international payments in the long run if all countries can add only 600 million dollars a year to their monetary reserves.

In my opinion, it is essential to modify the present international monetary system in order to assure an adequate but not excessive growth in monetary reserves and at the same time to strengthen the present structure of reserves. I start with the premise that a sound international monetary system cannot be established until the United States and the United Kingdom put their international payments in order. Furthermore, the great industrial countries must maintain a well-balanced pattern of international payments, avoiding large and prolonged deficits. I speak of a modification, not of a radical change, in the present international monetary system that has grown up in response to the needs of the world economy and under which it has functioned reasonably well. Any modification of the system must permit the continued use of gold, dollars and other foreign exchange as monetary reserves; and it must be based on the retention of the Bretton Woods system of fixed parities defined in gold. Furthermore, it should make use of the International Monetary Fund as the central monetary authority for the entire world.

There are two proposals related to gold that do not conform to these tests. The first is to raise the price of gold to 52.50 dollars an ounce, or to 70 dollars an ounce, or to some other price. This would increase the currency value of the stock of monetary gold, but it would undermine and perhaps destroy the use of dollars as monetary reserves. The increase in the currency value of gold reserves might be offset by so much liquidation of dollars that there would be little or no increase in aggregate monetary reserves. Furthermore, the gold hoarders and the gold speculators would be rewarded with a large windfall, while those who have placed their faith in dollars as reserves, to say nothing of those who hold assets denominated in their own currencies, would be penalized. The universal increase in the price of gold to enable the monetary authorities to overcome the worldwide depression of the 1930's was unavoidable. That cannot justify a rise in the price of gold in a period of worldwide boom. Nor is it clear how the monetary authorities could prevent the disruptive effects of expectations of recurrent increases in the price of gold that would be generated by such action.

The second proposal is that the United States should announce that it will sell gold at 35 dollars an ounce, but no longer buy gold at this price—at least, not from countries that have been converting their dollar reserves into gold. This proposal assumes that everything would be all right if only the European surplus countries were not insistent on gold rather than dollars in the settlement of their balance of payments. This is simply not true. Whatever justification there may have been for small U.S. deficits when the rest of the world was short of reserves, there can be no justification for the large and prolonged deficits of 1958 to 1964. Until the U.S. payments deficit is eliminated, the European surplus countries will continue to convert dollars into gold. The threat that the United States will not buy gold from them at a later date could not be enforced and is scarcely credible. The United States is committed by the Fund Agreement to maintain stable exchange rates and to buy and sell gold for this purpose. Apart from these legal obligations, would the United States really be willing to see the dollar appreciate in terms of the European currencies by refusing to accept gold from them when the U.S. balance of payments is in surplus? An appreciation of the dollar in terms of European currencies would depress the prices of U.S. agricultural products in world markets and greatly reduce U.S. exports of industrial goods. The refusal to buy gold from the European surplus countries could only disrupt the international monetary system without contributing to the solution of the U.S. payments problem.

The most practical way to provide for the orderly growth of money reserves is through the creation of a new reserve asset. This reserve asset should be fully equivalent to gold and have characteristics similar to gold. The new reserve asset should, therefore, be an ultimate reserve asset which could be used to convert other reserve claims, including dollars, as if it were gold. The new reserve asset should not be a form of reserve credit, itself requiring direct or indirect convertibility into gold. The gold base of the international monetary system is already too narrow to permit superimposing on it a new layer of reserve credit. By giving it the quality of an ultimate reserve asset, the new type of reserves could broaden and strengthen the existing gold base of the international monetary system.

The new reserve asset should not destroy the disciplinary effect of gold, although it should moderate it. The fact is that countries do respond to an outflow of gold by taking corrective measures to restore their balance of payments. It is essential to have such a disciplinary force, although multilateral surveillance by the OECD[1] countries could be very useful in improving the complementary policies necessary to attain a well-balanced pattern of international payments. At the same time, the world has become too sensitive to the outflow of gold, and as a consequence countries may not have sufficient time to put into effect appropriate corrective measures without resorting to harsh restrictions

[1] Organization for Economic Cooperation and Development.

that would deflate the national economy and the world economy. A study of the National Bureau of Economic Research[2] shows that from the peak to the low point of a cycle, the U.S. trade balance changes by about 3 per cent of total exports and imports. This would mean a reduction of the trade surplus by nearly 1.5 billion dollars, apart from movements of capital. If an expansion were to last several years, with two or three years in which the balance of payments is moving adversely for cyclical reasons, the resulting gold outflow might compel the United States to impose quite unnecessary and harmful restrictions. On the other hand, if the new reserve asset could be used with gold in the conversion of dollars, it would be possible to finance cyclical deficits (to be offset by later cyclical surpluses) without generating doubts about the adequacy of gold reserves.

Gold and the New Reserve Asset

In describing the characteristics of a new reserve asset, I have been advocating the proposal to create a reserve unit based on a collection of the leading currencies. This new reserve asset would be comprised of dollars, sterling, francs, marks and eight or ten other currencies of unquestioned strength and stability. Such a reserve unit, whose value would be guaranteed in terms of gold, could perform the functions of an ultimate reserve asset in conjunction with gold.

There are several proposals for creating a reserve unit based on a collection of leading currencies. Mr. Robert V. Roosa, the former Under Secretary of the Treasury for Monetary Affairs, has made such a proposal in his new book, *Monetary Reform for the World Economy*. The French Minister of Finance, M. Giscard d'Estaing, has been advocating such a plan for the past two years. And I proposed a composite standard of gold and reserve units

[2] Ilse Mintz, *Trade Balances During Business Cycles: U.S. and Britain since 1880*, Occasional Paper 67; New York: National Bureau of Economic Research, 1959.

to the U.S. Treasury consultants some time ago. I shall not argue the relative merits of these proposals which basically belong to the same family of plans. Instead, I am going to discuss the role they would assign to gold in the international monetary system.

One basic difference is in the relative proportions of the various currencies that would comprise the reserve unit. The French plan would base the composition of the reserve unit, and its allocation among participating countries, on their gold holdings. This seems to me to miss the essential point that the proportion of the different currencies in the reserve unit should bear some logical relation to their role in world trade and payments. I cannot see how it is possible to create a reserve unit which has a larger component of Swiss francs than of sterling or of Belgian francs than of yen. The Roosa plan claims to base the composition of the reserve unit on the significance of the various currencies in the creation of reserves, but the concrete illustration he uses seems to me somewhat biased. My own proposal is to determine the composition of the reserve unit, and its allocation among participating countries, on the basis of their quotas in the Fund and their commitments under the General Arrangements to Borrow. This is the measure of the obligation each country has assumed to provide reserve credit through the Fund. It would be only fair to allow any country to raise its quota in the Fund and its commitment under the General Arrangements to Borrow if either is too small at present.

In none of the plans is the reserve asset directly convertible into gold although in all of them there is or may be indirect convertibility into gold. In the Roosa plan, the reserve unit is convertible into the currency of any contributing country obligated to accept additional reserve units and each currency is to be made convertible into gold. In the French plan, a country holding excess reserve units (defined by the French as more than the average ratio of total reserve units to total gold reserves of participating countries) could require their conversion into gold by countries having a deficiency of reserve units. In my plan, a country holding excess reserve units (defined as more than one-half as much as its gold reserves) would be free to sell the reserve units for gold, for dollars or other currencies, or to have them redeemed into their constituent currencies.

There is an essential difference between the Roosa plan and the other two plans in the status given to the reserve unit to act with gold as an ultimate reserve asset. The reserve unit in the Roosa plan does not have unlimited acceptability within the group of contributing countries because it is not an ultimate reserve asset with legal tender quality. The reserve unit in the French plan and in my plan is an ultimate reserve asset and does have unlimited acceptability. This quality is imparted to the reserve unit by linking it with gold. As gold can be used without limit in the conversion of currencies, so reserve units can be used along with gold in whatever proportion the plan provides. Thus, the French plan and my plan are technically a composite standard of gold and reserve units. For this reason, the gradual addition of reserve units to the holdings of the monetary authorities of the participating countries will broaden the gold base on which the system of international monetary reserves is constructed.

Another major difference in the three plans is the role assigned to gold in international settlements. In the Roosa plan, the contributing countries can settle small deficits by the transfer of reserve units without any use of gold. On the other hand, when the surplus countries hold the limit of what they are obligated to accept in reserve units, and there must be some limit in the Roosa plan, any further settlements with these countries must be 100 per cent in gold. In my opinion, the Roosa plan gives us the worst features of the disciplinary and sensitivity aspects of gold. With a small deficit, there need be no gold settlements so that even the signaling effect of a gold outflow is lost. On the other hand, with a large deficit, there must be 100 per cent gold settlements, so that the present sensitivity of the world economy to gold movements is retained. The help that comes from moderating the outflow of gold is very great when there is least need for it—that is, with small deficits. But there is no help in moderating the gold outflow when there is great need for it, at a time of large deficits.

The French plan requires proportionate settlement in gold and reserve units. It retains the signaling effect of a gold outflow, but it exaggerates the sensitivity of the world economy to gold movements. That is because in the French plan, settlements are in the ratio of total gold reserves to total reserve units held by participating countries. It is generally agreed that in order to avoid an undue expansion of aggregate reserves, the creation of reserve units would have to be at a moderate rate—say, 1 billion dollars a year. This would mean that settlements would start with a ratio of 97 per cent gold and 3 per cent reserve units and decline gradually thereafter until in the fifth year (assuming an annual increase of 500 million dollars in the gold reserves of participating countries) the ratio would be 88 per cent in gold and 12 per cent in reserve units. Even in the tenth year, settlements under the French plan would be 80 per cent in gold and 20 per cent in reserve units. This does not seem to me to moderate in any way, at least for many years, the excessive sensitivity of the world economy to gold movements.

My own proposal is to establish immediately a ratio of 2 dollars in gold and 1 dollar in reserve units for all settlements —that is, for the conversion of the currencies of the participating countries among their monetary authorities. In all other gold transactions—in the purchase of newly-mined gold, in the sale of industrial gold, and in the purchase or sale of gold from or to the monetary authorities of nonparticipating countries and international financial institutions—the price of gold in national currencies would be the equivalent of 35 dollars at once. The two to one ratio in settlements would retain the disciplinary role of gold but would moderate the sensitivity of the world economy to gold movements. Incidentally, under the French plan and under my plan gold transactions with nonparticipating countries would be for joint account, much as is now done through the gold pool on purchases and sales in the London gold market.

There is one aspect of the French plan for a declining ratio of gold settlements that needs to be brought out. If a country had a deficit in the first year of the plan and settled in a very high ratio of gold to reserve units, it would be necessary thereafter to make annual transfers of gold for reserve units to that country even if it had no surplus or deficit thereafter. In order to achieve the same ratio of gold and reserve units in the reserves of each participating country, gold would have to be transferred to any country that previously made larger gold settlements whenever new reserve units are created and the ratio of gold to reserve units is decreased. It seems far more practical to avoid these subsequent gains and losses of gold, which have no purpose except to equalize the ratio of gold to reserve units for all participating countries, by establishing *ad initio* a fixed ratio of gold to reserve units, such as 2 dollars in gold and 1 dollar in reserve units, in all settlements among participating countries.

The French plan differs from those proposed by Mr. Roosa and by me with respect to the role of reserve assets other than gold—specifically, the dollar. Mr. Roosa and I would give countries complete freedom to hold reserves either in gold or dollars, as they prefer. In the French plan, at least in some versions, the holding of dollar reserves by the participating countries would be sharply restricted. Apart from the undesirability of limiting the right of any country to hold reserves in whatever form is suited to its economy, an imposed reduction in the holding of dollars would contract the aggregate of reserves. While the creation of reserve units in the future would add to reserves about the same amount that has in recent years come from the U.S. payments deficit, any reduction in present dollar reserves would offset a part, and perhaps a large part, of the increase of reserves in the form of reserve units. The right of countries to decide for themselves how much of their reserves to hold in dollars does not imply a continuation of U.S. payments deficits. Any increase in the holding of dollars as reserves would be matched by an increase in U.S. holdings of gold and reserve units. The increase in net reserves would still be equal to the amount of gold going into monetary reserves plus the creation of new reserve units.

The suggestion has been made that a composite standard of gold and reserve units could be established more simply by having the participating countries deposit 2 dollars of gold and 1 dollar of their own currencies in the Reserve Unit Account in return for an equal amount of reserve units. Thereafter, the reserve units would be full settlement in any conversion of currencies by the monetary authorities of the participating countries. From an economic point of view, such a system would not be essentially different from one in which conversions are made in gold and in reserve units in the same ratio. Perhaps something intangible would be lost in substituting a change in the holding of reserve units for changes in gold reserves. There are other objections to such a reserve certificate system of a more practical kind. The deposit of gold to back the reserve certificates would reduce U.S. gold reserves so that to nonparticipating countries it would seem as if the United States had less gold with which to maintain convertibility of their dollar reserves. Furthermore, if participating countries that do not hold large gold reserves—say, Canada, Japan or Sweden—had to deposit gold as well as their own currencies in order to secure reserve units, they would have to convert dollars into gold for this purpose—a problem that has already occurred twice in connection with increases in Fund quotas.

I shall summarize what I believe to be the appropriate role of gold in a new international monetary system. First, gold should remain the standard in which the parities of all currencies are fixed and countries should continue to keep exchange rates within a prescribed range above and below such parities. Second, gold should continue to be the principal form of reserves but not the only ultimate reserve asset. Third, the disciplinary role of gold should be retained, but the sensitivity of the world economy to large gold movements should be moderated. Fourth, a new reserve unit should be created based on the leading currencies and with a value guaranteed against depreciation in terms of gold. Fifth, each country should be required to convert its currency for the monetary authorities of other participating countries in a fixed ratio of gold and reserve units, say 2 dollars in gold and 1 dollar in reserve units. This ratio seems to me to provide the proper disciplinary effect of gold settlements while moderating the present excessive sensitivity of the world economy to large movements of gold.

CHAIRMAN HOADLEY: It has been my observation over the years that crises create the conditions for change. We have been discussing varying interpretations and degrees of crises. I think it is extremely useful that we can participate in a meeting such as this in order to set forth our deepest insights and express our most penetrating thoughts on a very complex problem of far-reaching significance to the world.

In my view it is essential that we define the problem as specifically as possible and consider carefully the degree of seriousness which we feel we must attach to it. Next, we must explore all possible alternative solutions, and make our recommendations for action. But as a realist, I submit that it is also important that we continually forecast what we think actually will happen, especially if no policy or procedural changes are made. Mr. Gainsbrugh, I am sure, will agree with me that we should not only try to foresee what will happen but try to see the problem sufficiently in advance to do something about it. Winning the passive forecasting numbers games is no longer a satisfying experience, certainly if we don't like the resultant numbers we have forecast.

Each one of us here no doubt has been doing some forecasting as to the future role of gold and the need for greater international liquidity. If we had not, I suspect we would not be here. Each forecast very likely includes some critical developments and challenges on the horizon. Obviously there is a great deal of difference in our interpretations as to just what these are and what they mean. Our individual thinking reflects our experiences as well as our research and analysis.

Nevertheless, I submit that my thesis still holds, namely, that crisis creates the conditions for change. When we find an actual crisis or widespread forecasts of a crisis, action almost certainly will be forthcoming promptly. But action is not likely to be well conceived in a crisis—so it is essential to prepare as much as possible either to avoid the crisis or take proper action to minimize its effects. Therefore, it is vital that we now have the benefit of extensive research, pursue rigorous analysis, weigh alternative programs, and try to crystallize thinking toward action recommendations. But the big questions still remain: Can we agree on a course of action? And when should action be taken?

There are those who have strong feelings that the time to act is now. Something must be done! Many others here believe with Mr. Bernstein that action is inevitable—but not necessarily at the moment.

I gather that there is no consensus yet that any real crisis exists or is imminent. Clearly there is some general feeling of uncertainty about the adequacy of international liquidity and that there is a problem concerning the adequacy of gold as a worldwide reserve unit which must be solved in due course. As Milton Gilbert, among others, has pointed out, it is important to distinguish between the domestic balance-of-payment adjustment problem and the need to provide supplements to existing international monetary reserves. These are interrelated but still separate problems. There is no easy solution to either, and the former cannot be solved indefinitely by the latter or vice versa.

Accordingly, I come back to the question—where is the crisis? Is it a U.S. domestic balance-of-payment crisis that is the real cause for concern, as a good many of our friends abroad in particular seem to believe? There seems to be a good deal of general confidence within this country that we are not facing a crisis in the United States at the moment and also that such a crisis is not imminent. No one, however, should minimize the U.S. balance-of-payments adjustment problem. If we may dare to generalize, it seems as though many people in the United States are most fearful about potential international financial developments beyond our shores, while those abroad are most fearful about impending American financial problems. So, all the more reason for us to meet together and at least to try to agree upon the facts and the dimensions of the problems now attracting worldwide interest.

Mr. Bernstein has focused attention on these main issues and given us an excellent paper. I hope that in his further remarks he will tell us a little more why he feels we can not get along with the monetary machinery which we now have. I am not suggesting that we should continue the status quo. He started, however, with the assumption that we can not get along with present monetary reserve mechanisms and defended this point to a degree. I think this is still an area for research and study. In addition, there are many questions regarding the details of some new reserve unit. But, I would ask what are the conditions —indeed, the crisis—which will bring about the adoption of a new reserve unit?

MR. HABERLER: The discussion indicates that the audience consists of two groups, those who defend the present international payments system and those who find it very bad and about to collapse. I agree with some arguments on both sides, but by the same token disagree with much of what was said. You cannot fully agree with people who disagree among themselves on many things. Let me stress the disagreements.

My friend Mr. Cortney believes that the present system is terrible, that it is just about to collapse and that the events of the 1930's will repeat themselves. Professor Triffin has repeatedly expressed the same gloomy view, although his reasoning and his policy recommendations are very different.

I must confess I cannot share these feelings of gloom and doom and I would plead for a little more realism and sense of proportion. If we look at the world economy as it has developed in the postwar period, we must reach the conclusion that it has done very well, especially—but not only—the industrial countries. Production, employment and international trade have grown by leaps and bounds as rarely before and we must assume that

the present international monetary system has contributed to this
excellent record. The situation is not nearly as bad as the extreme
critics of the present system would make us believe.

But this does not mean that everything is perfect and that
the present system does not need any reforms. Some reforms are
needed, but I believe that the dangers we are facing are not the
ones which the extreme critics have in mind. The system is not
about to collapse and I am not much concerned about the alleged
immediate inadequacy of international liquid reserves. At any
rate, I have the utmost confidence in the managers of the present
system of which we see several around the table—Mr. Emminger,
Secretary Dillon, Mr. Young and the ex-manager Mr. Bernstein.
If and when international liquidity really becomes scarce, they
will know how to provide additional liquidity and to prevent the
system from collapsing.

The real danger is, I believe, different from the one painted
on the wall, scarcity of liquidity and deflation. It is rather that
the reforms will supply too much liquidity and give rise to renewed inflation which will then intensify the real danger.

The real danger is a progressive drift towards controls. This
is already clearly noticeable. Whenever a country gets into
trouble, the first reaction is to impose controls on trade and capital, voluntary controls, involuntary controls. Our "voluntary"
controls on capital exports are voluntary only in name. In reality
they simply constitute exchange control on capital movements.
Now, if I had the choice between full-fledged exchange control
and the "voluntary" control on capital exports, I certainly prefer
the latter. But I do not think that the situation is really so bad
that we are confronted with that choice.

But how can we avoid the drift towards controls? I am afraid
I cannot agree with my friends here at the table who recommend
a doubling of the price of gold and reintroduction of the gold
standard. A sharp increase of the price of gold would have been
a very constructive measure when the world was engulfed by
deflation in the early 1930's. Today, in "the age of inflation" an

inflationary move like the doubling of the price of gold would be entirely out of place.

What should we then do to halt the drift towards controls? The answer is to improve the adjustment mechanism. We should not talk so much about liquidity. True, it is an important matter, but I am confident that our money managers will take care of that problem. More important and much more difficult is the adjustment mechanism. There is on the one hand the "internal adjustment"—working through domestic monetary, fiscal, wage policies—but I shall not discuss this further. There is on the other hand the external side of the adjustment. Here I would plead for a little more flexibility of exchange rates. I know it is a delicate subject and those of you who are close to the actual decision making cannot even discuss it. Still I think a modest step in this direction would be very desirable. I don't think of any radical proposal—introduction of complete exchange flexibility. I think of a widening of the gold points, the so-called "band proposal" and in addition, perhaps, of making the widened band a slowly shiftable one. I hope there will be a chance later on to discuss these reforms a little more.

MR. DESPRES: I would like both to say something about the background of the present crisis and to express some views about the possible outcome. In the first place, the whole period from 1950 to date has been one in which financial transfer from the United States has exceeded real transfer. Except in the time of the Suez crisis, our outflow of government aid and private capital exceeded the surplus on current account.

It is useful in thinking about this to divide this whole period into three sub-periods. The first was the period from 1950 to 1958, during which there was a quite pervasive, although mistaken, belief in chronic dollar shortage. The demand for dollars relative to gold was strongly in favor of the dollar, even though there was a small gold outflow from the United States.

The second period, from 1959 to 1964, was a period which can be described as one of contained crisis. The French financial stabilization, the restoration of convertibility at the end of 1958 dramatized the recovery that had taken place in Western Europe and very greatly increased the United States' willingness to lend and invest in that part of the world. At the same time the European desire to keep accumulating dollars was reduced. Now, this was a period of contained crisis because there was a general consensus among the central banks and governments, despite important disagreements about the international monetary system and in particular about the role which foreign exchange should play in monetary reserves, that the crisis should not be allowed to escalate. As a result, in addition to the Roosa bonds, the swap credits, etc., there was also more importantly a further accumulation of dollar reserves by European central banks, not because they wanted to hold additional dollars, but as an act of cooperation to contain the crisis.

The past year I think can be described as a period of either uncontained, or less-contained, crisis and, as Mr. Gilbert pointed out, the statement by President de Gaulle was a kind of turning point in this respect.

As to the future, there are a few things that I will stick my neck out to assert. First, no matter what happens, whether the existing less-contained crisis is brought under control or results in breakdown, the pure gold standard of the textbooks I feel quite certain will not be restored. An international monetary system linked to gold can be preserved only if in practice gold is not strongly preferred to credit money. The shift in preferences away from currency toward gold is in the last analysis a threat to the role of gold in the international monetary system. The future monetary system will be based on credit money, and the only question is whether gold will have a limited, symbolic role or none at all.

The second categorical forecast I'd like to make is that the general stability of exchange rates among the major currencies is likely to be preserved in any event. The major countries do not want an appreciation or depreciation of their currency.

There is one very simple way out of the present crisis, which is unlikely to be adopted, and a more difficult way out, which is in process of being adopted.

Mr. Cortney objected to the statement that the dollar is as good as gold. I object to that statement, too. In a fundamental sense in today's world the dollar is much better than gold. It is only the complete confidence that everybody has that the United States will stand ready to buy gold in unlimited amounts which makes gold a desirable and attractive asset today.

I think there are various ways of creating uncertainty in people's minds about this unlimited convertibility of dollars into gold, and in that way shifting asset preferences away from gold to dollars. I don't think this simple and direct means of ending the crisis is going to be tried. Instead the method which we are applying will be more difficult and harmful to the world economy. It has three parts:

1) The first step is to check the conversion of foreign official balances into gold. Perhaps an effort will be made to reach some agreement on the funding of those balances. Or, if they are to be converted into gold, to complete the conversion quickly so that the liquidation of the overhang either by funding or by conversion to gold is behind us.

2) The second step, barring a deterioration in the European economic situation, is that the capital outflow control will have to be permanent if the so-called deficit is to be eliminated. If one adopts the mistaken approach that the United States balance of payments must be brought into balance and held in balance, this means that measures in addition to higher interest rates have to be applied. Capital outflow must be controlled permanently and the problem becomes how to consolidate the present voluntary controls into permanent controls.

3) The least urgent task of all is to devise some kind of new reserve asset—"paper gold." The effects of permanent controls of capital outflow from the United States will be highly unfortunate for the world economy—not so much for the United States economy—but for the rest of the free world. I therefore regret that the idea of limiting United States' future willingness to buy

gold has not been seriously considered and that the United States is following a course which can only be harmful to the world economy and to its own foreign policy aims.

MR. TRIFFIN: Professor Haberler has performed a rare feat of acrobatics. It seems to me that he has succeeded to both agree and disagree, not only with the other speakers, but also with himself. He tells us that the present system is not so bad, but confesses at the same time his concern about its drift toward exchange controls. I think this drift is particularly alarming when it concerns the two currencies on which the whole present system of the gold-exchange standard rests. But this drift is not new.

I would like to point out that the gold-exchange standard which was established after World War I has been in existence now for about fifty years, but has functioned satisfactorily for only five years out of these fifty. After World War I, convertibility was not fully restored until about 1928. It then lasted three years, until 1931, and was followed by twenty-seven years of currency inconvertibility. After World War II convertibility was not restored until December, 1958. Less than two years later the flare up of gold prices in October, 1960, ushered in a new period of recurring dollar and sterling crises which are still plaguing us today. A formal collapse à la 1931 has been avoided so far, but at the cost of a radical and ominous transformation of the basic rules of the gold-exchange standard. Foreign central banks no longer retain dollar and sterling claims by choice, with full rights to convert them into gold whenever they please. Continuous negotiations (à la Roosa) are necessary to restrain such conversions and have subordinated central bank decisions to political considerations and bargaining which President de Gaulle brought to light in his speech of February last. Secondly, the very currencies which are at the center of the system—the dollar and the pound—are now protecting their formal convertibility through growing restrictions on the freedom of exchange transactions: on capital in both countries, and even on current account in England.

The events of the last six months have clearly demonstrated

the long-run unviability and the short-run vulnerability of a reserve system whose "satisfactory" functioning rests on large and persistent deficits of the two reserve currency countries, and on the continuing willingness of foreign central banks to finance a large portion of such deficits through their free accumulation of unguaranteed dollar and sterling IOU's as monetary reserves. The latter of these two prerequisites seemed to be vanishing in the first six months of this year. Calculated at an annual rate, central banks liquidated over these six months more than 4 billion dollars of their foreign exchange holdings instead of accumulating them at a rate of 600 million dollars a year, as in the decade of the 1950's, or of 1.5 billion dollars a year as in the five years 1960–1964 (see table, page 82).

I agree, therefore, with Professor Haberler that this system which he deems "not so bad" is in urgent need of a fundamental overhaul, and I am glad that the IMF and the Group of Ten unanimously agree on this point with both of us.

At the same time, I think we should put first things first, and try to avoid the collapse of world reserves which threatens us right now, before worrying too much about ways and means of providing for an adequate growth of world reserves in the future. The second question is less urgent and far more difficult to solve than the first. It raises a host of political and emotional reactions about national sovereignty, traditional attachment to gold, etc., which are highly divisive still and unlikely to be resolved in the very near future. A consensus of the first problem would be far easier to reach and seemed to emerge indeed at the last IMF meeting (see my paper: "La Banquise a enfin craqué!" published in Rome by *L'Espresso*, October 24, 1965).

Let me touch only very briefly on two other points. The mergers of national sovereignty which my long-term proposals —and indeed those of the IMF itself—for increasing world reserves through concerted international agreement are far less extensive and objectionable than the present blind and total surrenders of sovereignty to the hazards of gold production, gold sales by the Russians, gold purchases by the speculators, and

The International Reserve System: 1949–June 1965
(in billions of U.S. dollars)

Annual Rates of Change of Monetary Reserves	Ten yrs. 1950–59	Five yrs. 1960–64	First six months 1965
I. World Monetary Gold, from:	0.5	0.6	−0.1
A. USSR Sales	0.1	0.3	—
B. Western Sources, of which	0.4	0.2	−0.1
Hoarding and Speculation (−)	(−0.3)	(−0.8)	(−1.2)
II. IMF and BIS (Net)	0.1	0.2	3.3
III. Foreign Exchange:	0.6	1.5	−4.3
Dollars	0.7	1.0	−1.9
Sterling	−0.1	0.2	−1.1
Other and Discrepancies	—	0.2	−1.2
Total: Changes in Gross Reserves	1.2	2.3	−1.1
I. Reserve Centers (Net)	−1.0	−2.5	−0.6
A. United States	−1.2	−2.1	0.1
B. United Kingdom	0.2	−0.4	−0.7
II. Other Countries (Gross)	1.6	3.3	−0.2
III. Liabilities of Reserve Centers	0.7	1.4	−0.2

Reserve Stocks at the End of	1949	1959	1964	June, 1965
I. Reserve Centers (Net)	17.4	7.3	−5.0	−5.3
II. Other Countries (Gross)	17.7	33.3	49.9	49.8
III. Liabilities of Reserve Centers	10.4	17.0	23.9	23.8
Total = Gross Reserves	45.5	57.6	68.9	68.4

wide fluctuations in U.S. and U.K. balance-of-payments deficits. They are also far less revolutionary than Mr. Bernstein's proposals for "automatic" lending among the countries of the Group of Ten, irrespective of the policies followed by the borrowers.

As for the alternative solution of "flexible rates" so dear to Professor Haberler and most of my academic colleagues, I share the opposite view of the officials, for reasons which I have abundantly expressed elsewhere (see, for instance, my Princeton study on *The Evolution of the International Monetary System*, pp. 38–40). In brief, such a system would, in an open economy, sanction every expansionist ("inflationary") mishap or mistake with increases in foreign exchange rates, import prices, cost-of-living and wages, while opposite ("deflationary") mishaps and mistakes would be most unlikely, in this world of ours, to lead to any wage reductions. Flexible rates would be a one-way road to currency depreciation, which would be accelerated by the reactions of speculators to the expectations inevitably and correctly generated by the adoption of such a system. This is a subject that would obviously require far lengthier developments, but I am sure we shall have occasion to come back to it later in our debates. Let me merely put one more question to the proponents of flexible rates: Who would manage the dollar-sterling rate? The Federal Reserve or the Bank of England?

MR. MELTZER: I am not convinced that the central bank managers will fail to act in time of crisis. They have shown themselves willing, eager and diligent in looking for solutions to the problem of liquidity. What they have been slow and reluctant to recognize is the problem of the adjustment mechanism. It is widely believed, and Mr. Triffin just said so, that exchange flexibility is a completely unworkable system.

While we have cited the history of various world monetary standards, we have ignored a portion of that history in these discussions. There are two periods in which the dollar was permitted to float. In the 1870's, a period of great expansion in the United States economy, our problem was not one of economic expansion accompanied by inflation, it was a problem of economic expansion accompanied by deflation. Prices were falling during most of that period. In 1933–1934, when the world monetary system was in a state of almost total collapse, the United States allowed the dollar to float. No serious flight from the dollar occurred during that period. I find this evidence, to put it mildly, more reassuring than the constant repetition of the statement that a system of floating exchange rates would lead to the devaluation of the dollar or to substantial inflation.

We should remind ourselves periodically of the warnings in the late 1940's about the consequences of removing a peg from a fixed rate on government securities. Most of these fears were repeated frequently and widely believed. They turned out to be groundless.

I do not wish to argue here for a system of completely fluctuating rates. I would like to suggest that we try to design an adjustment mechanism under which each minor change in balance-of-payments position can be prevented from creating a major or minor crisis, or the appearance of one, in the world monetary system. If proposals to solve the long-run liquidity problems provide more flexibility in the adjustment mechanism, the amount of liquidity required to settle imbalances will be smaller.

The problem I think we should be discussing is not the question of providing more liquidity but of providing a better mechanism for exchange rate adjustments that will reduce the demand for liquidity.

MR. HEILPERIN: The Chairman said in his statement that crises create conditions of change. May I suggest the opposite of this: that crisis makes change inevitable because there are some changes in the crisis. It may not necessarily create the conditions for full change but some change. I would say that the crisis of the 1930's offers us a very good example. We are trying to brush the present crisis under the carpet. I am quite sure we have not been successful. From here on starts the search for solution.

Mr. Bernstein would like to see more paper gold than gold gold. I think his paper in general was extremely interesting and that is what everybody expects from him, but I have considerable doubt as to the paper gold being accepted in the same terms of confidence as gold gold.

CHAIRMAN HOADLEY: I would agree with much that you have just said. My point is principally that now is the time to intensify our research leading to some realistic solutions to the gold and liquidity problems discussed by Mr. Bernstein and many others among us. While we may disagree as to the existence or imminence of a crisis, we must agree that a significant challenge lies before us. The world must not drift into serious economic distress because of monetary deficiencies. Study and negotiation now should go a long way toward easing the practical problems ahead. It is my earnest hope that the threat of an eventual crisis itself will lead to a soundly conceived and enduring program of positive action to avoid any actual crisis. For, if an acute crisis does materialize, we're certain to get a crash program of action which we may not individually like or approve.

MR. HARWOOD: Mr. Bernstein referred to the gold standard's coming back to the fashion of the 1920's. We all know that the exchange standard was used then and that that was what failed so conspicuously. We have now created a much greater counterpart of the same system, which also is failing conspicuously.

He also referred to the universal increase in the price of gold to enable monetary authorities to overcome the worldwide depression. Five years after the devaluation of 1934 we still had the depression. I don't think they overcame it by devaluing the dollar.

And he referred to this reserve asset that should be fully equivalent to gold and have the characteristics similar to gold. I am going to predict when he or his successors in future generations find that asset, it will be gold.

MR. BERNSTEIN: I have little to add to what I said because anything reasonable my critics have said I have long ago accepted. What they have said that is not reasonable you would hardly want me to yield to at this moment. Maybe this summary will help.

I do not think there will be a crisis. There won't be a crisis because the present international monetary system has great flexibility and the will to cooperate is overwhelmingly great. The present system has worked well and I would not eliminate a single major feature from it. I do believe, though, that a further evolution of this system will be necessary and that we should

prepare for that. The next step in this evolution will be the creation of a new reserve unit that has the characteristics of gold as
an ultimate reserve asset. I don't care whether you call this paper
gold, as I have, or if you wish to say you are going to wrap the
gold in a paper wrapper. The point I want to make is that the
two must go together.

There is plenty of time to think through and talk through the
form of any new reserve unit and how it should be fitted into
the present reserve system based on gold, dollars and other foreign exchange as well as the International Monetary Fund.

But we should start on this process of thinking and talking
now and continue to plan so that we can deal with any difficulties that may arise even though I do not foresee any critical situation.

Chapter IV

Gold as the Ultimate Medium for International Payments

Chairman: SOLOMON FABRICANT
Position Paper: WILLIAM BUSSCHAU

CHAIRMAN FABRICANT: As we resume our discussion, I think it will be worth reminding ourselves, and then keeping in mind, the fundamental problem and dangers that we are confronted with, the problem of what to do and the dangers if these things we need to do are not done, or not done properly, or not done in time. I am very glad that Mr. Cortney, for example, emphasized the need not only for sound and better international economic policy, but also for sound and better domestic economic policy. These things go together. As for the dangers, the risk is not really of the 1930's type, in which we had a collapse in the volume of production and employment and a deflation of prices. Jules Backman was well warranted in emphasizing that. The dangers on the domestic front are rather those of inflation, and that in exercising its responsibility to maintain reasonably high employment, government will expand its role in economic life beyond what it should be—for example, drift toward controls of the sort that Gottfried Haberler referred to. On the international front, the danger is that the international division of labor, from

which the whole world benefits economically and culturally, will
be lessened.

The ultimate danger, if we and others fail to maintain a sound
domestic economic system here and in other countries—and a
sound international system as well—is political. Failure would
mean victory for socialism and communism throughout the world.

After this reminder, let me turn to our discussion leader. It is
not easy to put a label on William Busschau. He is listed, of
course, as Chairman of Goldfields of South Africa, Inc., which
we all know means more than just sitting back and letting a
president do the hard work. He is the active manager of the
company. Because of his wide business interests, he is also a
director in other enterprises. But his interests and competence
extend outside of business. He is also a member of the board of
the South African Central Bank. He is a trained economist—indeed, a former student of Sir Roy Harrod—with a Ph.D. in Economics, and he is even an Honorary Professor Emeritus. It is very
difficult to put a label on him, but let me put a label on him
anyway. He is a good citizen and a responsible citizen of South
Africa and of the world.

MR. BUSSCHAU: I would like to be called a good citizen of
the world, and I will try and get this discussion back to our
mutual international problems. I know some of you are good
internationalists, and that you have been arguing your differences
and looking through your national windows at the world, and I
want to look at the world as a whole.

When I started writing seventeen years ago about the subject
of this conference and then used the terms "international liquidity" and "international banking liquidity," I defined them carefully as relating to the ratio of gold to money supply. This
appeared to me to be a legitimate definition since it gave the
relationship of universal money, gold, to the "money supply"—
in other words, this related the units which were capable of
such conversion to the object of the conversion. On such a
definition the international monetary system's liquidity could,
if all the national currencies were expressed in one common

currency, be measured by the ratio of gold to aggregate "money supply," both magnitudes expressed in the same currency at different dates.

Other writers and the financial press came to use this definition and the reduced accessibility of gold to national currencies and the greatly reduced "international liquidity" of the international system came to be recognised by many competent observers.

In relation to the international system it should be obvious that the national holdings of each other's currencies would in the summation of the system's liquidity (in the defined sense) have to be excluded, because as Patchouli knew when he invented double-entry bookkeeping and any student of his system knows today what is a debt payable in one person's books is a debt receivable in another person's. It is not necessary to develop this idea as events have clearly shown that the holding of other's paper currencies in one's national reserve can be a source of danger if there is a general demand for payment in universal money, i.e., gold. Gold in a national reserve is an unencumbered asset, while a holding of another currency is simply an unrequited debt. Gold cannot depreciate in terms of itself, but modern currencies have shown a regrettable tendency to do so.

In the summation of the international system the intercountry exchange holdings cancel out as the system as a whole cannot be either debtor or creditor to itself, and gold alone remains as the reserve of money.

Defining International Liquidity

What happened next was that those opposed to our point of view sought to prove that there was no shortage of international liquidity. This was done by using a new definition which made liquidity a quantitative concept and not a relationship. Thus an IMF staff report defined international reserves as "a country's holdings of gold, dollars, sterling and other foreign-exchange assets on a gross basis, i.e., without taking account of short-term assets that might be considered to be offsetting." In other words, each country's reserve would be equal to its international money, gold, plus its debts receivable on international account, but ignoring its debts payable. This might be a formula appealing to a spendthrift undergraduate, but not one likely to be used by a prudent businessman. Since then the opposition's definition has been expanded following the Roosa operations to become equal to: Gold + Debts Receivable + Overdraft Facilities on international account (again ignoring debts payable). In this sense let us accept that there is no lack, but rather an excess, of "liquidity," but it is quite indisputable that in our sense of accessibility of paper money to gold the world's system has shown an alarming diminution in international liquidity.

According to our ideas the increase in the amount of foreign currencies held in so-called "monetary reserves" has staved off a collapse, but not avoided it, and each further round of borrowing (by "swap arrangements," multicountry agreements to borrow or increases in IMF quotas) simply increases the size of possible balance-of-payments deficits and makes no difference to the basic liquidity of the system as a whole.

In this context the various plans to "create" reserves are also expedients to avoid final reckoning without solution to the problem. In so far as the "units" created contain national currencies they simply in the hands of others represent debts payable by the countries providing the currencies underlying the units. This means that, as with present provision of facilities by the IMF, the bookkeeping is complicated, but at any given moment a certain number of countries would show an aggregate of debts payable which is equal to the aggregate of debts receivable by certain other countries. In this manner, no doubt in the present mood of the money-planners, the improvident will continue to borrow cheaply from the provident. Against this background, I believe it will be useful to attempt to bring out the basic difference between the Cortney and the Bernstein theses.

Now Mr. Bernstein has admitted, "The present international

monetary system is based on the undertaking of the members of the International Monetary Fund to establish fixed parities for their currencies in terms of gold and to maintain the foreign exchange value of their currencies within 1 per cent of the agreed parities. This system is a form of the gold standard. It differs from the classical gold standard, however, in the relative importance attached to fixed parities, and to other objectives of economic policy."

Let us accept this. The IMF system is a kind of gold standard whose aim is to make currencies freely convertible into each other *and into gold*—into gold at any rate in official intercountry transactions. When I first argued with Mr. Bernstein on these matters, back in 1950, he would not have it that the United States could in the foreseeable future not be able to cover its dollars with gold without limit in amount or time.

Now that this is no longer so, he apparently believes that the deficiency in the IMF system's aggregate gold holdings (at the current parities) to allow free conversion into gold can be met by the "creation of reserves" through intercountry borrowing and lending.

Here I believe lies the real difference of opinion between Mr. Cortney and Mr. Bernstein. Mr. Cortney, it appears, does not believe that foreign debts can, in relation to the monetary system as a whole, properly be regarded as "reserves," as do Mr. Bernstein and other monetary planners.

The growth of foreign exchange holdings as "supplement" to reserves, whether they are direct single-country holdings or composite Bernstein-Roosa- or Triffin units, makes no change to the over-all liquidity of the system (in the sense of the gold-to-money-supply ratio). The growth of foreign exchange holdings as a "supplement" to gold reserves is in fact evidence of the general illiquidity and not a cure for it.

While foreign exchange holdings can be regarded as "supplement" to a single country's national reserve this is so only if there is no doubt that the currency can be turned into gold—as John Law explained, "Confidence is nothing but the certainty of being paid." Today, certainly, holders of sterling and U.S. dollars can legitimately feel diffident about the chances of being paid in gold and there is as yet no substitute. Indeed, some United States' spokesmen have implied that because the United States cannot pay, their debtors should not demand payment.

Changing the Price of Gold

Obviously a large increase in the gold price in a uniform revaluation of gold would immediately remove the present difficulties in making international payments in gold, since to meet a given debt in the national currency only half the previous amount of gold would be necessary to repay the foreigner. All countries would, as it were, compromise with their creditors in terms of gold, but for the future they should then be able to make payment in gold, instead of avoiding payment as many now do. It is quite clear that at present the United Kingdom and the United States cannot meet *in gold* the equivalent of 27 billion dollars that they owe to others, and this hard fact is not obscured by the euphemistic talk regarding their "burdens" of providing reserve currencies—the fact is that they have borrowed value which they cannot repay. In such circumstances it is sensible business practice to compromise with one's creditors to allow trade to flow freely in the future.

The belief that in some magical way new reserves for the system as a whole can be created by an expansion of internation debts is a futile one. In the system taken as a whole the reserves consist of the commodity money, gold. Proper money is a material thing, which one wants to hold when one does not wish to buy, nor to invest, nor to increase one's holding of debts.

In the past the United States' authorities have refused to consider the gold revaluation proposition on its merits, and have usually simply condemned it without reasoned argument on the ground that the magic of 35 dollars per ounce was an element of stability. Perhaps hope is breaking through.

Mr. Martin of the Federal Reserve in his famous speech of June 1, 1965, did present some reasoned argument. After showing many points of similarity between the position in the early 1930's and now, he accuses advocates of a higher gold price of confused thinking without supporting proof. He then gives his positive objections, which I quote from the report in *U.S. News and World Report*.[1]

True, most advocates of an increase in the price of gold today would prefer action by some international agency or conference to unilateral action of individual countries. But no international agency or conference could prevent gold hoarders from getting windfall profits; could prevent those who hold a devalued currency from suffering corresponding losses; could prevent central banks from feeling defrauded if they had trusted in the repeated declarations of the President of the United States and of the spokesmen of the U.S. monetary authorities and kept their reserves in dollars rather than in gold.

To this day, the French, Belgian, and Netherlands central banks have not forgotten that the 1931 devaluation of sterling wiped out their capital; and much of the antagonism of those countries against the use of the dollar as an international reserve asset should be traced to the experience of 1931 rather than to anti-American feelings or mere adherence to outdated monetary theories.

Most importantly, no international agency or conference could prevent a sudden large increase in the gold price from having inflationary consequences for those countries that hoarded gold, and deflationary consequences for those that did not. And the gold-holding countries are precisely those whose economies are least in need of an inflationary stimulus, since they are most prosperous—not prosperous because they are holding gold, but holding gold because they are prosperous. In contrast, those that do not hold gold are most in need of further expansion.

Hence the inflationary and deflationary effects of an increase in the price of gold would be most inequitably and most uneconomically distributed among nations.

While I have the highest respect for much of Mr. Martin's thinking and for his integrity, my replies to this profusion of unrelated ideas would be:

[1] Issue of June 14, 1965.

1) There is no good reason why the nationals of other countries should act to their own disadvantage to keep inviolable statements made by United States' politicians and monetary authorities, which later events may prove to have been ill-considered.

2) The objections relating to the sterling devaluation of 1931 do not relate to a uniform revaluation of gold. As all currencies would be devalued to the same degree they would not suffer losses on their holdings of dollars. They would indeed not receive a premium on the amounts held in dollars instead of gold, but in the devaluations Belgium, France and the Netherlands have themselves undertaken since 1931, they have not been deterred by any such objections. Before sterling was devalued in September, 1931, France and Belgium, through separate devaluations, had already increased their national gold prices by 393 per cent and 39 per cent, respectively. If the dollar were "as good as gold" the objection would be removed by encouraging them to convert dollars into gold. In any case, central banks that hold foreign currency instead of gold deliberately expose themselves to the risk of foregoing profits on a gold revaluation.

3) The mere act of revaluation need be neither inflationary nor deflationary. Indeed, the enhancement in the value for gold in the balance sheets of central banks could be neutralized by a similar allocation to capital reserves. The new gold figures would then justify the inflation which had already taken place. If central bankers were then to embark on a new bout of inflation, they would by their own choice add new sins to their old ones.

4) On Mr. Martin's own argument the prosperous countries hold gold. The enhancement of gold's value would then be a reward for their good management, particularly for their thrift and prudence. Are these virtues no longer so regarded, and is virtue now only to be attributed to those with unbalanced reserve positions?

5) If Mr. Martin is worried that other countries, particularly the less developed countries, now hold dollars instead of gold, he could easily pass on to them the premium they would have

obtained on the gold they could have drawn if they had converted their dollars before revaluation, and he could, perhaps, couple this with agreement limiting their propensities to inflate. Indeed, on the ground of equity, there is much to be said for such an arrangement.

6) The biggest profit on hoarding would accrue to the United States as it still holds a bigger single physical hoard than any other country. This assumes that it can continue in the meanwhile to persuade others not to encash dollars into gold.

7) It is now clear that the scramble for gold could set in motion similar contractionary tendencies to those existing in the 1930's. There is, therefore, no confusion in the contention that a revaluation of gold need be neither inflationary nor deflationary, since it could justify the level of bank credit which now exists and avoid the contraction of bank credit which can grow alarmingly if the present scramble for gold continues.

If it is accepted that the revaluation of gold is required to allow for the smooth functioning of the international monetary system, the question arises as to how much this should be raised in a uniform revaluation as envisaged in the IMF charter.

In my first published comment on this (in *The Measure of Gold*) in 1950, I was of the opinion after examining the relevant banking figures after the devaluation of sterling and other currencies, that the price of gold should be doubled in order to give a workable relationship between gold reserves and the world's money supply.

The Supply of Gold

Since 1950 the proposition of doubling the gold price has appeared in many texts, often with no supporting calculations. Much has happened since 1950. On the one hand the free world's supply of gold (i.e., including Russian sales) has increased from around 25 million fine ounces per annum to a level around 50 million fine ounces (50.6 million fine ounces for 1964). Recent

official statements that gold production has provided a slow rate
of addition to reserves, have ignored the fact that the rate of
physical production of gold has actually shown a large increase.
On the other hand the proportion of the annual supply going into
non-monetary uses has also increased while inflation has continued. Unfortunately, there exist no published official or authori-
tative studies of what would be the change in world production
consequent upon increases in the price of gold, or of what re-
leases there would be from hoards if the price of gold were
raised. In the absence of such studies, we can only make a rough
"guesstimate."

If we accept that the figure of a 100 per cent increase in 1950
was reasonable, and that since then money supply had increased
in the order of 40 per cent, then the current value of gold stocks
should be 140 per cent of the end 1950 figure (at 70 dollars per
ounce). Monetary gold stocks at the end of 1950 stood at 1,125
million ounces valued (at 35 dollars per ounce) at 39.4 billion
dollars. The required figure of 1.4 times the 1950 figure of 1,125
million ounces at 70 dollars per ounce, would be approximately
110.2 billion dollars. The actual monetary gold stock at the end
of 1964 was 1,347 million ounces which, at 70 dollars per ounce,
would amount to about 94.3 billion dollars. This means that the
required figure would be reached if the monetary gold stocks
were to receive 15.9 billion dollars as a release from the private
hoards, which I believe is too high a figure to expect.

On the experience over the years 1890 to 1929 the amount
of newly-mined gold going into non-monetary use was around
40 per cent and it is assumed that this is a more normal figure.
If it is assumed that after revaluation money stocks would be 60
per cent of the total stocks, then money stocks would be in the
order of 1,500 million ounces, i.e., the release from hoards would
be only 153 million ounces valued at 70 dollars per ounce at
10.7 billion dollars (which is short of the required figure).

These calculations are full of assumptions and are presented
with diffidence. In the absence of detailed estimates of the
amounts that could come from hoards and of the production on

different gold prices, it appears to me that the required increase should now be in the order of 110 to 120 per cent—say, 75 dollars per ounce. This should be enough to convert the foreign exchange holdings of 28 billion dollars in reserves into gold, and release enough gold from the hoards.

On the basis of 75 dollars per ounce the revalued money gold stocks would become worth 101 billion dollars. The release from hoards required would then be only 9.2 billion dollars, or only about 123 million ounces at 75 dollars per ounce. (Union Corporation estimates that at the end of 1964 the amount in private hoards was approximately 480 million ounces.) The release of 123 million ounces would require then a fall in hoards of only about one-quarter, which seems within the possible range.

With a revalued gold stock of about 110 billion dollars, annual gold production at the rate of 50 million ounces, of which, say, one-third went into hoards and non-monetary uses, would represent a 2.5 per cent annual increment—a rate consistent with maintainable growth.

World monetary reserves at the end of 1964 were about 75 billion dollars (gold 47 billion dollars and currencies 28 billion dollars). With gold at 75 dollars per ounce the gold reserves would be 110 billion dollars and the figure would be large enough to retire the existing foreign-exchange holdings from their tired role of pretending to be genuine reserves. The United States' reserve position would come out of the red. Sterling would still face difficulty but no doubt a long-term loan could then be arranged from its friends to secure its eventual stabilization.

The facts do not support the view that the present monetary system has worked well. The rate of growth has been high owing to magnificent scientific achievements but the failure to achieve the full result is apparent from the restrictions still impeding economic progress. Instead of embarking on hazardous schemes of creating further credit, it would seem sensible to improve the existing imperfect IMF gold standard, which instead of being an outstanding success has simply limped from crisis to crisis.

MR. ROCKEFELLER: As a commercial banker, I was somewhat

disturbed by what I understood to be Dr. Busschau's statement that any government or central bank would be taking improper risks in holding foreign currencies as reserves on the ground that they might not be 100 per cent backed by gold. If we as commercial bankers couldn't have depositors who did not have 100 per cent cash backing in their deposits we would be in a bad way.

It seems to me that the important thing is that we as commercial bankers have assets which over a period of time could be liquidated to take care of our depositors. And I would think that this was much the same sort of requirement that central banks or governments should look to in their currencies. Certainly in that sense the United States is a pretty good risk because of our long-term investments overseas and our short-term liabilities in the form of deposits which are really in central banks as reserves. So I am a little bit baffled and troubled by this statement.

MR. BUSSCHAU: I am glad you asked that question; I have heard it before. I respectfully would like to suggest a point. As a commercial banker you have to give your customers acceptable cash, and that acceptable cash comes back into the bank. You provide an acceptable cash by giving the depositor United States notes. But you have got to understand that you cannot apply this analogy to the international scene. Up until a few years ago you could convert the dollar completely into gold, and there was no question of lack of confidence in those things that you could pay the foreigner in what was to him acceptable instead of gold.

I grant you that to some extent you can operate below such a working balance. But in commercial central banks, central working balances are indeed quite small, and much of the physical borrowing was due to involuntary holdings. So I don't think you can argue that this is the same thing as the commercial banks. The foreigners needn't accept the dollars or sterling or any other currency and, therefore, I don't believe this is an analogy you can hold at all.

MR. TRIFFIN: I wonder whether Mr. Busschau could say a word about the impact of the increase in gold prices over gold production because by implication his paper seemed to say there would be no increase.

MR. BUSSCHAU: I think I did say that it is very hard to make predictions regarding future gold production. It is difficult to predict the gold production of a single mine with all its own individual technical problems and it is similarly much more complicated to predict the future gold production of the world. One really has to examine each separate single source of production, existing and potential, and then to add them all together. The supply of gold to the free world is now in the order of over 50 million ounces per annum as compared with an annual average rate in the five years before devaluation of under 25 million ounces.

As regards South Africa, the production for 1964 was over 29 million ounces as compared with under 12 million ounces in each of the three years before 1949.

One has, however, to examine these increases as consisting of the addition of two curves, one relating to the old industry as it existed in 1939 and this curve shows a rapid downward fall so that this sector of the industry now produces only one-third of what it produced in 1939. The other curve relates to the new sources of production which mainly came into operation after the end of World War II and this rapidly rising curve is steep enough to out-balance the decline in the other curve.

The new mines have played an increasingly important role in South Africa's gold production as is evidenced by the fact that twenty-one companies (out of the existing sixty-three gold-producing companies) which started operations after 1950 contributed 66 per cent of the total gold output in 1963–1964. The twenty-one mines which commenced crushing between 1930 and 1950 contributed 21 per cent, while the remaining mines, which were already operating before 1930, accounted for 10 per cent. In other words, the upward sweep of the total production curve is entirely due to the new sources of production while old sources have largely been eliminated as a result of the unfavorable price/ costs relationship.

On the basis of present factors, the prospect is that the peak of the physical production in South Africa will be reached in 1966 or 1967 and will then decline fairly rapidly as further older mines are closed down.

MR. GAINSBRUGH: What would happen to the production curve if the prices were raised? How much influence would the price of gold have on production?

MR. BUSSCHAU: The shape of the future growth would be altered in that the peak of production would be reached after 1967 and the decline would then be more gradual.

MR. GAINSBRUGH: What per cent would this increase be, 5 per cent or more?

MR. BUSSCHAU: With 100 per cent increase in the price of gold I would say that the immediate fall would be in the order of a 10 per cent drop, but there would then be, with the opening up of new plants, a later rise also in the order of 10 per cent of the 1964 figure. These are rough estimates relating to South Africa, but I should think it is likely that in the rest of the world there would immediately be increases in production because old mines that are now dormant would again soon be brought into production. The Californian picture would be something like this but Mr. McLaughlin can tell you about that better than I can.

MR. GILBERT: I am rather disturbed by the way some of the speakers here have been talking about whether the dollar is as good as gold. You might get the impression that this is a philosophical question. Somebody says the dollar is as good as gold. Somebody else says it isn't as good as gold. Professor Despres has said that it is even better than gold. But, as you know, that's what makes a horse race.

We have a market economy and so we have to see what the market tells us. The price of gold today is around 35.13 dollars, and at that price there are a lot of people quite willing to hold dollars at 4.5 per cent. Many of them are quite free to take their dollars and buy gold if they want to, and if the price of gold were different and the rate of interest different, there would undoubtedly be some shift in the holdings of gold and dollars. The point is that you cannot talk about the question in absolute terms.

Now it would be nice, perhaps, if the price of gold was the sort of economic magnitude which we could move up or down in accordance with other variables in an econometric model. But all of you know that cannot be done if we want to keep gold as a monetary metal. You have seen here that we can hardly even talk about the price of gold because we are afraid of the speculative forces that might be set in motion.

As the matter now stands, there is one man in the world who has the power to say what happens to the price of gold. He lives in Washington at 1600 Pennsylvania Avenue. He could bring about a rise in the price of gold; he could bring about a demonetization of gold. He happens to be in the hospital today, so I don't think he is going to take any immediate action. But I would like you to reflect on what it means that one man has such concentrated power over the role of gold.

It means that in an operating, functional sense we are more on the dollar standard than we are on any other kind of standard. It is the dollar that is in the center of the international financial world. This hasn't come about by law or by international agreement. It has happened because the trading community of the world, the banking community of the world, and the central banks, I might add, find it convenient for it to be that way. In my opinion it is going to stay that way as long as the United States takes enough care of the dollar and acts sensibly enough to make the dollar worth their trust.

I would like to emphasize that this is what the criticism by the Europeans of the United States in the monetary field is all about. They are not objecting to the role of the dollar. What they are practically begging the United States to do is to keep the dollar sound—to assure the exchange stability of the dollar. And as long as the United States does assure the exchange stability of the dollar, the monetary system is going to remain much as it is.

Now, you can disagree with the European advice about how the United States should maintain the stability of the dollar, or what measures the United States should take. But I don't think you can disagree with that fundamental objective because it is as much in the interest of the United States as it is the rest of the world.

MR. WALLICH: It was an impressive presentation that Mr. Busschau gave us. Before taking issue with it in a more economic way, I would like to run down shortly what I think are the main objections to his case. The main practical objections are the uneven distribution of benefits, the injury to dollar holders at the present time, the destruction of the existing reserve currencies and the reserve currency system, and the subsequent speculation on future rounds of gold increases. To the economist this proposal lacks appeal because we are invited to apply resources to the creation of something that can be created more efficiently with less input of labor and capital.

I think this speaks against the use of gold as the sole international asset. Nevertheless, the doctrine that Mr. Busschau produced about the netting out of all monetary claims and liabilities is one that has received a good deal of attention by economists in the domestic sphere. It has been talked about in terms of inside and outside money. "Inside money" is money created by the banking system against private claims, and the claims and the money wash out. "Outside money" is created on the basis of government debt and foreign exchange, and gold. It remains after you wash out debt and credit.

A few economists attribute certain virtues to "outside money." Nevertheless I don't know anybody who says that "inside money" doesn't increase the liquidity of the economy. By the same token the international "inside money" that consists of international monetary claims and liabilities also generates liquidity. It just happens not to generate as much as international outside money, which is gold, would generate.

Finally, if we really want a hard international money produced by sweat and labor, I submit there is a more attractive alternative. I don't like it, but it has been proposed, and that is the commodity reserve currency. This would mean creating a bundle of commodities against which money would be issued and extinguished. As compared to gold, it has at least the following advantages. There would have to be no increase in the price of any particular commodity. The procedure would stabilize the incomes of producers of various commodities in a great many countries. And if the system should ever be abolished, as I think it speedily would, at least we could consume the commodities it would have stored.

MR. BUSSCHAU: I want to comment on what Mr. Milton Gilbert said about the consensus being against the proposition. This might be so. I could give him testimony and examples where the decision was made by consensus, but I am unconvinced that it was the right decision.

As regards the other remarks, he wasn't really dealing with what I was talking about regarding the dollar being as good as gold. He was talking about the market here. I would believe this proposition that the dollar is as good as gold if you give me double eagles for my dollars any time I wish to. If you believe this is true, why don't you try it out? Your Treasury has given an effective answer to that.

As to the rest of his remarks, I think Mr. Bernstein dealt with them earlier, and I agree with Mr. Bernstein's analysis, though not with his remedy.

As regards the commodity standard, of course, you can do it. I wasn't arguing that in my paper. In the final analysis you have to have a commodity. I must say I was worried when Mr. Young said he didn't care how the gold got there. There seems to be, I must say, some kind of lack of respect for the lessons of history.

As regards this question of money as something you can eat, you should read John Locke, who gave a perfect definition of money. Money is some useless thing that men desire, but which is useless in relation to living needs. You mustn't take something you can eat because you are subtracting from world welfare.

As for Mr. Triffin and others who are making slanderous remarks about gold, the difficulty about the annual increment in relation to growth of credit is it is hard enough to work with gold, and much more difficult to do it with two currencies. You find it even more difficult if you try to manage it in a mixed bag of commodities. This is really something I know the central bankers, like my friend Ralph Young and sometimes I, with my other hat on, get very worried about. When you try to do it not against one commodity but the whole mixed bag of commodities which are fabricated, it is hard to believe that gold is as useless a commodity as some might claim. I don't know of any people who eat gold, but I know some people who eat with gold.

MR. OLSEN: Listening to the papers Mr. Busschau and others have presented, I can't help feel we may be overlooking the fact that in the final analysis we must always depend on the rational behavior of men. There is some feeling that if we were to enlarge the role of gold along with an increase in the price of gold, somehow this would reduce the risk of irrational behavior on the part of men. I don't find any great comfort in this because the degree of latitude for irrational behavior even under the enlarged role for gold is still quite considerable. Indeed, an increase in the price of gold, and this has been said before and answered before, could very well confirm in the minds of many people the wisdom of hoarding gold. After a period of time, and most likely a short time, the cycle would repeat itself once again with people hoarding gold feeling completely justified by past events.

We are at the present time at a very important crossroads in determining whether gold is going to dominate, or whether it is going to play a role as it has along with paper currency. In this respect I suggest possibly that the gold mechanism or return to gold would kill off the key reserve currency. If this occurs the function of money (then being gold) would become more of an end unto itself rather than serve as means of exchanging goods and services. When money becomes largely a means unto itself it provides poorly for growth in trade and investments. Indeed we are beginning to see this already in the stepped up hoarding of gold.

This morning Mr. Hoadley made a remark about creating a crisis condition in order to obtain change. There are some who tend, sincerely, to express fears that create a synthetic sense of crisis. This can serve a useful purpose, I think, in some ways to get things done. But, of course, I always feel when it comes to forecasting disaster and persuading people to take a course of action in their personal affairs of those institutions with which they are associated, we must realize that being wrong can be costly. Somehow a notion has arisen that there is little risk in forecasting disaster year after year despite the fact disaster never comes.

Those who heeded the threat of imminent disaster in the 1929 period were saved great loss. But those in the postwar period who may have acted on the advice of those who insisted that complete collapse was imminent paid a terrible price.

MR. BUTLER: I just want to make two fairly brief points. First, it seems to me that one of the problems in this area is to differentiate clearly between the real world and the money world. That is the idea that you can do something through the route of money that will solve real problems, and this seems to me to have little merit.

On the other hand, our objective is to have our monetary system domestically and internationally work reasonably and fairly to support the things we do in the real world. To support transfers between countries has seemed to be desirable. I think in these terms we have a problem today. For financial reasons the United States cannot do as much in support of defense and development of the free world as I think it should. We need to move in an evolutionary way to improve these financial mechanisms and facilities and encourage the real transfers about which we are genuinely concerned.

Emile Despres made a very important point in saying that U.S. financial transfers have exceeded our real transfers in recent years. One of our problems is to correct this situation so that our financial transactions are supporting the transfer of real resources in support of the development and help of the free world and are not transfers in response to purely monetary or liquidity demand in the rest of the world.

I am also impressed with the talk of the importance of adjustment rather than liquidity. It seems to me that this is the nub of the problem. However, most of the talk is in terms of adjustment on the part of deficit countries. While that is a problem, the problem of presenting some incentives or compulsion to make the creditor countries follow the rules of the game may be as important as the adjustment process on the part of the deficit countries. One of the drawbacks in the plans that have been put forward is that they do not pay enough attention to providing enough incentives or compulsion to make the creditor countries go along. This is an essential part of any program that is developed.

MR. BERNSTEIN: I had a debate with Mr. Busschau and Mr. Cortney in 1953, as you no doubt have heard. This debate ranged over the whole question of gold, and it was under the sponsorship of The National Industrial Conference Board.[2] I wish everybody here could have heard that debate.

It is true that I could not foresee that the United States would run a deficit in its balance of payments for a long time, although I was always a non-dollar scarcity man. But these gentlemen were predicting imminent collapse of the monetary system, and I venture to say fifteen years later this hasn't shown any signs of occurring.

To my mind Dr. Busschau is making a serious mistake in underestimating the strength of the dollar. He cites the short-term liquid liability of 27 billion dollars against our reserves. But this exaggerates one international banking position. Many of these liabilities are to countries that owe us on short term a good deal more than their claims on us. For example, if you look at the liquid liabilities of the United States you find liabilities of 2.6

[2] See National Industrial Conference Board, *Studies in Business Economics*, No. 43, "Shall We Return to Gold Standard—Now?," discussion by the Economic Forum and guests, with revisions, New York: National Industrial Conference Board, 1954.

billion dollars to Japan, but the short-term banking claims of the United States on the Japanese government, the Japanese banks and Japanese businessmen is more than 2.7 billion dollars.

The difficulty about the dollar is not that there is no confidence in it; there is in fact great confidence in the dollar. You merely have to hear the very sophisticated Euro-dollar bankers discuss the dollar to see how strong it is. The difficulty about the dollar is that some of the surplus countries of Europe have said that they cannot absorb the influx of external money arising from our deficit and they would like to have us put our balance of payments in order. So they have converted dollars into gold.

As the French Minister of Finance said, the sole purpose of these conversions was to mark the limit of how much they are willing to accept in this form, not because they have no confidence in the dollar but because they don't want the repercussionary effects on their economy. The dollar is strong. The willingness to accept and hold dollars as prime assets is exceedingly great. The increase in private holdings of dollars and even holdings of official reserves in dollars will begin to resume once it is clear that we will maintain the balance of payments in order.

Having said all this, I want to agree once more on one point and one point only. It is not desirable to keep building up the international monetary reserves of the world solely in the form of one currency or even very largely in the form of a number of currencies because in a period of political or economic uncertainty there is a danger that these foreign exchange reserves will have to be converted into gold.

My solution to that problem is not doubling the price of gold, certainly not raising it each time the ratio of the world money supply to gold changes, and this seems to be implied in Dr. Busschau's argument. My suggestion is that in a sensible and reasonable way we provide another reserve asset different from the dollar and having more of the final settlement characteristics of gold. This I think we can do with great safety and confidence that it will be well managed and that it will meet the real problem much better than a change in the price of gold.

MR. BUSSCHAU: I am quite willing to reply to things I said, but not to things I didn't say. I didn't say one should keep putting up the price of gold. I didn't talk about the gold standard. I didn't say the rise in the price of gold would cure everything.

MR. HABERLER: I must say I find it difficult to discuss the paper of Mr. Busschau for one reason. He seems to have different standards of evaluating the success and failure of the system as, for example, when he says it is not true that the present system has worked well, that we have limped from one crisis to the other.

In a sense, of course, we have limped from one crisis to the other. But if you look at the world at large during these years, when we limped from crisis to crisis, the standard of living has risen enormously, the volume of trade has increased, convertibility of currencies has been introduced, and that has contributed to the increase in output and employment and trade.

If you take as objectives the increase in wealth and standard of living and volume of trade and so on, then I say let's go on limping from crisis to crisis, and in twenty years we shall all be better off than we were with the volume of trade being larger than it is.

So I think that it depends on the values you adopt.

Now let me report on an imaginary experiment which I made for myself. I had not seen Mr. Busschau's paper at that time, but I think it fits very well. I asked myself, suppose in 1950 we had introduced the gold standard and we had doubled the price of gold exactly as we are told we should do now, and as we should have done in 1950. At that time our gold stock was 23 billion dollars, our liabilities to foreign official dollar holders was about 5 billion dollars. So we would have found ourselves with 46 billion dollars of gold instead of what we have now. Now, suppose the United States had pursued the same internal financial policy no more inflationary, no less inflationary than it actually did. Suppose, too, that other countries had also pursued the same policies as they actually did. Then the American deficit would have been about the same as it actually was and the difference would have been that we could have paid out our deficits in the form of gold rather than in the form of accumulating liabilities, and now we would have a much better ratio between gold stock and liabilities.

I grant Mr. Busschau and other advocates of the gold standard that that would be a much healthier situation than the one we have now. But now I ask you, is it reasonable to assume that the United States would have pursued the same policies, if it had had all along a much larger gold stock and nothing to worry about the balance of payments? Is it not almost certain that the United States would have pursued, let me say, somewhat less austere and more inflationary policies? Would not countries like South Africa have increased their expenditures? Isn't it reasonable to assume that these countries and many others would have taken a different attitude and would have spent more? Isn't it pretty sure that if we had done that we would have had much more inflation in the world than we actually had?

The lesson of this little mental experiment is that you can have a lot of inflation with the gold standard and that the reintroduction of the gold standard could be a highly inflationary move.

MR. BUSSCHAU: On the first point about gold, I think that the increase in physical production of gold in recent years represents a very wonderful form of scientific achievement. But I wasn't aware the credit for the physical growth belonged to the bankers. We are not living in a world with free trade and movement of goods. Even the almighty United States now has exchange controls on capital movements. To me as a responsible citizen of the world this is a most regrettable fact. You are so big that when you do things you influence others. I think it is not real to make assumptions about what would have happened. We know there was inflation even though they didn't make the adjustment. I never advocated the full gold standard. I said this consistently: Let's make this system work. But making it work means that you have to have currencies convertible into each other and into gold. You should try to remove all the restrictions. That was the objective of the IMF, if I may so remind each of you.

MR. VINER: But may I turn to Mr. Milton Gilbert and ask a question. Is it really realistic to speak of a foreign bank and a merchant bank in particular as being the same as a central bank, or in other words, as acting as does a central bank when it holds some dollars and some gold in its reserves? Is it realistic to speak of commercial banks as showing, by the degree in which they keep their holdings on gold and in dollars, their preferences as between the two? A more realistic view is that they are willing in some quantities to hold dollars rather than gold if they get something like a 4 or a 4+ per cent annual insurance premium on their dollar holdings.

MR. GILBERT: There is a market at 4.5 per cent. If you couldn't get any interest on holding dollars, nobody would hold dollars in preference to gold.

MR. VINER: There was a period in the United States when the short-term interest yield was very nearly zero and yet even then there were important dollar balance holdings.

MR. GILBERT: The conditions were different. The market conditions were different.

MR. VINER: Once again the analogy doesn't seem to work. Then about the central banks: Central banks are, I take it, in the main holding dollar reserves without getting any interest yield on them. I may well be wrong on that; I would like to know. Am I wrong?

MR. GILBERT: Absolutely wrong.

MR. HARWOOD: Mr. Rockefeller, would you advise any of your depositors to take their money and buy gold either here or abroad?

MR. ROCKEFELLER: I wouldn't in the United States because it is illegal.

MR. HARWOOD: I understood Mr. Gilbert to say the President could raise the price of gold. Am I mistaken in assuming that the Congress has reserved to itself the right to do that?

MR. GILBERT: Of course, the legal position is that the change in the price of gold would have to be brought about by Congressional action. I was speaking somewhat figuratively. However, if the President thought it was in the interest of the United States and the interest of the world to have a higher price for gold, I have no doubt that he could arrange matters so that such a result would be highly probable.

MR. CORTNEY: I am afraid I shall need more than two minutes to refute some arguments produced here against my ideas.

Mr. Gilbert stated: "There is one man in the world who can say what the price of gold is going to be. He lives at 1600 Pennsylvania Avenue. He can raise the price of gold. He can demonetize gold."[3] From this statement Mr. Gilbert draws the conclusion that it is the dollar that counts in the world and that gold is in a subservient position.

Now, of course the President has the power to do many things, both wise and foolish. There are, however, a few things in the monetary field which he cannot do. For instance, in the present circumstances he cannot lower the price of gold. At this moment he has not the power to prevent a rise in the price of gold much longer, unless the free world is prepared to accept a plan, like that of Mr. Bernstein, for the creation of "synthetic" reserves.

Mr. Gilbert asserted that whether the dollar is as good as gold is a "philosophical question." Yet he refuted his own assertion with his following statement (page 110): "If you couldn't get any interest on holding dollars, nobody would hold dollars in preference to gold." Why is that? The answer is as simple as it is obvious: You are always certain to get dollars in exchange for gold while the reverse is not always true. The dollar would be as good as gold, if it were freely convertible into gold.

Whatever one may think of central bankers, they are certainly no fools and each central bank is conscious of the interests of his bank and his country. If dollars are as good as gold, or even better than gold according to Mr. Despres, why are central

[3] See page 101.

bankers holding gold which does not earn any interest in preference to dollars which presently earn 4.5 to 5 per cent per
annum? The answer is very simple: A central bank holding gold
incurs no risk, while it runs a substantial risk if it is owning
dollars.

Mr. Gilbert also asserted that my plea for the gold standard
means that I am forgetful myself, and that I am advising others
to forget, about full employment. I submit to him first that he is
wrong as to my position on this question (to convince himself
he may wish to read my book *The Economic Munich*, pp. 100–
116). Furthermore, I hope he has not espoused the false view
that there is any incompatibility between the gold standard and
full employment, or the wrong diagnosis as to the causes of the
Great Depression which broke out in 1929. I maintain that monetary stability, by which I mean essentially stable exchange rates
and a relatively stable level of prices, is a *sine qua non* condition
of sound economic activity and expansion. Such stability is ob-
tainable only if there is no inflation of money and there is a limitation to credit expansion. The gold standard means above all a
determination to put an end to inflation and permits a quasi-
automatic coordination of the movements of prices in the different countries, and thus an international monetary system.

I was glad to hear Mr. Bernstein state that it is not desirable
to keep building up the international monetary reserves of the
world very largely in the form of currencies, because in a period
of potential or economic uncertainty there is a danger that these
foreign exchange reserves will have to be converted into gold.
His solution is not a doubling of the price of gold, but the creation of a "composite reserve unit" which is as good and acceptable
as gold. Now, this is the rub, and probably a problem without
solution.

MR. SACHS: With regard to this whole attempt to justify the
advocacy for a doubling of the price of gold on the basis of
relationships between money supply and the current value of
gold stocks, there are two challenges—one from the economic
history of the 1920's and the other from the simplism of assuming

a uniformity of relationships between any single measure and the complexities of our economic order. The lesson from economic history is that in the later 1920's, eminent economists like Gustav Cassel argued that because the rate of growth in gold production was below the great expansion in the decade prior to World War I, the commodity price level was too deflated and needed inflation. And on grounds independent of the rate of gold production, but merely the shortcomings of British export, the great Keynes argued, as late as 1928, in the *Manchester Guardian's* "Commercial Review," that it was commodity prices that needed reflation. That was at a time when the technological changes in manufacturing and the excessive rates of commodity production so obviously called for downward readjustments, though admittedly the magnitude of commodity deflation in the Great Depression was excessive.

Whether or no the consensus of economists' opinions discerned it at the time, there were a few among us practical economists who from the later 1920's stressed that the malfunctioning of the political settlements of Versailles in the Balkanization of Europe and that the dissatisfactions revolving around reparations were great obstacles to the continuability of the postwar reconstruction. In this context the cliché-distinction in our economic-statistical textbooks between the internal economic or endogenous factors and the external or exogenous factors misses and distorts the fundamental deliverance of economic history that the extra-economic forces, particularly after a great war, are integral to the functioning of the economic order.

As to the attempt to reduce the complexities of the interlinked gold exchange and monetary orders to the simple and single composite of the gold price and money supply, I am reminded of a question that was addressed by the great French mathematician Henri Poincaré to a student body of which it was my privilege to have been a member. The question was what would happen if all things in the world were, say, doubled in magnitude or size. The preponderance of attending students responded with a resounding chorus, "Well, if all things were

changed by the same magnitude it would not make any difference." At that point the eminent mathematician and physicist
bade the student body to reflect on the manifold diversity and
differentialness in our world. "Think of it," he said. "It's an
elementary principle of aeronautics, whether for planes or bal-
loons, that the minimum speed needed to keep an airplane of a
given shape in the air varies as the square root of that plane's
length. So if the linear dimensions were increased four times,
it would have to fly twice as fast. Then the power needed for
the minimum speed also increases more rapidly than the weight
of the machine. This requires of the larger plane, weighing sixty-
four times as much as a smaller one, an increase in the horse-
power by one hundred and twenty-eight times. It is this which
has put limits in nature on the size of birds: the eagle like the
kite cannot keep in the air mainly by moving its wings, but must
balance itself on rising columns in the air and thus gives the
impression of soaring. That soaring becomes more and more difficult with increasing size." Then with a twinkle and a smile, he
said, "It is these considerations that would prevent angels from
remaining aloft on clouds, singing psalms to the Good Lord, as
in order to house the muscles in working the enlarged wings their
chests would be projected more than correspondingly by the
increase in weight."

The just narrated lesson from Poincaré bears *a fortiori* on our
monetary and economic systems. Changes in the price of gold
would bear hardest on nations, like the British, whose economic
structure is so dependent on imports, not merely of food but of
the products for their manufacturing. For such an economy which
finds it so difficult to balance imports and exports, the markup on
exports is necessarily a fraction of the multiplier of the markup
attaching to imports under normal conditions of world prosperity
as contrasted to what was the still continuing world price deflation in the 1931 gold suspension. Coordinately, economies like
Sweden, which deliberately prefer to have productive reserve
assets to gold, would be disadvantaged over against economies
that embarked—as has been the case with France—on the neo-

mercantilism of accumulating sterile gold. Still coordinately, the divergences in the ratios of gold to total reserves would exert differential impacts with exponential power on the several economies of the world.

In sum, not only must these disparities in impacts be taken cognizance of and adjusted for, but the clear lesson of it all is that readjustments must follow an evolutionary instead of drastic *simpliste* blow, whose consequences would not only produce a new Great Depression for the free world but expose that free world to political chaos from the anticapitalist powers.

CHAIRMAN FABRICANT: Mr. Busschau, would you care to make any final comments?

MR. BUSSHAU: I would say I did try to convince you all that this was an international problem. I made no secret about where I come from. And unhappily my country has difficulties in its relations with the rest of the world. I would only urge on you that we should all try very hard to be citizens of the world. This matter should be looked on as an international problem and not only as one of domestic problems such as the United States' balance of payments.

Chapter V

Fluctuating

versus

Stable Exchange Rates

Chairman: ROBERT TRIFFIN

CHAIRMAN TRIFFIN: Gentlemen, may I call this parliament to order to listen to an exchange of ideas on the exchange rate flexibility solution advocated here by some of my professional colleagues. I think the debate might be most usefully opened by Professor Haberler who has very definite views on the problem.

MR. HABERLER: Let me state as briefly, concisely and simply as I can this case for some flexibility. Let me repeat one thing I said this morning. I think the adjustment mechanism is much more important than the liquidity problem. If the adjustment mechanism doesn't work, no amount of liquidity is enough. And on the other hand, if the adjustment mechanism works well, then you need have little liquidity. So we should try to speed up and make more efficient the adjustment mechanism. Now if we look at the adjustment mechanism as it has operated during the postwar period, I think it is not unfair to say that it consists in differential rates of inflation. The surplus countries inflate more than the deficit countries, but not a single country in the whole world has had a falling price level, at least for a long time.

I assume that we want to avoid direct controls. If that is accepted and if you also wish to avoid inflation, then you have to introduce some flexibility in the exchange rates, because the adjustment mechanism nowadays operates only through controls or differential rates of inflation.

If we assumed as some writers still do—it would be easy to cite examples, although nobody around the table this afternoon takes that position—that wages and prices are flexible in both directions, then the adjustment would be easy, also with fixed exchanges, and there would be no point in making them flexible.

It is, however, a fact of modern life that money wages are not only entirely rigid in the downward direction, but also that it is almost impossible to prevent an upward push of wages. The very best we, or any other country, seem to be able to do is to contain the wage push to the level of the increase in average labor productivity so that the price level can remain approximately stable.

If we could do a little better and keep the wage rise below the rise in average productivity so that prices would gradually fall in the deficit countries, it would be possible to get adjustment without inflation and direct controls and without creating unemployment.

Since we are unable to do that and unwilling to accept unemployment that would be needed to keep wages from rising as fast as (or faster than) average productivity, some flexibility of exchange rates and a wider margin, say 4 or 5 per cent on either side of parity, would be desirable.

Let me explain how it would work. Take the Italian case: When Italy had their great balance-of-payments crisis two years ago, the lira would have gone down a few per cent, the German mark and the French franc would have risen a few per cent and that would have helped to adjust the Italian balance of payments, by stimulating exports of goods and services and checking imports.

Actually, under the system of fixed rates, the Italians adjusted their balance the hard way. They applied drastic classical medicine—credit restriction. As far as the balance of payments was concerned, the cure worked beautifully. The balance shifted within a year from a large deficit to a large surplus. But they had to pay a high price in terms of a sharp decline of the growth rate and a rise in unemployment. If there had been that little margin of flexibility, the adjustment would have been less painful. This is the basic case for flexibility.

for

One more remark. The only valid argument against flexibility that I can see is the one which was most persuasively stated by Professor Viner: If you give up the fixed exchange rate you let down the guard against inflation. If central bankers in particular, and the country in general, need not worry about the international reserve, the most important resistance against inflation will crumble.

against

This is a serious argument but I would argue that a declining exchange rate would be as strong a deterrent against inflation as a vanishing international reserve. (Rising internal prices and erosion of the purchasing power of money and money savings remain, of course, just as much a deterrent under the flexible as under the fixed rate system.)

for

You may be interested, Mr. Chairman, in the story which the late Arthur Marget once told me. In the 1930's, Belgium had a short period of floating rates. The President of the Belgian National Bank then was M. Maurice Frère (still alive), a most conservative central banker. Margret (who was not an advocate of flexible exchange rates himself) asked Frère what he, as a central banker, would regard as a stronger inducement to put on the credit brakes—a declining monetary reserve or a falling exchange rate? To Marget's great surprise, the answer was, "Of course, a falling exchange rate would be the strongest possible inducement to contract credit!"

We have little experience with floating rates (except under high inflation). But Frère's answer suggests that central bankers, if they operated under a system of floating rates, would behave differently than they say they would when they are asked under a system of fixed exchanges how they would react in case the rate were flexible.

CHAIRMAN TRIFFIN: Could I now call on Mr. Bernstein, who I

think has as much or more experience than any of us with this type of policy.

MR. BERNSTEIN: I hadn't expected to get into the discussion so early, but the Chairman always looks out for my interests.

I start with the premise that the facility of adjustment in the past was exaggerated. My authority for this is Dr. Samuel Johnson. You remember he said that when wages once go up they will never come down. I want to say the difficulty of adjustment in the present period is exaggerated. Obviously in a postwar period when countries haven't yet recovered their postwar capacity it will take time to restore the balance-of-payments position. When you have uneven inflation as a heritage of the war it will be difficult to restore the balance-of-payments position. But when you get communities in which monetary discipline has established reasonable stability then in my opinion the adjustment process as evidenced by some of the cases mentioned is not really as difficult as it seems.

I am going to take the United States as an illustration, although I know of other countries you could use. In this country, when we stopped the inflation in 1959, we were able to keep wages and manufacturing costs down so that the labor cost today per unit of output in manufacturing is lower than it was, say, four years ago.

The consequence of that has been along with other factors— I don't want to take this alone—that the U.S. export surplus of goods and services has risen from something like half a billion dollars in 1959, which was a cyclical peak, to around 8.5 billion dollars last year, which was almost a corresponding phase in the cycle.

Of course, a depreciation of the dollar, whether through fluctuating rates or wider margins would have reduced our costs and increased our export surplus. I doubt, however, that the export surplus would have risen as much as it actually did. With fixed exchange rates and monetary discipline we probably had an even greater improvement in the trade balance.

MR. HABERLER: Unemployment is not excessive.

MR. BERNSTEIN: I will come to that in a moment. The first thing I want to show is that in fact the adjustment process does work. The argument that this requires unusually large unemployment is simply not true. It does require keeping the level of employment a little below the point where in fact you can't get any mobility of labor anyway and where, in my opinion, the pace at which the economy is running might actually interfere with the rate of growth. Our rate of growth has been much better, and I think it will continue to be much better at a 4 to 4.5 per cent level of unemployment than it would be at a 3 per cent level of unemployment. I do not mean that the GNP would not be high in the year we get down to 3 per cent unemployment, I am merely saying the rate of growth between one year and succeeding years at 3 per cent unemployment will be less than it would be at 4 per cent, and that is precisely because there is a waste of labor, labor hoarding and a halt to the mobility of labor. Under such terms it is true the United States was not able to restore its balance of payments. But that was for reasons which are not related, in my opinion, to fixed exchange rates.

It is not an easy thing to bring down your long-term foreign investments to the scale you can pay for out of your export surplus after you have had twenty years of subnormal or negative investment. And that was our case from 1930 to 1950. It is very difficult to do it when your companies find that the rest of the world is in fact growing in the very fields in which they have the greatest advantage.

If the world is becoming Americanized in the structure of its economy, who can best take advantage of that kind of growth if not American companies? I am not sure what is going to happen to our foreign investment. If it stays at the levels of recent years we are going to have difficulty in restoring our balance of payments.

I do believe this, though: changing interest rates would help, of course, on the short-term capital movements, bank lending. It might help in the bonds, although it takes a lot of change in interest rates. But how can it do very much on the direct investment when a company like General Motors has invested a billion dollars to establish a position for its cars in Europe? Higher interest rates cannot deter it from investing another 100 million dollars if the purpose of that 100 million dollars is to maintain its position in established markets.[1]

If you want to see the true return on additional investment, you have to take not the increase in their earnings compared to the increase in their investment; you have to find out what their earnings would have been without this 100 million dollars' worth of investment.

My proposition is a simple one. The adjustment process will work if the monetary authorities will start in good time and work with it. My proposition is that insofar as our problems are unique we can't depend on any adjustment process, including flexible exchanges. And I am very much afraid that if we have a system of flexible exchange rates the pattern of behavior will be this: In a period when our balance of payments is bad we will go down to the bottom of that scale. When our balance of payments improves, there will be great objection from our exporters to losing the 5 or 6 per cent benefit in relative costs that would be involved in an appreciation to the previous level of exchange rates.

I think we do have to try and see whether the adjustment process, which I think is reasonably good, can be further improved. But I think we ought to try it within the framework of what we have. Incidentally, just for the record, I was for flexible exchange rates in the 1930's. It was not for balance-of-payments reasons. I believed it was a good way for the United States to get more employment.

SIR ROY HARROD: I was asked by Mr. Gainsbrugh to incorporate something about flexible rates in my paper before this rump session was arranged. So I am now proposing to transfer a few

---

[1] Editor's note: See Judd Polk, Irene W. Meister and Lawrence A. Veit, *U.S. Production Abroad and the Balance of Payments*, National Industrial Conference Board, 1966.

remarks, and under the circumstances I hope I shall be allowed a little latitude.

Now, personally, in the abstract field, I am not unsympathetic to the idea of flexible rates as sort of a scientific optimum. I would say first that I think that this scheme is *out* for the time being for reserve currencies and for near reserve currencies, perhaps for all the more important currencies, as it would lead to unmanageable movements of private short-term funds.

Now the main point I want to make is that, whatever the merits of flexible versus fixed rate, I do not believe that the flexible rate entails an economy in reserves. The subject of this whole session is to discuss the adequacy of world reserves, and I do not myself believe that flexible rates are a way out of the need for adequate reserves.

I'd like just very briefly to go over the question of the use of reserves in relation to a change of position. I will take in the first instance an adverse change in position. Something happens which would under a logical flexible-rate system call for a somewhat lower rate; and in due course that becomes known to people.

Now I want to think in terms of the flexible rate. But I will say hurriedly in passing that, from the point of view of the short-term capital movements, the worst thing you can have for provoking perverse movements is a fixed rate in which there is no confidence, or in which there is some lack of confidence. That is the worst thing you can have. In what follows I shall only compare flexible rates with fixed rates in which there *is* confidence.

Now, under a fixed rate in which there is confidence it is assumed that there will be some adjustment by which the fixed rate will be maintained, and people have confidence in that. But under the flexible system there will be the belief that there will be an adjustment by means of a change in the flexible rate; otherwise what is the meaning of the flexible rate, unless this is something that changes if an adverse factor occurs? So the opinion forms that there will be a downward movement.

Let us suppose that there is substantial reason for people to think there has been an adverse development and that there will in consequence be a turndown in the rate. Often people refer to what follows in terms of "speculation."

The point I want to put strongly is that the major part of the short-term capital movement due to the belief that the exchange rate may go down is not of the kind that we ought to regard as speculative.

I would suggest that, while the really large firms, very well organized, with foreign exchange departments, will normally, as a matter of business routine, cover all future commitments, there are a great number of firms of medium and small size who do not normally cover all future commitments in all circumstances. But as soon as there appears on the horizon any suspicion the rate may go against their own currency, they will be advised by their banks, one after another, to cover future commitments expressed in other currencies. This was the experience of my country last November. The vast mass of medium and small concerns who didn't normally cover began covering. They did so under the fear that sterling was going to be devalued. They would likewise do so if they feared that a flexible rate was going to go down. Under adverse circumstances it is also expedient for foreigners to cover receivables invoiced in the suspect currency by selling them forward right away. These leads and lags were certainly a very big aspect of the British situation last November. With a flexible exchange rate system, when an adverse factor happens, you get a lot of people who don't normally cover their commitments covering, and conversely you may get lags in payments.

I believe that the "speculation" that my academic colleagues talk about is a very minor aspect in this situation. The movements that I refer to should more properly be called precautionary. When you have adverse factors in the foreign exchange market operating, and the currency is moving downward, the leads and lags will not be reversed until the currency falls to a point at which these forces begin to operate in the reverse way, i.e., more people begin to think that the currency will move *upward.* But that won't happen as soon as the currency reaches its new equilibrium point. If the underlying forces are such that the currency ought to go down by 5 per cent, then, when it has gone down by 5 per cent, people won't begin to say at once that it is likely to go up. It will have to go down by, say, 10 per cent or more before people covering future commitments begin to take reverse action. If there is an adverse action requiring a fall, the currency has got to fall somewhat below the equilibrium level before the reverse movement sets in.

But before this point is reached, the authorities will have regard to what is needful for steady investment and trading operations. They will say, "We cannot allow the rate to go down by 10 or 15 per cent, when we are absolutely convinced that 5 per cent is enough for the long-term equilibrium." Therefore they will think of giving support when it has gone down by 5 per cent; and that means they have got to have reserves for this support operating. My contention is that the central banking authority will have to have bigger reserves to support a fluctuating rate within what are regarded as reasonable limits than it needs to support a fixed rate, because in the former case it has to counteract perverse private movements, while in the latter case, so long as there is confidence, private capital movements will be on the whole helpful.

My conclusion is that, whatever we may think of the fluctuating rate, in the long run we should not think that the fluctuating rate is a substitute for adequate reserves.

MR. GILBERT: I would like to make a few remarks on the proposal to widen the margins. It sounds attractive as a means of giving more flexibility, but as a technical matter I do not believe it would work.

When the currency isn't under pressure then the rate doesn't move much. But when the currency is under pressure, the central bank is forced to peg the rate right at the point where it is.

Take the recent case of sterling. The rate went down below 2.79 (U.S. dollars per U.K. pound) and a lot of money was flowing out. The Bank of England entered the market at a favorable moment to try to get the rate up a little so as to show there was a strengthening of confidence. The rate moved up to 2.79. As money was still flowing out, the Bank could not let it go down a quarter of a cent for fear that the outflow would be accelerated.

Or look at the Swiss case. Switzerland is not a member of the IMF and it has wider margins. I think their range is something like 4.28 on the upper side and 4.25 on the lower side, Swiss francs to the dollar. The operating range of the Swiss National Bank, however, is between 4.30 and 4.35 and the bank does not let it go outside that range. Again the reason is that experience has shown that a wider range increases speculation.

Another problem is that the persons who have the job of operating in the various markets must have a precise understanding about the rates at which they are going to operate; otherwise they would find themselves working at cross purposes.

MR. EMMINGER: I wouldn't have asked for the floor if it hadn't been for a provocative remark made by Mr. Haberler. He expressed the opinion that this subject of fluctuating exchange rates is unmentionable in central banking circles, and I must say I have encountered this myth very often. Some academic economists seem to hold the belief, for instance, that the Group of Ten, or all these official people, were prevented from even thinking about the exchange-rate problem. This is not true. We were having our own discussions on it inside the Group of Ten. We were even considering putting something on it into the report of the Group of Ten. In the end it was left out because we thought at that time it would require so much space that it would be out of proportion to the rest of the report.

I do not believe that we get very far if we put the question into the simple and generalized form. What system is preferable: a system with fixed or with flexible exchange rates, or one with widened margins? We have to differentiate and to split up the problem.

If somebody says the adjustment in case of disequilibria does not work satisfactorily with fixed exchange rates, and therefore we ought to have flexible rates, does he mean to say that every currency should fluctuate (or at least fluctuate within a wider margin than at present) against all other currencies? I firmly believe that such a generalized system for all the major currencies fluctuating against all the others is unworkable and would not last very long. It seems technically and economically very difficult, to say the least, to conceive of a system in which all the major countries' currencies would fluctuate against each other. Very soon countries would try to realign themselves. Some countries would peg their exchange rates to the dollar and others would try to peg to something else, so there would be some clubbing together. Therefore as a generalized and universal alternative to the present adjustment system with fixed exchange rates, fluctuating rates are out. If, for example, we pegged our rate to the dollar we would then have to march in step with the dollar club, and this clubbing together would soon be followed by some sort of an arrangement.

Moreover, if we had a generalized system of fluctuating rates, we would not have any reserve currency, or let's say any currency in which we could reasonably hold a larger amount of foreign exchange as working capital for exchange transactions and interventions. Even leaving aside currency reserves proper, we need working capital and what Mr. Roosa called "vehicle currencies." The central bank in nearly all cases has to have one foreign currency with which to operate in the exchange market, or against which it measures its operations in the market. We have the dollar as an intervention and vehicle currency. All the European currencies use the dollar for this purpose. Therefore we hold our working balances in the dollar. We could no longer do so if we were fluctuating against the dollar in a generalized system of fluctuating exchange rates.

The central banks could try to even out some of the fluctuations in the market. But it is difficult to conceive of stabilizing short-term operations in the market if you have all the major currencies fluctuating against each other. In such a case the central banks would very often operate at cross purposes against each other because we have no anchor, no peg to which we finally pin our actions. As long as we have the par value, we have more or less such a peg on which we can orient our actions.

Therefore, as I said, a generalized system of all the major currencies fluctuating against each other would very soon resolve itself into a de facto system of stable exchange rates at least among certain groups of countries, or clubs; and then you might have just two or three of these groups or blocks of currencies fluctuating against each other. But inside the groups you would have all the present adjustment problems again.

The question of flexible versus fixed exchange rates should rather be put in a more specific or selective way. In what cases —or for what countries—would flexible rates be more appropriate than fixed rates? I leave aside the question of whether, under certain circumstances, there might be something to be said for two (or three) currency blocks—e.g., the dollar (and sterling) block versus the EEC block—to fluctuate against each other within a wider margin. You may remember that this was advocated, although only as second-best solution, by the Brookings Institution in 1963.[2] It has already been mentioned that reserve currencies, i.e., the dollar and the pound sterling, are under a special constraint in this sphere. This constraint does not only make a devaluation of the pound, and much more so of the dollar, appear as only a very remote last-resort measure; it also would make it a little difficult to envisage free fluctuations of the dollar against all other major currencies as long as we have an international reserve system based so largely on the dollar. This special position of the dollar, as one of the mainstays of the whole international system, carries with it, of course, a special obligation, namely, not to let the dollar fall by domestic inflation, etc., into a position of persistent fundamental disequilibrium where an adjustment in exchange rates might become necessary.

The next particular case to be considered is that of a country which has brought itself into just such a position of fundamental

[2] Walter S. Salant, *et al., The United States Balance of Payments in 1968.*

disequilibrium and which should, therefore, adjust its exchange rate according to the IMF's Articles of Agreement. In cases where such a country has not yet been able to get its house fully in order and that inflation of demand (and/or costs) is still going on, it may be advisable to use a flexible exchange rate until the time comes when a newly-established exchange rate can be maintained with some certainty. This, incidentally, is the case of many marginal countries, Latin America for example.

Another special case is the one to which Mr. Haberler's argument refers. He says that nowadays deficit countries are no longer able to deflate effectively, so the whole adjustment process would consist only in different degrees of inflation. This, in itself, would not constitute an argument for a permanent system of exchange rate flexibility, quite apart from the fact that I would wholly subscribe to Mr. Bernstein's view that we should not be too pessimistic for the future possibilities in the adjustment sphere. Mr. Haberler's case may, however, be relevant to a country which is less prone to the inherent inflationary tendencies of a modern economy and which, moreover, very much resents the inflation forced upon it by other countries under a system of fixed exchange rates ("imported inflation"). Such a country may have to appreciate its currency, either by a once-for-all revaluation or by letting its exchange rate fluctuate. Germany did the former in the spring of 1961 by an upward valuation of the DM by 5 per cent. There is, however, a lesson in this episode. Mr. Haberler advocated a wider margin of, say, ±4 per cent around the par value instead of the present ±¾ per cent or 1 per cent. This may lead, in an extreme case, to an upward valuation of a currency from −4 per cent to +4 per cent, that is by +8 per cent. Now we have seen that already a modest appreciation of 5 per cent produced such a shock on the exporting community that nowadays all German industry has, so to speak, sworn that this should never occur again. Thus, the wider margin of Mr. Haberler may occasionally facilitate a required modest devaluation of a currency—which would represent an involuntary appreciation for the other currencies—but there would certainly be great practical difficulties in letting a currency also appreciate deliberately by a sizable amount, just as Mr. Bernstein explained it.

As to Mr. Haberler's and Mr. Viner's decisive question, what is more likely to act as a deterrent against domestic inflation: a loss of reserves in a fixed rate system, or a decline in the exchange rate in a flexible rate system, I think there is no definite and watertight answer to it. The answer will vary according to different cases and circumstances. But one must not forget that the defense of the exchange rate—which on Mr. Haberler's account Governor Frère of Belgium seemed to consider such a powerful argument—is really at work not only in a system of flexible exchange rates but even more in a system of fixed exchange rates. Thus, in Great Britain one of the major reasons for fighting domestic inflation has been, over the last ten years, the defense of the pound, meaning the existing exchange rate (and the position of the pound as center of the sterling area, connected with that exchange rate). This has certainly been the one argument that has been best understood by the British public. There are other cases which could be quoted here. So I would also say that in many countries defending one's own currency's parity is a stronger incentive for putting one's house in order than is the mere loss of reserve. But that is no argument against a system of fixed rates; quite the contrary.

Finally a remark on the Italian case quoted by Mr. Haberler in defense of his argument for more flexibility. I would have reasoned just the other way round. Italy had a domestic inflation in 1962–1963. If, at that time, it had had a wider spread in its exchange rate, the lira rate would have declined against the other currencies. What would have been the effect? Italian exports would not have come so quickly under pressure as they actually did; imports would not have increased so much in volume, but much more in price. Hence the Italian economy would have been exposed to additional inflationary influences from the external account (increase in import prices, incentive for exports), and would not have been exposed (or not nearly to the same extent) to the "dampening" influences that under the present exchange rate system came about through an outflow of foreign exchange (monetary effects!) and a vast increase in the import surplus of goods (real resources effect!). By partly shielding the Italian economy off against the effects of their inflation on the external side, the domestic inflation would have been "bottled up" inside Italy (to use Mr. Triffin's expression), and been so much stronger. Inflation could have gone on longer, because it would not have so immediately shown up in the reserves. After some time, of course, this bottled-up inflation would have had to be brought under control anyway.

What would then have happened under Mr. Haberler's system? The exchange rate of the lira would have strongly appreciated, say from 4 per cent below par to 2 per cent above par. This would have very much hampered the recovery of Italian exports. Now it so happens that an effort to fight inflation lands an economy quite often in a stagnation (stabilization crisis); this has nothing to do with the exchange-rate system, but with the difficulties of finding the right dose of anti-inflation, particularly in a case where, like in Italy, political and psychological factors played such a big role. In the Italian case, this stagnation was lessened, and in the end overcome, largely through an enormous upswing of exports to the tune of 50 per cent and more; at the same time the concomitant large inflow of foreign exchange expanded the cash base of the Italian banking system and the liquidity of the whole economy, and thus provided the monetary base for the later recovery.

In summing up, Mr. Haberler's more flexible rate system would certainly have lessened the swings in Italian foreign trade and in the reserve flows. It would, however, thereby have greatly lessened the "dampening" and equilibrating effects of these large swings of the external accounts both in the phase of domestic inflation and in the subsequent phase of stagnation. Thanks to their fixed exchange rate, the Italians "imported stability" during the phase of domestic inflation, and they "exported unemployment" during the subsequent phase of stabilization. The Italian case has always seemed to me to be an illustration of the good equilibrating effects of a fixed exchange rate.

MR. DESPRES: I want to contrast the flexible exchange rate not with the present system, but, like Sir Roy, with a situation in which there is general belief in the permanence of the exchange rate structure. Moreover, I want to talk about the truly flexible exchange rate case, not merely some widening of the gold points. And I would classify the Canadian flexible episode as one of widening the gold points because there was a general belief that the range of possible fluctuations was rather limited.

The orthodox theory of the adjustment mechanism is that of the adjustment of the current account to an autonomously generated capital inflow or outflow. If the problem were one of the prompt adjustment of the current account with no give in capital movements, I would agree with Mr. Haberler that the flexible exchange rate is the indicated solution although I don't like it. However, I think that the main contrast between the two cases, and one widely overlooked, is in the mobility of long capital. All international lending involves the assumption of an exchange risk on the part of somebody. Usually the loan is denominated in the creditor's currency, so it is the debtor who assumes the risk; if the debtor hedges in the forward market, his risk is merely transferred to someone else.

A system of permanently stable exchange rates makes it possible for countries with good credit standing to finance large savings in the trade balance through international borrowing and lending. These savings in the trade balance largely neutralize the inflationary or deflationary effects of fluctuations in domestic demand.

Under a system of really stable rates, where the permanence of the rate structure is taken for granted, the debtor accepts the exchange risk without thinking of it as a risk. Foreign currency and domestic currency are regarded as nearly perfect substitutes. Loan capital is far more mobile than under conditions of uncertainty regarding exchange rates. As Mr. Bernstein has pointed out, and as just pointed out in the Italian case, the system of fixed exchange rates permits rather wide variations in domestic aggregate demand without too much domestic inflation or deflation because the current account is able to move. And so long as the country's credit standing remains strong, and the domestic expansion does not get so large as to raise doubts in the minds of lenders, there is a built-in kind of stabilizing device that limits purely national inflations and deflations. Under a flexible exchange rate system we would lose most of this built-in stabilizing effect because loan capital would not perform the same role. We might lose more than 100 per cent of it, as a matter of fact, if capital movements were perverse, as they might very well be. The case for flexible rates, as a business cycle matter, was developed when people thought of outside forces as highly unstabilizing; flexible rates were proposed to stabilize the domestic economy. It is much more realistic today for most countries to consider that there may be fluctuations in domestic aggregate demand and that the foreign trade balance on the whole can serve as a compulsory stabilizer provided they can finance these compensatory fluctuations in their current account. It is only in the fixed exchange rate system that capital movements will behave in a way that permits this.

I would like to add that one of the big mistakes in most discussions of the adequacy of reserves is that they overlook the fact that under conditions of general confidence in the stability and permanence of existing exchange rates, movements of private capital for many countries, for the countries with credit standing, very greatly reduce the need for reserves.

MR. MELTZER: An alleged advantage of the present system of fixed rates, in addition to those so cogently put forth by Mr. Bernstein, is that fixed rates promote trade. Those who argue against flexible rates usually discuss this advantage at some length. However, they fail to point out that to meet the desirable end of increasing trade, restrictions are imposed either on the volume of trade, as in the U.K., or on capital movements and the financing of trade as the United States has done.

Mr. Bernstein talks about improvement of our current account. But how much of our recent improvement is the result of U.S. grain sales to the Communist countries, of the Canadian grain sales with their favorable consequences for the U.S. balance of payments and of de facto controls imposed by the United States? How much of our adjustment in the past four years may be regarded as permanent or long-run?

Like Mr. Haberler I believe that initially we don't have to go from completely fixed parities to completely fluctuating rates. But we do have to permit responses to cyclical fluctuations in the various domestic economies. Widening the margins and providing an adjustment mechanism to supplement, though not necessarily to completely replace the adjustment mechanism that has already been established, is a useful step in the right direction.

Let us suppose the dollar is floated now, so that the gold-dollar price becomes freely fluctuating. How much would we expect the dollar to depreciate or change? Since I am not an expert on this question, I took a poll of some experts and came up with the answer—you may have your own answer which may different substantially from the experts I have asked. The poll shows that the dollar would change by anywhere from +5 per cent in the personal opinion of some of the experts to an extreme of −3 per cent in the opinion of others.

Since the majority of us expect the United States balance of payments to be in balance within the next few years, the question that we must answer is, how do we expect the adjustment to take place? Is it to be accomplished by imposing additional restrictions on trade and capital movements? Or is it to be accomplished by some other device that has not been clearly specified before this, or to the best of my knowledge before any other group?

It is difficult for me to understand why it is that those who express fear and suspicion about the national monetary managers and their asserted proclivity to engage in inflationary actions are so optimistic about the prospect of asking these same people to function as international monetary managers and to manage an

international currency unit. First, I think that despite my criti-
cisms in the past of central banking, the one criticism I would
regard as most unjust is that the United States Government in the
postwar period has been on a rampant inflationary binge. Second,
if inflation is the great fear of those present, it would seem to
remove almost completely every basis for the argument that the
solution to the international monetary problem is going to be
achieved through international monetary cooperation. Third, let
me try to answer very briefly those who seem so certain that the
system of fluctuating exchange rates or limited fluctuations will
always be designed to push the rate to the minimum rate.

First, I would cite the highly relevant experience of the
United States when it pulled the peg on bond yields in 1951. For
years it had been said that removing the peg would immediately
produce a substantial increase in interest rates. Almost nothing
of the kind happened immediately after the peg was pulled. In
fact, surprisingly little happened to interest rates in the following six months. This result must be called surprising not only
because of the predictions that had been made prior to the event
but also because the peg was pulled when the United States was
engaged in fighting the Korean War and was financing a reasonably large deficit in the public sector.

Second, we should not ignore the much more adequate forward foreign-exchange market that would develop if we move
to a system of limited flexibility in the exchange rate. A forward
market would, of course, remove some of the problems about
which Sir Roy spoke. Most of the arguments I hear presented
presume that the existing system of fixed parities would in every
other respect be maintained and that intelligent members of the
international financial community would not be capable or intelligent enough to observe changes in domestic interest rates
and to make decisions regarding the future movements of the
exchange rates. I expect that the contrary is more likely true, and
that an active forward market would develop within the limits
imposed by the 4 or 5 per cent margins. Our own experience in
the United States, the tremendous changes that have taken place

in the domestic financial market—the negotiable certificate of deposit and the Federal funds market—surely speak very loudly and clearly in support of my view.

And third and very last, let me repeat again the experience with flexible rates in the United States in the nineteenth century. This was the only prolonged period during which the country was on flexible rate and it reinforces my conviction, as it should reinforce almost anyone élse's conviction, that flexible rates are not inconsistent with falling prices, increasing output and expanding trade.

MR. SACHS: The foregoing advocacy by Mr. Meltzer of a flexible dollar exchange rate and his invocation of what he calls "the experience with flexible rates in the United States in the nineteenth century" are challengeable, first of all for their causal role in the post Civil War crises that culminated with the Great Depression of the 1890's. The United States was then a debtor economy that, even with its preponderance of agricultural exports, needed capital imports for the completion of its railroad transportation network. It suffered from the legacies of the depreciated currency and the inflation-accentuated costs of railroad construction in the ensuing prolonged agricultural and correlative price deflations. That reference, then, to the nineteenth-century experience looms forth as a warning against the evils contributed by and associated with the instability in exchange rates in that long and tough epoch of economic disruption and social distress. The end of that epoch and the re-entry on recovery and cumulative prosperity happened to have been signaled by the defeat of Bryan in the 1896 election. That defeat applied not to just a person but to the chronic uncertainties regarding the stability of the currency and lack of confidence in the panaceas of silver and manipulative monetary standards. In the wake of the clarification of the monetary and exchange rate outlooks after 1896, the European investor-creditor interests financed the reorganizations of our railroads that had been thrown into receiverships during that prior combination of economic depression and monetary instability.

In reinforcement of this condensed recapture of the economic-financial history, we can adduce the strengthening of our economic system, now the major creditor power of the world, in this decade after the abandonment of the complacence in the mid-1950's with the Sumner-Slichter doctrine of the feasibility of an annual 3 to 4 per cent inflation rate. One of the novel and constructive developments since entry on this decade of the 1960's is our synthesis of stable exchange rates and stable prices with efficient management of inventories through stability of the turnover of inventories in relation to sales and orders. Whereas in the previously accepted theory and patterns of business cycle progression, once passed from the recovery into the expansion stage, inventories uniformly entered on progressive accumulation measured by sales and orders, in this expansion up to and through this very year 1965 the inventory turnovers have remained stable with the conditions at the beginning of the recovery and expansion. *This condition of stability has been signally manifest in all sectors of the economy, durable as well as nondurable, and within manufacturing by all stages of fabrication; and for the economy as a whole by the stages of distribution.* Under the earlier and presumed structured pattern of the short-run business cycle, the tendency to the buildup of inventories in the expansion at rates faster than the distribution tied up capital not merely for the interest cost of carrying but for the insurance and the management of the excesses, and thereby this diversion of internal funds and credit led to strains on the working capital position of the economy. Hence the altered trend in the measures of inventory turnover to orders and sales served as lead-indicators of the topping-out of expansion and prospective entry on recession.

The economic mutation in this expansion instead of parallelism with the old order has been aided and accentuated by the adoption and diffusion of computerized management of inventories, not merely in the recording but in the ordering and alert keying of stocks of goods and the utilization of the stocks into sensitive registry of demand at all stages of fabrication and distribution. That clustering of techniques could not have been put into as effective use if business managers had to be worrying about exchange and money value instabilities from flexible international rates with their inevitable disruptive repercussions on the domestic price system. Having confined myself to featuring the character and the functioning of this economic mutation in the instant expansion, this participant in that transformation of inventory management submits the results of an estimation by him to authorities here and in Britain that the monetary savings from this new inventory management over the period 1961–1964 aggregated savings for durable manufactures alone in a range of 15 to 30 per cent, which worked out to be a cumulative economy even greater than the tax reduction in its benefits for the manufacturing economy.

MR. BERNSTEIN: Mr. Meltzer points out that the fears of many people that the interest rate would rise sharply once the peg was removed did not materialize. Let me explain why interest rates did not rise immediately after the removal of the peg by the Federal Reserve. So long as there was a pegged rate on government bonds, the Federal Reserve had to create enough money, through the purchase of the bonds, to match the liquidity, the cash balances, the public wanted to hold at that interest rate. As the public, therefore, held all the cash balances related to the pegged rate, the removal of the peg should not have resulted in a sudden rise of interest rates. That would happen gradually as the cash position of the public tightened with reduced purchases of government bonds by the Federal Reserve System.

MR. MELTZER: I am shocked at the fact that all the predictions about what would happen to the interest rate turned out to be false.

MR. BERNSTEIN: Of course not everybody thought that there would be a sharp rise in interest rates immediately. If investors and government bond dealers had thought so, there would have been such a sharp rise merely on the basis of expectations. The real fear of informed persons was that the continuation of the peg would cause inflation. The consequence of having kept the peg on government bond rates so long was precisely what the

Federal Reserve said it would be. The money supply was expanded to the level the public wanted to hold at the lower rate. With the excessive cash balances—excessive relative to the needs of a community with stable prices and costs—the excess reduced itself gradually through a further rise in prices and costs. That is part of the explanation of the inflation from 1951 to 1958.

Now, as to Mr. Meltzer's interpretation of what I said on the current balance, I am afraid his figures are wrong. Our balance on goods and services went from 500 million dollars in 1959 to 8.5 billion dollars in 1964. The first point is that no capital movements were involved in this. The second point is that the part played by sales of wheat to the Russians and other countries were quite moderate. Suppose it was 400 million dollars, you still have to go from 500 million dollars to 8.1 billion dollars.

CHAIRMAN TRIFFIN: Much of what I wanted to say has been said already, and I shall avoid repeating it. Let me merely add that I would agree very largely with Milton Friedman—and with his answers to the objections most frequently raised against his flexible rates proposal—if the main cause of balance-of-payments disequilibria were always the previous development of international price and cost disparities, making a country uncompetitive, or overcompetitive, in relation to its trade partners. If this were the only problem, floating rates à la Friedman would be appropriate to preserve equilibrium, and speculation might help to accelerate readjustments rather than aggravate maladjustments.

But international cost disparities are not the only problem, and no single panacea can cure all problems. It could often aggravate them, and this is eminently true of floating rates. Most of the major balance-of-payments disequilibria of recent years have their roots in capital movements rather than in current account transactions. This has certainly been the case in the United States, for example.

Another major factor, particularly for the open economies of Europe, has been disparate rates of monetary and financial expansion, spilling out from the more expansionary to the less expansionary countries, and leading directly to balance-of-payments disequilibria well in advance of price or cost disparities. (See my article with Herbert Grubel in the November, 1962 issue of the *Review of Economics and Statistics.*)

Take a very simple case to illustrate this point. Assume that the Dutch have preserved full equilibrium, internally and externally, for the last ten years, but decide suddenly to distribute a bonus of 1 billion guilders to the veterans of the last war, or engage in a wild credit expansion. With stable exchange rates the inflationary forces unleashed thereby would spill out in foreign spending and losses of monetary reserves. Domestic price rises would be kept in check by import competition from other countries, particularly from those of the Common Market. When losses of reserves force the Dutch to correct their policies, their price and cost structure will have suffered only minor damage. If, however, they had had instead floating rates à la Friedman, the inflationary potential would have been bottled up inside the economy, and caused large increases in foreign exchange rates, import prices and domestic costs. Under modern conditions wages would have been adjusted upward to the rising cost of living. And by the time the Dutch corrected their policies, it would be too late. Wages would not come down. In brief, every expansionary mistake would be sanctioned by wage rises, irreversible under modern conditions, while deflationary mistakes would not be expected to produce compensating declines in wage rates.

These one-way movements of wages would definitely impart an upward bias to foreign exchange rates. Speculators would be aware of this, and accelerate the movement.

As for James Meade's proposal for managed flexible rates, it raises in addition two other problems. Who will manage the dollar-sterling rate? Who will decide? The Federal Reserve or the Bank of England? I need not pursue this point which has been emphasized already by Mr. Emminger.

The second problem is that of internal management. The rate will not be managed by economists, but by politicians subject to powerful lobbying pressures. The experience of Latin American countries in the nineteenth century and of France under Poincaré is most illuminating in this respect. Exporters will welcome exchange rate depreciation, but fight tooth and nail any substantive appreciation cutting down the proceeds of their sales abroad, converted in domestic currency, especially if they are confronted with wage costs which can easily move upward, but never downward. Exporters will be in favor of flexibility when foreign exchange rates move up, but will plead for a return to stable rates whenever they tend to move down.

Chapter VI

A Central Banker's
View of Gold

Chairman: JACOB VINER
Position Paper: OTMAR EMMINGER

CHAIRMAN VINER: Disraeli, in the House of Commons—in a
House of Commons heavily infested with enthusiasts for one version or another of monetary reform—said that he had come to the
conclusion that more men have been knocked off balance by gold
than by love. I don't know what statistical basis his statement has.
My interpretation is that he wasn't comparing love of gold with
other species of love but hatred of gold with one particular
species of love. The persons I think he was referring to were
early monetary reformers who felt that gold as money was an
incubus which was checking the progress of England and should
be rapidly ejected from the monetary system.

Our speaker, Otmar Emminger, is one of the governors of the
Bundesbank, a very high official in that bank. He is relied upon
heavily by the Bundesbank to represent them at international
agencies and in international negotiations. He is at present
Chairman of the Deputies of the Group of Ten. He was edu-
cated at the University of Berlin, the University of Munich, the
University of Edinburgh and the London School of Economics.

Although he apparently would not want this to be too widely
known in Germany, and I didn't get this information from him,
he is an economist. He belongs to our union, although I don't

think he feels knowledge of that is a useful asset. He is universally regarded by all accounts as a man of extreme judgment, of extreme knowledge and with just the right experience for his present post.

He is also by all accounts a magnificent negotiator on the range of problems with which this conference is dealing. I pass on to you the opinion which has been transmitted from a good judge who knows him well that he is the greatest brain in Europe on monetary questions. We at this conference have already seen evidence of the quality of the man. For me it is a high honor to have the privilege of introducing him to you.

MR. EMMINGER: Thank you, Mr. Chairman, for that extremely kind introduction which slightly embarrassed me. I may perhaps, by way of introduction and also by way of excuse, just say a few words on how my position paper, which you have before you, came about. When I was asked if I would come forth and prepare something in the nature of a position paper, I did not know what other contributors there would be for this conference. So I just sat down last week in Washington, during a very busy week, and wrote down some things which had come to me in European discussions. What you see in effect in this paper is not a very systematic or deep-going discussion and dissertation on all the many aspects of gold in our monetary system. Fortunately for me, but especially fortunately for you, we have the benefit of Mr. Bernstein's brilliant paper. He did a great service to us, and especially to me, because he really went systematically into the problems of gold and the role of gold in our system.

When the deputies of the Group of Ten delivered their first interim report on the functioning of the present system they wrote, "Gold remains the basic reserve asset of the system and the common measure of par values." The French Minister of Finance, in his statement at the annual meeting of the International Monetary Fund in Tokyo last year, expressed this idea more forcefully when he said, "The international monetary system must be thought of as consisting of concentric circles . . . the center is constituted by gold. . . ." Indeed, gold is in the center of the international monetary system—but in some ways also in the center of present controversies about this system. There are some who want to enhance the role of gold in any future world monetary system; there are some who want to increase, some who want to lower its price. Others again who foresee a growing shortage of gold in the future, want to create substitutes for gold and lay down rules for the use of gold and its substitutes.

There is a school in Europe who want to enhance the role of gold in our system by a return to the so-called classical (or "automatic") gold standard. Currency reserves should, in principle, consist only of gold (apart from small working balances in foreign exchange); settlements of residual balances between countries, except when they belonged to the same "monetary zone," should be effected only in gold.

What is behind such proposals? In a very general way it is a nostalgic longing for the "good old times" (which in reality were not so good after all). It is also a vague distrust against the management of money by government, by politicians. Some people prefer to let money be governed by the hazards of gold production, gold hoarding or Russian gold sales, rather than by the whims of politicians. Or as George Bernard Shaw put it in his own witty way in *The Intelligent Woman's Guide to Capitalism and Socialism,* "You have to choose (as a voter) between trusting to the natural stability of gold and the honesty and intelligence of the members of government. And, with due respect for these gentlemen, I advise you, as long as the capitalist system lasts, to vote for gold."

The economist will build his case for a return to a pure gold standard rather on the deficiencies of the present gold exchange standard: 1) that it is unfair and inflationary in that it exempts the reserve-currency country from balance-of-payments discipline; and 2) that the growing volume of dollar balances in foreign hands makes the system sensitive to waves of mistrust in the dollar and, therefore, threatens its stability.

In the eyes of the most influential living proponent of a return to the pure gold standard, President de Gaulle, there comes on top of it the aversion against basing one's currency on another, extra-European, currency. "The international payments system," he said in February, 1965, "must be established on an unquestionable monetary basis which does not bear the mark of any individual country. . . . It is difficult to envision in this regard any other standard than gold. Yes, gold, which does not change in nature, . . . which has no nationality, which is considered, in all places and at all times, the immutable and fiduciary value par excellence. Furthermore . . . it is fact that even today no currency has any value except by direct relation to gold, real or supposed."

The Role of Gold Today

It is a pity that this glowing picture of the role of gold does not quite correspond to the sober realities of our time. Gold is not the immutable value par excellence, standing above any governmental arbitrariness. We have seen in our own lifetime— in 1934, to be exact—that its price could be changed overnight in terms of nearly all currencies by the decision of one government —and what an arbitrary decision was the increase in the U.S. gold price in 1934! And even today, the price of gold is dependent on the attitude mainly of one country, namely, the U.S., together with a handful of other countries. If they were no longer prepared to buy gold at a given price in order to hold it for monetary purposes, then its price would quite certainly fall drastically. Nor is the purchasing power of gold the immutable value from which the other currencies derive their value. It is the other way round: gold derives its value from its relationship to some national currencies. As over the last thirty years gold was principally tied to the dollar, it has had to share the fate of the dollar, losing more than half of its real value vis-à-vis commodities since 1934. Some one hundred sixty years ago the French philosopher Rivarol said, "Gold is the sovereign of the sovereigns." But today it is more like a useful servant, a well-honored and above all well-paid servant of the monetary system.

Professor Rueff, the well-known French economist and gold protagonist, fully realized this when he recently said in an interview, "The price of gold is not in itself something given by God; it's the result of a policy." But Rueff himself occasionally seems also to fall victim to the widespread belief in something magic about gold, e.g., when he asserts that as long as we have a gold exchange standard, based mainly on the dollar, the U.S. will inevitably have large balance-of-payments deficits; while as soon as the gold exchange standard would be abolished in favor of a pure gold reserve standard, to quote him, "the deficit of the balance-of-payments of the U.S. will disappear in less than three months."

I would not disagree with Professor Rueff that the gold dollar standard initially gave the U.S. much more latitude for financing its balance-of-payments deficits than its own reserves would have allowed. The gold exchange standard gave the U.S. access to a large amount of supplementary foreign short-term credits. But it is, of course, not true that a reserve-currency country has no other choice but to utilize this additional margin for deficits. Nor do I believe that the gold exchange standard provides the reserve center with an unlimited margin for perpetuating its deficits. On the contrary, from a certain point onward, the burden of accumulating dollar liabilities toward foreign countries has begun to exert a growing pressure on the U.S. to balance its external accounts, so that this disciplinary effect by now far outweighs any remaining margin for further deficits.

Or to put it in different words, it is hard to understand why and how the present gold exchange standard should prevent the U.S. from taking the necessary steps for correcting the imbalance in its external accounts; and on the other hand also, why and how an outflow of gold would have such magic powers that it would make automatically disappear within three months all the various domestic forces making for inflation of demand and costs or, for that matter, the special burdens weighing in particular on the U.S. balance of payments. We have just had a nice practical illustration to support our theoretical reasoning. The U.S. has had, in the first eight months of 1965, a gold out-flow to the other countries of 1.3 billion dollars, several times the amount of its actual balance-of-payments deficit. It has, so to speak, over-fulfilled the norm which a full-fledged pure gold standard would have imposed on it. And yet, even after nine months of more than 100 per cent gold settlements, the under-lying U.S. deficit has not yet magically disappeared, but on the contrary is showing signs of increasing again.

The Gold Standard

This just goes to show that those who want to put our inter-national monetary system back on the basis of a pure, or so-called "automatic," gold standard, cannot rely on any magic au-tomatism of gold flows alone. We have regretfully to admit that the nineteenth century is over. And monetary historians will probably tell us that even before 1914 the gold standard did not work so automatically, nor that it was any such pure gold standard at all, without reserve currencies nor additional credit facilities, as the gold advocates of today would have us believe. Dr. Vocke, former president of the German Central Bank and himself a stanch adherent of the gold standard, once said, "The so-called automatism of the gold standard is nothing but a schoolbook legend." Most of the advocates of a pure gold stand-ard, indeed, would therefore not only prescribe that reserves should be held entirely in gold and that deficits in the external accounts should be settled entirely in gold, but they would sup-plement this with a firm commitment to the effect that coun-tries should conduct their policies in such a way that they cor-respond to the "rules of the so-called classical (or automatic) gold standard." Countries should, in other words, pursue a re-strictive monetary and fiscal policy in case of deficits and an expansive policy in case of surpluses.

Now I am all in favor of persuading countries to have their domestic policies oriented more toward exterior factors than they do now; otherwise our present system of fixed exchange rates may have difficulty of functioning in the longer run. But if it is not the automatic force of gold flows alone that brings this result about, but rather the deliberate adjustment policies of governments and central banks, then we might as well try to improve these adjustment policies within the framework of the existing gold exchange standard. This is exactly what the Group of Ten has begun trying; and a few days ago the ministers and central bank governors of the Group of Ten, assembled in Washington for the annual meeting of the IMF, have reaffirmed their intention of searching for a better balance-of-payments discipline with the help of agreed rules.

Some of the advocates for an enhanced role of gold plead for an increase in the price of gold, a doubling for instance, as has been proposed by Rueff and others. What are their reasons?

1) They consider it unfair or unjust that the price of gold in dollars should be kept where it was put by the U.S. in 1934, while nearly all other dollar prices have in the meantime more than doubled. In my view, this is an extremely weak argument, especially as the price of gold is an entirely artificial one, determined largely by the decisions and interventions of monetary authorities.

2) Some adherents of the pure gold standard want to double the price of gold in order to increase the nominal value of gold reserves in the world, and thus to compensate for the destruction of international liquidity that would be bound to follow from the abolition of the present gold exchange standard, that is to say of the practice of holding dollars and pounds as reserves.

3) Some among them would see the particular merit of a doubling of the gold price in making it easier for the U.S. (and also for the U.K.) to repay all or a large part of their short-term liabilities to other countries. As Professor Rueff declared a few months ago, "I consider it a crime to speak of a change in the price of gold without speaking of the reimbursement of the

dollar claims, because the change in the price of gold has no other justification."[1]

It is not surprising that such proposals have been sharply rejected by American officials. Mr. Deming, the Under Secretary for Monetary Affairs in the U.S. Treasury, a few months ago categorically rejected an increase in the price of gold, because "this would repudiate the implied and stated commitments of the gold exchange standard to the advantage of a few and the disadvantage of many," and would be discriminatory against those countries that had kept faith with the dollar and continued to hold a substantial fraction of their reserves in dollars. To which I would add that it would be disruptive (and would probably in the end lead to a demonetization of gold altogether) if one began tinkering with the price of gold in order just to alleviate one's debt burden. Furthermore, it would probably not contribute to monetary discipline in the world if the world's reserves (apart from international institutions) would be suddenly increased from their present level of 64 billion dollars to 82 billion dollars—as they would be if the gold reserves of 41 billions would be nominally doubled to 82 billion (even if all the foreign exchange reserves of 23 billion would be wiped out, which is, of course, an unrealistic assumption). As to filling the world's need for reserves, there are better and less arbitrary methods at hand than such an increase of the nominal gold price. I would agree with Mr. Pierre-Paul Schweitzer, the Managing Director of the IMF, who recently stated, "Raising the gold price would be a poor way—and an unjust way—to increase world liquidity. I do not see any good in it and I see a lot of harm in it."

The case against an increase in the price of gold—I have not enumerated all the reasons here—seems to me absolutely convincing. But not all people seem to be convinced by it, as we see from the recurring waves of gold hoarding, in spite of its relatively high cost in terms of foregone interest or investments

[1] See Jacques Rueff and Fred Hirsch, *The Role and the Rule of Gold: An Argument,* Essays in International Finance, No. 47, June, 1965; New Jersey: Princeton University Press, p. 11.

profits. Speculation about the gold price is inevitably a one-way street. While people may believe that at some time in the future the price of gold might be increased (or that a big crisis might even force such an increase on unwilling authorities), hardly anybody believes that there is the slightest risk of a fall in the gold price. There has of late been a discussion in the U.S., and in particular in the Subcommittee on International Exchange and Payments of Congress, of whether one could not break this one-way psychology by the U.S. suspending purchases of gold at the fixed price of 35 dollars per ounce, or lowering its purchasing price below 35 dollars. Without going into the details of this discussion here, let me just state my conviction that this suggestion is probably unrealistic, in short, a non-starter.

The Future Role of Gold

After having briefly outlined what should not be done with gold—it should not, and could not, become our sole reserve asset, and its price should not be increased—let me say a few words on what the future role of gold in our international payments system might possibly be. The Subcommittee on International Exchange and Payments of the U.S. Congress, in its recent guidelines for international reform, came to the following conclusion:

> Gold should continue its present role as a universal medium of international exchange. The United States should not seek to undermine it. But nothing must be done to enhance its value in relation to other forms of reserve assets; no arrangements can be acceptable that provide incentives to convert reserve currencies into gold.[2]

In my view this is fine as far as it goes. The problem, of course, is how to implement this guideline in actual practice. At

[2] U.S. Congress, Subcommittee on International Exchange and Payments of the Joint Economic Committee, *Report: Guidelines for Improving the International Monetary System,* 89th Cong., 1st Sess., 1965, p. 8.

present, there are no rules laid down for our international reserve system. Contrary to what many people believe, and some professors write or teach, the Bretton Woods Agreement contains no rules on the composition of national currency reserves; it is up to every country whether it wants to hold only gold, or gold and reserve currencies, or any other reserve medium it considers suitable. The competition between gold and the reserve currencies as to their place in national currency reserves is determined by the advantages and disadvantages of the different reserve assets, and also, of course, by the varying appraisals of the risks involved in holding either gold or reserve currencies. This competition has produced, up to now, what I would call "an uneasy balance" between the various reserve media. If we don't want to upset this "uneasy balance" two points have to be kept in mind:

First, in any future reform of our international monetary system, we should be careful not to create incentives for increasing gold reserves at the expense of the dollar. I mention two examples: The French have proposed to create a new Collective Reserve Unit (CRU) which would be distributed to member countries in proportion to their gold reserves. This would not only be inequitable but may also create a scramble for increasing gold reserves at the expense of reserve currencies (except if special safeguards were taken). The same might also be true for a proposal of Mr. Roosa. In his recent book, *Monetary Reform for the World Economy*, he suggested that all member countries taking part in the creation of a new "fund unit" should agree to buy and sell gold at a fixed price against any amounts of their currency tendered by the monetary authority of another member. At first sight, this looks like a sort of equitable burden-sharing, as it would relieve the U.S. from being the only country that has to convert its currency into gold. But I cannot help feeling that this would induce all members to hold most of their reserves in gold in order to be on the safe side against such requests for conversion into gold. Thus this proposal may backfire.

Second, we should devote more attention to the question of

whether we should not try and agree in the future on some general rules for the composition of reserves at least among the major reserve-holders, practically the members of the Group of Ten who account for about 85 per cent of the total gold reserves of the western world. It looks as if a sort of dilemma may be shaping up. On the one hand, gold should represent in the future a decreasing share in the total currency reserves of the world, as the additions to world reserves that can reasonably be expected from new monetary gold will, at least in the longer run, be only a minor part of the total increase in reserves. On the other hand, the present propensities of monetary authorities seem to go, on an average, rather in the direction of slowly upgrading the proportion of gold in their total reserves. Now, even if the average gold proportion in the world's reserves is increased by only one percentage point, say from 60 to 61 per cent, this would be tantamount to an extinction of international liquidity of about 700 million dollars, or just about as much as gold production and Russian gold sales together have, over the last few years, added to monetary reserves on an annual average. There appears to be a sort of conflict between what in the longer run appears to be necessary, and what is actually taking place.

All the present talk about "international liquidity" starts from the assumption that the additions to the world's monetary gold stock—which, on an average, would raise world reserves at best only by about 1 per cent per annum—will in the longer run be inadequate for the world's need for reserves. To me it seems slightly odd that we discuss all sorts of artificial reserve supplements to gold to be created by common agreement, but that at the same time we entirely neglect changes in the composition of reserves which might actually provoke greater changes in total international liquidity.

Mr. Schweitzer, the Managing Director of the IMF, spoke recently about the necessity of making the development of international liquidity a matter of deliberate control. This view has been widely acclaimed, most recently by the British Chancellor of the Exchequer at the annual meeting of the Fund. To me, deliberate control of international liquidity would mean not only control of new liquidity, but should also encompass some common supervision of the existing volume and composition of liquidity. I know that this raises difficult questions, such as the effectiveness of "multilateral surveillance" and the freedom of choice among the various kinds of reserve assets and the free convertibility between them. But we have, in fact, already internationally accepted a reserve medium where there is no such absolute freedom of choice and convertibility, and whose variations are governed by rules laid down in the Fund, namely, the member countries' reserve positions in the Fund. They amount already to about 5 billion dollars, which is one-third of the present total of official dollar reserves.

I don't want to go into any further details here. But it may well be that we are in the transition from the old gold dollar standard—a loosely-based system that has grown up and expanded in a half-conscious way—to a new gold exchange system where the insufficiency and the vagaries of the supply of monetary gold will be evened out and compensated by a conscious provision of other reserve assets, and where the relationship between gold and other reserve assets will be governed by agreed rules, thus assuring our international monetary system the stability which we need for a stable and expanding world economy.

CHAIRMAN VINER: I think the statement of mine about Mr. Emminger's qualifications, based in past on secondhand information, was confirmed in a surprisingly few minutes by his presentation. I am sure we are all pleased with Mr. Emminger's very sober, sane and judicious statement.

A great German philosopher in the eighteenth century preached what was known as the optimistic doctrine, that this was the best of all possible worlds, and a fellow German said, "How sad!" The discussion I have heard here and elsewhere has indicated to me that we have now about the worst possible of all international financial structures, and also that it is not very bad. I am inclined to both views, leaning toward Mr. Haberler, who I believe this morning managed to work both sides of the street with great agility.

But I have only one fairly substantial conviction on the matters that we have been discussing and that is that we are bound for the indefinite future to have an international financial structure which doesn't have any precise shape and does not conform to any well-defined blueprint. It will show signs of roughness, of gaps, of over-supply of machinery. But it will operate. If it operates even with tolerable success, it will in large part do so because of the character, the wisdom, the experience and the judgment of the aggregate of responsible officials who will have the deciding voice both in shaping the pattern of the system and in operating it.

Sitting beside our speaker during this conference, and reading his paper, and now listening to him, I felt in all sincerity that he seems to be ideally fitted both to participate actively in the process of designing the system and of operating it. I appreciate especially the sense of realism, the good judgment, and the flexibility by which his fine presentation was marked. It has been for me, and I am sure for most of us, a very satisfying experience.

MR. WIDENMANN: Mr. Chairman, I take my cue from you. You said last night that in the contemplation of the problem of what to do with the monetary mechanism we should bear in mind what we expect to evolve in international finance, international trade and international capital movements in the years ahead—in other words, in what environment the problem is going to arise. Many of the things I had in mind were covered by the brilliant statement we just heard from Mr. Emminger.

I would ask you to consider Mr. Emminger's remarks against the background of the following, namely, that the world is in a phase of unusually rapid change, more rapid change than we have ever experienced in our lifetimes. This rapid change constitutes a basic change in environment and hence shifts the frame of reference of our technical international monetary problem. The world is moving more and more rapidly. We are in fact in a technological revolution, gentlemen, which is dynamic. It is the most dynamic thing that has happened in the economic and financial world since the industrial revolution of the early 1800's. It requires enormous amounts of capital, enormous amounts of research and development, and wide markets. I ask you to consider what Mr. Emminger told you in the light of this. This is part of the pound-dollar problem.

I agree one hundred per cent with what Mr. Emminger had to say about expecting too much of the mechanism, not confusing this mechanism with adjustment, and the necessity of adjustment. And this is more important than liquidity. And maybe if you had this adjustment you wouldn't need as much liquidity. He didn't say that, but this is my judgment.

I agree you can't expect the surplus countries in this kind of environment to bail you out. The surplus countries have problems of their own. They are in a phase of rapid growth which presents very attractive investment opportunities on the one hand and on the other exposes them to severe wage pressure which create difficult domestic monetary pressures. Under such circumstances what is the incentive to invest abroad just to reduce a balance-of-payments surplus, particularly when there is a question of when and whether you are going to get your money back? This is the second phase of the problem. This gap cannot be bridged by additional central reserve bank credit. These conflicting pressures reflect the enormous demands for funds arising out of the technological revolution which should not be confused with a lack of central bank reserves which in turn should not be confused with capital.

In the third place, the demands of the underdeveloped countries are creating problems because their demands are becoming more and more strident. The thought that you can solve this by tinkering with the mechanism of the IMF if you could only find the formula—this is also an illusion. What the underdeveloped countries really require, are really asking for, is additional capital. Although from their point of view they are not so much concerned whether the additional funds are capital or credit. They lose sight of the fact that the developed countries also require capital, that they don't necessarily have a surplus thereof, and that in terms of the amount of money that can be profitably invested in a viable economy with no political risk, the United States is the most underdeveloped country in the world.

I had the pleasure of talking about this problem with Mr. Emminger and we agreed that this dilemma is not one that can be resolved by changes in the IMF mechanism or devices to economize gold. This problem comes down to a question of national policy, of determining what the national, political, financial and economic priorities should be, determining how much money is required by the domestic economy and how much domestic demands can be put back so as to make room for foreign commitments deemed to be in the over-all national interest —how you adjust your internal economy to whatever you think its demands ought to be and how much productive facilities you ought to go ahead and allot to satisfy the external demands.

The technological revolution, as I said, requires enormous amounts of capital. And when the U.S. was finally forced in January to go ahead and put on the voluntary controls, temporary controls, because technically the dollar was more important than anything else we had to do, the sudden cutoff of the supply of dollars was very revealing. The rest of the world is also in a technological revolution and must keep pace with us. Japan, the continent, Germany, they all must keep pace with this thing, and they haven't got the capital to keep pace. The result is that while we were having the outflow of dollars they were borrowing these dollars to keep pace with the technological revolution. When we cut it off, we created all sorts of difficulties and we also uncovered all sorts of misinvestment. I could give you a catalog of these misinvestments all over the world, but this would carry me too far afield.

The technological revolution is creating new problems for us right now in the balance of payments. It explains the pressure to make additional foreign private investments which have risen so substantially this year. This is the important facet. This is what Mr. Sachs referred to, the problem of the pressure to invest and relating it to the problem of the monetary mechanism—that is to say, the huge investments that are necessary in the Common Market, in the Persian Gulf, in the North Sea, and in the Far East. These are the real problems which must be related to the problem of the monetary mechanism and how you deal with it.

Let me just leave you with one final thought, namely that while this enormous demand for capital creates its own problems and at the moment has aggravated the near-term outlook for the balance of payments because of the enormous investments we are making and have to make, at the same time in this technological revolution we have an enormous advantage over the rest of the world. We have the capital, we have the know-how, we have the facilities, and we have the enormous investment in research and development.

I see in that the prospects of the continuation of a cost differential in our favor. This is, I think, the most important and the most constructive thing that can be said about the future of the dollar.

MR. HITCHINGS: Mr. Emminger's position paper and remarks dealing with the role of gold, international monetary reserves and balance-of-payments discipline are particularly helpful in providing a clear understanding of the problems and policies involved. Much of our previous discussion in this conference has highlighted the wide divergence of opinion on how serious the problems are and what should be done about them. These discussions have stimulated thinking and explored possible courses of action. There is also a need, however, for narrowing these differences in terms of what policies are feasible for the world as it exists today. Mr. Emminger has made an important contribution toward meeting this objective.

To develop somewhat further what policies are necessary and feasible, I would like to direct some questions to Mr. Emminger. The first questions deal with U.S. dollars as international monetary reserves, assuming that the price of gold is not increased. If the United States holds to its firm commitment against raising the price of gold, as appears likely, is there a need to inject some other form of international claim as a substitute for dollars? Are the existing dollar claims already too large, or is the problem primarily that of preventing a future excessive buildup of dollar claims? Would present holders of dollars be willing to keep these claims in dollars if they were satisfied that steps were being taken to close the gap in the United States balance of payments?

The next questions deal with policies to close the gap in our balance of payments, assuming that the United States Government continues to oppose a rise in long-term interest rates. This also is a rather firm policy at the present time. If this policy is continued, what steps should be taken other than the current voluntary program to control capital flows? Can more be accomplished in terms of making it easier to purchase U.S. goods and services in countries that have built up a surplus of U.S. dollar claims?

MR. EMMINGER: I would not have to say very much, or to add to what Mr. Widenmann said about the very important role that the United States has to fill as regards capital development all over the world.

When it comes to considering whether U.S. capital exports should be further increased or whether they should be restrained, one has to keep one fundamental principle in mind. In the longer run, the U.S. can export only as much capital to other countries as can be covered by a surplus in the movements of goods and services. In so far as net capital outflows from the U.S. are not covered by an equivalent surplus in goods and services of this country, this country does not contribute real resources to the rest of the world but contributes only monetary liquidity. Now, sometimes that may be useful, but not always. So in the end these two things must be brought into some sort of a balance. This, in a nutshell, is your present situation.

With this I come immediately to the questions of the second

speaker. First he said the United States is committed to the present gold price. I mentioned the same idea when saying that changing the U.S. gold price would really run counter to firm commitments of this country on which other countries have based their own policies, including my own country, including my own bank. Now the question was whether under these circumstances of an unchanged gold price there would be a serious need for additional reserves.

I would refer back to what was said on that question last night by my friend Ralph Young. He had a surprisingly optimistic view and estimate on the possibility of future monetary gold supplies. I haven't been that optimistic. I am taking a slightly less optimistic view in order to be on the safe side. I would say not immediately, but over the longer run, it is likely that we shall need something additional, whatever that may be. Whether it will be a new "fund unit" according to the Roosa Plan or some other kind of reserve, is an open question and is now under consideration and negotiation in the Group of Ten.

Ralph Young said yesterday that we ought to have a contingency plan because we are not certain about the future supply of gold. I would say we are uncertain not only about the future of the supply of gold, we are uncertain about a number of other things which may be very important. Among these, I have listed tonight the uncertainty about the future composition of reserves, and uncertainty about the existing volume of reserve currencies, like the dollar and the pound, in the reserves of major countries. So my answer would be that for such contingencies we should plan ahead in such a way that we work out the plans fully and realistically.

The second question was whether, under the assumption that the United States would achieve and maintain full balance-of-payments equilibrium, foreign dollar holders would not become willing dollar holders while today some of them are unwilling dollar holders. In my personal opinion that would do a great deal to convert unwilling holders into willing holders. But I am not certain that it would solve all the problems before us. We have not only the dollar problem but also the pound problem. And when I alluded to the probability of maybe thinking out some arrangement against the run on reserves in order to safe-guard it against destroying liquidity, I had primarily sterling in view.

I would not be concerned at all about the dollar. As soon as this country really maintains or achieves and maintains a bal-ance-of-payments equilibrium, and by that, of course, I mean balance-of-payments equilibrium which is not only achieved by controls but also through underlying forces, I would have no concern about existing dollar balances in the hands of foreigners. But such an equilibrium in the U.S. balance of payments would, of course, mean at the same time that the U.S. would no longer contribute anything to the reserves of the rest of the world (which it did to such a great extent over the years 1958–1964).

The question of U.S. external equilibrium is, I think, related to a point, a third point of Mr. Hitchings', whether higher in-terest rates might be an important instrument for achieving and maintaining such an equilibrium on the basis of the underlying market forces. Well, on that I am uncertain. I have been mis-quoted on that point in a newspaper lately, and I guess it gives me an opportunity to set the record straight.

I am quite uncertain whether interest rates would achieve market equilibrium at the present time. What I was saying in the meeting where I was misquoted was only that in the long run, because I would not willingly envisage or gladly envisage the continuation of "voluntary restraints" or outright controls over capital movements indefinitely and permanently, one must look to some other forces more in conformity with real market forces to achieve equilibrium. This would probably mean that some-thing has to be done in order to bridge the present gap in in-terest rates between the U.S. and Europe both on this side of the Atlantic and the other. So in the end I would hope that some interest rates in Europe would come down, and also that investment opportunities in Europe would not be as affected by creeping inflation as they are now. On the other hand, this country might have an upward adjustment of interest rates. I don't foresee, however, any early solution along these lines. So if you ask me in what other areas something can be done, I must say I am not qualified to give you good advice on your own balance-of-payments policy. That is a highly political question which every country has to solve by itself. The only thing I can say is that we in Europe hope for an early and for a lasting and full equilibrium in the U.S. balance of payments. I may also add that my personal conviction is there will be no real progress in the negotiations on future monetary reform if there is not a very firm conviction on the part of everybody concerned that this country has full control over its external account.

I just see from my notes I have skipped one point that was mentioned by Mr. Hitchings, whether surplus countries couldn't do more to facilitate this adjustment by importing more. To this I would answer they are already importing much more. My own country has increased imports this year by 21 per cent, and that is quite a lot. We have gone into very heavy deficit on current account now, primarily because of this rapid increase in our imports.

MR. DILLON: I had originally thought that I would be able to come here and listen and learn so that I might be able to better carry out the duties I have been given in trying to advise our Treasury on questions they are interested in in the international monetary field, but I have been told by higher authority here we must all contribute.

So I am going to contribute by giving you a little of the background of our position up until last April. Certainly we always agreed that there could be, and should be, no serious consideration of international monetary reform as long as the United States balance of payments was in deficit. Now, this is not a very acceptable position to some of our academic colleagues because they saw the need for reform and didn't think it should wait. But we felt that it would be misunderstood, as it would have been, as long as the United States was in deficit. So for that reason over time, and right until recently, our position in Washington has been that we did not favor international monetary reform; there was no need for it, and we didn't want to talk about it. We did move to strengthen the existing arrangements in ways that were clearly needed. It was on our original initiative that the general arrangements to borrow were negotiated. They provided the IMF with the resources it needed to live up to current commitments in the new circumstances where they could no longer use the United States as their chief source of assets.

We also last year favored an increase in quotas of the International Monetary Fund. That was worked out more or less successfully although the special increases by strong countries were not as large as maybe we would have liked. Meanwhile we did our best with the balance of payments.

In spite of some of the thoughts that have been heard here, that consideration was always at the very front level. I must say I agree wholeheartedly with what Mr. Wallich said, that it was good to have this discipline because it might serve as a certain discipline on the domestic side. That certainly was true. It was and is true. The balance of payments in certain fields was given overriding priority right from 1961 on. We felt that we could move up short-term rates very considerably, which we did, although we were not at anywhere near full employment. This is something quite different from the monetary policy that we had had during the 1950's in this country. Some people objected to it because they felt it slowed up our move toward full employment. But we thought there was no real conflict and it could be done—and we did it.

On the balance of payments we followed the more classical concept and moved and worked on the current account. We were fairly successful. The current account improved very dramatically in the last four years, but this was accompanied by an equally rapid and almost equal-sized deterioration in capital account.

So finally, as that became evident for all to see, we suggested certain rather gradual moves in this area. First the interest equalization tax, and then when that proved not to be enough, last

February finally a complete move in that area with a voluntary control program which for the first time provided a complete and rounded program of balance of payments that had no real loopholes left.

One might say that certain parts of it were not as effectively enforced as they could be and so forth, but there was no longer any complete gaps or holes. At long last there is no reason to believe that this couldn't be completely successful because it is quite different from any program we had before it. For the first time it covered all aspects of our balance of payments.

Certain people have felt that we could have moved sooner, or should have moved sooner. I don't think we could have, because in a democracy you can move no faster than public opinion and I don't think public opinion would have stood for that sort of move earlier. So we didn't.

We were worried about the capital account as early as 1962. We hoped it would settle itself. I made a statement about it at a meeting of the American Bankers Association in Rome in the spring of 1962, talking about what might happen if capital outflow grew too rapidly.

Well, it grew even faster than I feared at that time, and we had to move even further. But it wasn't that we weren't aware of it. It was just that the public was not ready, and we could not move. When we did move I think it was accepted more or less willingly and generally. And the banks who have been the chief contributors to this new program have done so patriotically and willingly although I don't blame them for not being too happy. But they recognize the reason for it.

The result has been that since the middle of last February, when that was announced, the United States has been continually in surplus—on the official settlements basis—for seven and a half months now. But no one can look ahead. We have all learned that.

With the ability to make this more effective if needed, and the President's statement that this will be done if necessary, the fact that for seven and a half months, ever since the program has been in effect, we have been continually in surplus, there is, I think, good reason to think that we have at least found a partial answer. The statement has been made that we want to continue forever. We certainly don't. But it does give us breathing space until the adjustments Mr. Emminger was talking about can take place between our capital market here and those in Europe. Our action was, of course, stimulated and brought about by the loss of gold that began earlier this year. We began working on it even earlier because of the large balance-of-payments deficit in the fourth quarter of last year.

I would like to make one comment. There has been a lot of semiacceptance of some statements that have been made that the French purchase of gold, their change in policy this year, influenced a number of other countries, and there was sort of a general movement in that direction. I don't think that the facts as I know them bear that out at all. I don't know of a single country that adopted the French action or imitated them in this way.

During the first half there were two other countries, Spain and Austria, that were continual gold purchasers. Those have been reported in our six months' statement. But both of those purchase programs were given to us before the French statement, before the French change in policy. They were a natural concomitant of the surpluses these two countries had during 1964 when neither of them bought any gold and it merely built their ratio back to about 50 per cent.

Aside from that the only other purchase of any size was a modest purchase by Italy which restored in full the 200 million dollar gold loss which they had the year before. They succeeded in restoring the substantially greater part by their own means and they bought the modest extra amount, about 75–80 million dollars, from the United States last spring. But this was in no sense a copying of the French pattern. I think this has been a remarkable example of the generally cooperative spirit that has been engendered in conversations among countries in the last few years. There was nobody who followed this French lead.

Certainly I think that the fact that our payments seem to be in balance—and it is the determination of the United States to keep them there for a substantial period and really indefinitely, subject to minor swings—opens up the whole question of international reform.

I don't believe, and I don't expect the other countries of the world to accept the fact that our payments are really in balance and are going to be in balance until this has been proved for a longer period of time. But our policy assumes this to be the case, since we know what our own policies are. So, therefore, we felt free for the first time to look ahead and see what should be done to the over-all system. For that reason last March 31, when I had my final press conference before turning over the job to my successor, I said that in my view the chief job of my successor would be to strengthen the international monetary system because the other major problems were on the way to solution and only needed continued attention to keep the programs under way.

My successor, Secretary Fowler, followed that up by his speech in July. This was designed not just immediately to have an international monetary conference, for he very carefully qualified his call for that. It was designed primarily to show that the United States was now ready to negotiate seriously to strengthen the international monetary system.

We feel it has to be strengthened. We feel that the problem will be the needed growth in reserves to make all the major countries feel happy and comfortable. The growth in reserves needed to keep pace with the growth in the world economy cannot be supplied by gold alone, and it will not be supplied by excess dollars in the future. Therefore some other means have to be found. I think Mr. Gilbert's thought, which he developed a month or so ago in a paper, is very pertinent here. He said it is not entirely, it is not really, the question whether there are enough or too many reserves at any one moment. You can never decide that. But the real question is there has to be a continued increase in reserves large enough each year to make enough to go around so that the major industrial countries will be happy and will not feel that they have to adopt unduly restrictive measures.

I think that the invention of the phrase "contingency plan" was a master stroke. I don't know who invented it, whether it was our Secretary Fowler or someone else, or whether it just grew like Topsy. But it in one stroke got over the major hurdle that has stopped any serious conversation on this subject, which was the argument that had not been settled, and could not be settled possibly by any reasoned discussion, whether there was at the moment, right now, too many or too few reserves. By talking about contingency planning some time in the future everybody agreed, without having to face the problem whether there was too much or too little. There are some very intelligent people, representatives of various countries who think there are too much, and there are equally intelligent ones who take the other view. So you can take either side you want. But this was avoided by the use of the words "contingency planning." I feel certain that this will be successful.

I don't worry too much about this overhang of dollars that some people have been talking about. There has been some talk about action. I think that depends on where the dollars are. As far as we can see, there was one really large unwilling holder of dollars which was the Republic of France, and they now have reduced their holdings to something like 900 million dollars. We must also realize that of that 900 million dollars they owe some 400 million dollars to the United States, or possibly a little more, for the assistance that the United States gave to France in the form of foreign aid—low-interest long-term loans right after the war of 2 per cent or 2.5 per cent—loans which the French are still paying off rather gradually even though they have speeded up their payments schedule. But they have always agreed to the concept that these loans were a form of foreign aid and that they should keep a similar amount of dollars offset against these debts. So if you leave that out, all France has left is 500 million dollars out of about 900 million dollars. And in conversations I have had with the French as to what the proper working balance would be they have been very insistent that because of the importance of the French franc the working balance they would have to hold would be as large, and slightly larger, as anybody else's. They have said that 300 million dollars would be on the small side.

So you can see that that doesn't leave very much left for them to feel that they are now holding in an unwilling fashion—maybe 100 million dollars, at the outside 200 million dollars. Beyond that the Swiss, the Dutch and the Belgians are approximately 100 per cent in gold except for necessary working balances. You then come down to Germany and Italy. The Germans have always believed in cooperation. I don't know any country that has cooperated better, not just with us, but as a surplus country by unilateral reductions in their tariffs, by changes in their taxation policies that affected capital investment portfolio, and by a number of other measures. As a result they are now running a deficit which this year has very sharply reduced this problem, if it ever existed in Germany, by reducing the amount of dollars that they have free. They had to use these dollars to pay off their deficit.

Italy is another country, and Italy has always been cooperative. They have also been on the receiving end of cooperation and they understand the problem.

Finally, I don't think there is any danger from the other dollar holding countries like Canada and Japan, who have always held dollars, and Sweden, which has always held dollars by preference. So I don't see any great problem in the so-called dollar overhang, provided we stay in balance, which is our assumption and our intent—a very serious one.

I think the problem is to work out in time the means of providing additional assets. I don't know what "in time" is. I am sure that if our balance is positive as we expect it to be and if we kept it there for two or three years that would begin to have a very real effect on the rest of the world. As a result I feel that agreement will be reached that will provide some form of additional asset, whether in the IMF or a special asset such as in the Bernstein, Roosa or French plans. I am pretty sure that some plan will be generally accepted in the relatively near future.

MR. WALLICH: It is not easy to comment after such a beautifully balanced, vintage Emminger.

I share the feeling that this is a period of transition. And while I am told that that is a remark that Eve made to Adam during the incident with the apple, I nevertheless think it is appropriate to our situation. That gets me to the problem Mr. Emminger touched last, the problem of the balance of payments. It is a cause of reasonable preoccupation that we finally had to descend to direct control. We may descend further.

If one thought that these controls were going to be permanent rather than transitional, there are many alternatives one would prefer. But we are in a transitional period, one of merging international capital markets. Capital is becoming international on a scale on which it has not had this characteristic since before World War I.

When reservoirs of credit with widely different levels of interest rates are connected up, it is not surprising that imbalances emerge. It is perhaps not reasonable, therefore, if for a while we contain this merger of reservoirs by direct controls. In the long run we have no alternative but to let interest rates in the various reservoirs reach a common level, separated only by risk premium. That means some rise in U.S. interest rates. I hope it does not mean an immediate rise. We cannot, however, indefinitely maintain what amounts to an import duty on the importation of foreign securities. Right now we seem to be inefficient producers of securities. Foreigners produce better, that is, higher yielding securities. Eventually we ought to be allowed to buy them.

On the matter of burden sharing in balance of payments adjustment, I am sure I don't say anything new to Mr. Emminger. The Europeans have suffered their inflation. We have suffered our unemployment. The more lasting contribution has been by the Europeans, because when the unemployment is over, that part of the "contribution" that has taken the form of lower aggregate demand and hence lower imports into the U.S. will be over too.

Some lasting contribution has been made by unemployment nevertheless because it has helped us to keep prices down, thus it may in the long run have contributed as much as inflation did on the European side.

How we can move toward a better adjustment mechanism is something that hoptfully we can discuss later, Mr. Chairman.

Now I would like to say a word about the role of the dollar in the evening picture. The gold exchange standard has been good to the United States, and it has helped us in our travels of the last seven years. It has clearly now reached an impasse. We have over-used it and we have converted what really should have been a monetary system into a credit system. The Europeans rightly are drawing a line at present levels of credit. We have no alternative but to straighten out our accounts. I hope that eventually the dollar can again function as an increasing reserve unit.

I don't think we ought to aim at that in order to create resources for ourselves. With the GNP approaching 700 billion dollars, we don't have to scrounge around for one billion to borrow abroad each year.

I do think the possibility of being able in an emergency to rely on other countries' temporarily holding our IOU's is an important one. We should not give that up if it is at all possible to maintain. But clearly, for the time being, these credit facilities have run their course.

Looking forward to the future perhaps one can take off from the last paragraph of Mr. Emminger's paper. He speaks there of the proportion of several assets. I think this seems to be clearly what we are moving toward, gold as a reserve asset and dollars. The exact forms in which this will be done are up to the present time before Mr. Emminger's committee.

The Ossola Report has made clear that the many brilliant and ingenious plans that they have constructed are really particular models of a general species. The Ossola Report contains a sort of do-it-yourself kit for monetary reform. We can all put together our own bits and pieces here, inside or outside the IMF—own reserves, borrowed reserves, automatic or conditional assistance, the developing countries, the reserve unit's relation to gold, riding piggyback on gold as it were or standing on its own feet, and finally the manner of reserve creation.

Let me simply wind up with a note on timing. We have moved early with our proposal for monetary reform. We ought now to press for speed. The term "contingency planning" very admirably described the attitude we should take. The deliberations of Mr. Emminger's committee will take time, and I wish him good luck with it.

MR. TRIFFIN: Mr. Chairman, since my academic colleagues and I have been so harsh on our gold-loving friends, I would like to soothe them somewhat by confessing that they have two valid, and even powerful, arguments in favor of their thesis.

The first is that gold is the only anonymous debtor in international finance. If you do not hold your foreign assets in gold, you have to hold them in some specific currency or currencies. And if the debtor country, in its sovereign wisdom, decides tomorrow to devalue its currency or make it inconvertible, you cannot send the police—or the Marines—to collect your claim in full. Gold will, therefore, retain its attraction as a "safer" reserve asset, as long as international negotiations are unable to devise an alternative asset, endowed with sufficient guarantees to inspire as full confidence in it as in gold itself. Failing the development of such an alternative and adequately guaranteed asset through international agreement, an upward revaluation of gold prices may well prove the only alternative to world deflation or restrictions.

The second argument is the one associated with the name of Professor Rueff. It is that gold reserves—or even gold money in internal circulation as well—is the only possible barrier against the inflationary proclivities of governments. One may doubt, of course, that new gold production, plus gold sales by the Russians, minus private gold purchases for the arts, industry, hoarding, and speculation, will automatically adjust available supplies of monetary gold to the legitimate monetary requirements of an expanding world economy, and guarantee us automatically either deflation or inflation. Monsieur Rueff, I must say, shares these doubts also, but considers that the possible inflationary or deflationary consequences of his proposed gold automaticity are still far less in magnitude than the dangers attendant to the use of the printing press by governments or central banks.

In the course of a recent academic debate at the Sorbonne, he admitted that his case for a return to a pure gold reserve system rested on this automaticity argument. I asked him then how a man so sincerely concerned with inflation would not hesitate to open the gates wide to inflation by doubling the price of gold and throwing thereby overnight 40 billion dollars of additional gold reserves into his automatic gold machine. He countered this argument by saying that, of courst, simultaneous agreement among the major countries concerned would be necessary to sterilize the inflationary potential of these 40 billion dollars of revaluation "profits." The United States, for instance, should agree to use such profits to repay immediately its indebtedness to foreign central banks. And since the revaluation profits of the U.K. would be far insufficient to enable it to do the same, other countries—particularly continental Europe—which have no such debts of their own to repay should sterilize their own revaluation profits by financing, on a long-term basis, the liquidation of Britain's indebtedness to foreign central banks.[3]

Where is the automaticity in all this? The governmental agreements required by Mr. Rueff to exorcise the inflationary impact of gold revaluation would be far more difficult to negotiate successfully than the agreements needed to make such revaluation superfluous and unnecessary. Extensive and continu-

---

[3] See *Travaux du Congrès des Economistes de Lange Française, 1963* (Editions Cujas, Paris, 1964), particularly pp. 22, 27–39, and 110–117, and the transcript of Mr. Rueff's intervention in a debate at Federal Trust, London, May 24–25, 1965.

ous cooperation will remain indispensable, in any case, to assure in the future a reasonable adjustment of reserve supply to reserve needs. Gold revaluation, penalizing those countries which have been most cooperative in moderating their gold demand in recent years, and rewarding those which have refused such cooperation, would be the worst possible preface to the type of reforms needed for the successful functioning of our international monetary system.

Gold revaluation would make sense if the only problem we faced were that of a liquidity shortage. It does not if we recognize, with Governors Holtrop, Blessing, and others, that the present system can be—and has been in recent years—inflationary, rather than deflationary, and that its basic defects are its haphazardness and vulnerability. The doubling of the gold price will not cure these defects, especially if Mr. Busschau was right in his excellent presentation of the problem, and if gold production were—as his figures imply—so irresponsive to a price change that it would remain at 50 million ounces even after the price of gold has been more than doubled and set at 75 dollars rather than 35 dollars an ounce. I would appreciate from him a word of explanation about this rather puzzling forecast.

MR. HABERLER: I shall not try to argue with the views of Professor Rueff or of anyone else who is not here. Instead, I shall comment on the paper presented by Mr. Emminger which I admire greatly.

Let me take up only two points. The first refers to a passage where I think he was a little unjust to my gold standard friends on this side of the table. He says, "The U.S. has had, in the first eight months of 1965, a gold outflow to the other countries of 1.3 billion dollars, several times the amount of its actual balance-of-payments deficit. It has, so to speak, over-fulfilled the norm which a full-fledged pure gold standard would have imposed on it."[4] In spite of that the deficit is still there. Surely this is not refutation of the gold standard theory. The theory does not say that the outflow of the gold by itself, automatically and miracu-

[4] See page 148.

lously, brings about the adjustment. What the theory says is that
it tends to bring the adjustment, if it is accompanied by at least
an equal reduction in the circulation of money. This latter condition was, of course, not fulfilled. The money supply has steadily
increased. There remains the fact that the observing of the
gold standard rule would have created unemployment. The
gold standard advocates can be criticized for not coming to
grips with this crucial problem. But this is another matter which
I cannot discuss at this time.

The other point is this: In reply to my earlier complaint to
the effect that the adjustment mechanism was greatly neglected
as compared with the liquidity problem, Mr. Emminger points
out that the Group of Ten in their well-known report mentioned
adjustment; in fact, they stressed right at the beginning, before
going into the liquidity problem, that there must sooner or later
be an adjustment of the balance-of-payments disequilibria.

Yes, there were a few sentences to that effect—you cannot
discuss the balance-of-payments problem without mentioning
adjustment—but there then followed forty pages or so on liquidity. I don't think it is unfair to call that a comparative neglect of
the adjustment problem—compared, that is to say, with the
liquidity problem. I could go beyond the statement of the Group
of Ten and mention, if I had time, ten books on liquidity, but
hardly a single one on adjustment!

CHAIRMAN VINER: Mr. McLaughlin asked me if he could
speak even though he was a gold producer, and I said I am not
prejudiced.

MR. MC LAUGHLIN: I realize all too well that I don't hold a
union card in this rather closed shop of economists and bankers,
but I can't refrain from making a little comment on the subject
before us, for a gold miner can't help being interested in how
his product is used.

One of the reasons advanced here why we should not raise
the price of gold is the alleged waste of resources in mining
gold. Many of you seem to forget that gold is not merely a
monetary metal. It is an element of growing importance in the

industrial world. In the past two years the industrial consumption of gold in the United States by licensed and legal users of the metal has been nearly twice the production from our domestic mines. In the previous five years, consumption about matched production. This development clearly indicates that there is a market in industry and the arts in our country for gold beyond the monetary agencies and that it is growing. Abroad, it is not as simple to distinguish between gold so consumed and the gold that is acquired by those seeking protection against inflation of currencies, but it is perhaps worth noting that in recent years less than half of the new gold available to the free world is being added to its monetary stocks.

Gold is an extraordinary element with very distinct properties. Many are unique and when better appreciated are likely to ensure gold a continuing market. In this great age of science and technology, I may be so bold as to predict that before many decades go by the demand for gold for industrial uses is going to be so much larger that gold for this reason alone in a truly free market would command a price higher than that currently defined in depreciating dollars. What is happening in silver may well happen in gold. When the attempt is made to tie a valuable metal to a depreciated and still depreciating currency, something has to give.

I would, however, like to add that revaluing gold to twice or even three times its present level as defined by the gold content of the dollar—which would merely bring it in line with its prewar status in relation to paper currencies—would not result in a flood of new gold from the mines. Indeed, the first effect would actually be a decline in annual production as measured in ounces for lower grade ore would certainly be milled wherever possible in order to prolong the life of the mines. Prospecting for new gold deposits and development of new mines would, of course, be stimulated and eventually the output of the metal should increase, but it would be a slow process and unless some truly spectacular discoveries were made—which is possible though not very likely—the increase would be orderly and not out

of balance with the needs for industrial uses and monetary stocks
(even with convertibility of currencies and with removal of restrictions on ownership). It might also be noted that for a limited time a substantial outflow from private stocks of gold, sometimes called hoards, could be expected that would promptly
ease the situation in the interval during which mine output was
picking up.

MR. EXTER: I am here partly because of the powers-that-be.
Martin Gainsbrugh looked at me as much as to say, "Here we
have given you three meals and a night's lodging and you haven't
earned a cup of coffee." I am not here because Dr. Emminger's
excellent talk provoked me to reply to it. In fact, it didn't provoke me as much as the opening statement of Ralph Young, my
former boss, provoked me.

I am always accused of over-simplifying and over-mecha-
nizing, especially by Chairman William McChesney Martin, who
has told me several times that I do. I have always replied that I
can't understand complicated things. So, if you will forgive me,
I'm going to over-simplify and over-mechanize for just a few
minutes.

I should like to go back to the way in which money is created in this international monetary system of ours. It is created
every time a central bank acquires an asset. We have fractional
reserve systems, of course, so we all know that on the basis of
those central bank assets additional money is created as commercial banks in turn acquire assets.

The first asset that central banks acquire is gold. If central
banks acquire only gold, we shouldn't be sitting here tonight.
We shouldn't have this problem. We should have the automatic
gold standard system and there would be no chronic balance-of-
payments problems in the world.

The second kind of asset that central banks acquire is domestic assets—any domestic asset—and this is the problem.
Different central banks acquire different quantities of domestic
assets. Some central banks in the world have acquired none at
all, others a great many. The National Bank of Switzerland has

none. The Netherlands Bank has none. And, by the way, those central banks have no balance-of-payments problems, as you might guess.

On the other hand, those central banks that have acquired domestic assets in quantity, the Federal Reserve System in recent years, and the Bank of England, have balance-of-payments problems. When central banks acquire domestic assets they create money, have balance-of-payments deficits, and their currencies get into the hands of other central banks. If the other central banks hold their currencies, then they create money, for this is the third kind of asset held by central banks.

So a central bank can create money by buying gold, by acquiring domestic assets, or by acquiring foreign currency assets. As the central banks of the world have acquired not only gold, but also dollars and sterling, we have built up what we call the gold exchange standard.

The trouble is that central banks will acquire foreign currency and the gold exchange standard will grow, only as long as they have confidence in the foreign currency acquired. But a point can be reached, particularly if the central bank goes on acquiring domestic assets, when foreign central banks will no longer willingly hold the foreign currency of that central bank. This I think is the stage at which we are today.

Money can be created and it can also be destroyed. It has already been pointed out that the gold holdings of central banks and also the foreign currency assets of central banks have shrunk, so that we are now beginning to see some actual destruction of international money, of international liquidity, because of this reduction of gold and foreign currency assets in the hands of the central banks.

Interestingly enough neither the National Bank of Switzerland nor the Netherlands Bank holds foreign currency assets. So these two central banks hold neither domestic assets nor foreign currency assets. Most of us think that it is stimulating to an economy if a central bank acquires domestic assets. Yet the economies in the world that have been most stimulated have been those whose central banks either acquired no domestic assets, or destroyed or reduced their domestic assets.

In recent years the principal economic problem in the world, to my mind, has been that the Federal Reserve banks have acquired too many domestic assets. In the first year of the present economic recovery they acquired about 1.2 billion dollars of domestic assets, chiefly U.S. Government securities. In the last year they acquired 4.2 billion dollars, and in addition acquired about 600 million dollars of foreign currency assets.

Incidentally, these foreign currency assets have been acquired not because the Federal Reserve banks earned them through a balance-of-payments surplus but because they created them in the process of making swaps, principally at the instance of the Bank of England. So the Federal Reserve has created four times as much money through the acquisition of domestic assets and foreign currency assets in the last year of this recovery as it created in the first year of the recovery.

I should now like to direct a question to Mr. Emminger. I have noticed that his central bank, the German Bundesbank, has acquired domestic assets on a substantial scale in the past year. If I read the figure correctly it has been something like a billion dollars. As he has pointed out to you, Germany has had a deficit in its balance of payments and the Bundesbank has lost foreign currency assets. This, as I have observed the world, is typical of what happens in this type of system—one of free convertibility of one currency into another at fixed exchange rates. So if a central bank acquires domestic assets, it is certain to lose gold or foreign currency assets, and vice versa. So I should like to ask Mr. Emminger to comment, if he will, on this acquisition of domestic assets by the Bundesbank in the past year and its loss of foreign currency assets. I should also like to ask him whether he thinks the United States can correct its balance-of-payments deficit while the central bank goes on acquiring domestic assets and foreign currency assets at the rate of about 4.8 billion dollars a year.

MR. GAINSBRUGH: John, we got a high yield from those three meals we gave you.

MR. EMMINGER: I would first like to go into those questions or remarks where I can be relatively brief. I would begin with the remarks by Mr. McLaughlin about the wasting of resources. His argument is that gold has also become a very important industrial commodity and will become even more important as an industrial commodity.

What I said was in no way intended to mean that we are now wasting the resources that go into gold mining. I only wanted to support fully what Mr. Wallich said on the effects that an increase in the price of gold would have. An increase in the price of gold would, of course, increase the resources going into gold mining. If this were done merely with a view of increasing international liquidity, this might be wasteful because we might get the desired result much more cheaply in other ways. I am not against the present scale of gold mining but against an increase that would only be provoked by reason of an artificial increase in the price of gold.

Secondly, a very brief remark on what Mr. Haberler said on the relative evaluation of the adjustment process versus international liquidity in the Group of Ten. He certainly misunderstood me if he took from my remarks that there was just one sentence in the report of the Group of Ten on this point. I just looked up what the relationship was. We had a full chapter on the necessity for an improved adjustment process and better payments discipline, altogether six long paragraphs. And we had a smaller chapter consisting of only five smaller paragraphs on future reserve needs. The whole report is only eleven pages, and it dealt with many other subjects, including gold, the International Monetary Fund and other things.

As to the comments regarding the lack of literature on the adjustment process, I throw this ball back to the economists because it is not us who have the time to write books. It is the economists who have to do that.

CHAIRMAN VINER: You win on that one.

MR. EMMINGER: My next point would also be in reference to
a remark made by Mr. Haberler, namely on the outflow of gold
from the U.S. in 1965, where he, I think, interpreted a remark which I had made somewhat facetiously on the small adjustment effect of the large outflow of gold from the U.S. in 1965,
in a correct manner.

What really was behind my remark was that in modern times,
to have a fully automatic international system of payments adjustments was neither possible nor even so desirable. It usually
doesn't work because there are so many compensating influences on the liquidity of the economy, and a gold outflow
can, usually, not have a fully automatic effect on the domestic
monetary circulation, because circumstances will nearly always
make some compensating policies by central banks inevitable.
Nothing in the world can bring back the happy old time automaticity which would bring balances of payments into line
quite automatically.

This leads me directly to the last remark made by my old
friend John Exter. In his two questions, if I understood him
correctly, he was visualizing a world where the central banks
would hold nothing but gold, neither foreign currencies nor—
and this was the main point—domestic assets. Now, I would not
like to even visualize such a world, where the whole supply of
central bank money was only determined by gold supplies. I
must say this is a terrible world to visualize with all due respect
to gold. It would be extremely inflexible and outright deflationary. It would certainly affect unfavorably most of the other goals
of economic policy, if this were accepted willingly or willy-nilly.
I think we should not envisage such a world.

I come to his two or three examples. It is correct that the
Swiss Bank and the Netherlands Bank hold relatively small
working balances of foreign exchange currencies, between 10,
12 or 15 per cent of their total reserves. It is also correct that
usually they don't hold very much in the way of domestic as-

sets, but not because this is their policy. They are fully authorized to do it and they sometimes do hold domestic assets.

What I would not accept is that thanks to their policy of not
holding domestic assets they have no balance-of-payments problem. It is exactly the other way around. Because they have
been having surpluses in their foreign exchange balance for
a number of years, they have acquired such a large amount of
foreign exchange assets or gold and foreign assets and don't
need to acquire much domestic assets. But there was a period
when the Netherlands, for instance, had a balance-of-payments
deficit, in 1957, and at this time the Netherlands Bank, the central bank, had to acquire domestic assets. So it is just the other
way round. As long as these central banks have a balance of
payments in surplus they don't need to acquire domestic
assets because the increase in their foreign assets amply provides for the necessary increase in their domestic obligations. As
soon as they have a balance-of-payments deficit, which they
might have just like other countries—and Switzerland, too—as
soon as they have a balance-of-payments deficit they will need
to acquire domestic assets. And this has been exactly the situation in my own country.

It is not because the Bundesbank has been acquiring domestic assets that Germany is now having a deficit in the balance
of payments. It is again exactly the other way around. We have
had a balance-of-payments deficit because of our general increase in imports and our deliberate attempt (e.g., through a
devaluation of the DM) at restraining a further expansion of
exports. The consequent deficit in the balance of payments has
led to an outflow of foreign exchange which has diminished
pro tanto the cash base of the banking system. As the money
circulation could not possibly shrink suddenly in a corresponding amount, the central bank had to take over some domestic assets from the commercial banks in partial compensation of the
outflow of foreign assets.

I was asked by Mr. Reierson to give some more details on

what is often called the Blessing Plan. I cannot now go into great detail. The major point in the whole plan is that we suggest some sort of loose agreement or understanding among the major central banks on the composition of reserves, that is, as to the proportion of gold and other foreign assets. This does not necessarily mean laying down any fixed rules of a definite percentage of gold versus other assets to be kept, but some sort of margin of, say, between 60 and 70 per cent of gold so that there is not too violent a change in the composition. The whole world would be subject to continuous multilateral surveillance so that the situation can be continuously adjusted to varying conditions.

Now this brings me to a further point that was, I think, very usefully made, namely, the inevitability of cooperation in the modern monetary system. It was Mr. Triffin who very nicely brought that out by telling us about his discussion with Professor Rueff. It is quite clear whatever one does, whatever reform plan one accepts, even if one goes over to the so-called automatic gold standard, you cannot get anywhere in the modern monetary world without a great deal of international understanding, agreement and other forms of co-operation. I have come to accept this fact although it entails a great deal of international meetings for, and consequent personal hardship for, people like myself. But it is a fact of life which you have to accept under modern conditions. This is really the consequence of what Mr. Haberler rightly calls the very complicated nature of our international monetary system.

I will tell you as briefly as I can why I think this has become inevitable. First, in a general way, we live in a very complicated world in which everything has become much more complex than it was in the good old times. Second, there is a special reason of its own why our monetary system has become so complicated. It is because we try to combine two goals that are very difficult to pursue simultaneously. On the one hand we want to preserve external stability, international stability in exchange rates and all that combined, of course, with free trade and free movement of capital, because in an integrated world we need this external stability and freedom of movement. On the other hand we want to pursue full employment and the social welfare state and similar things domestically. To try to achieve these two things together inevitably creates great complications for our monetary system. I think it is likely that we shall be moving into ever more complex situations, and also institutions.

Finally, I may say one word on this very useful expression of "contingency planning." I, too, think this phrase is extremely useful. It has really opened the road for the joint work on future reform. Maybe I contributed a little bit to the origin of this expression. It turned up for the first time about ten days after Secretary Fowler's speech in Hot Springs which was, I think, the ninth or tenth of July. There he indicated the United States Government's willingness to take part in an international monetary conference which, of course, was nearly equivalent to taking the initiative for such a meeting. About eight or ten days later I visited in Washington with the Secretary of the Treasury and Mr. Deming and others, discussing how all this would fit in with the already existing mandate of the Group of Ten, or how to fit the Group of Ten into this whole framework. I happened to be chairman to the deputies of the Group of Ten. I explained to Secretary Fowler and his associates that some European countries would probably feel some difficulty in going along with such an accelerated pace of preparing for international monetary reform. They were of the opinion that other matters were much more important, such as the stability of the pound and the equilibrium of the U.S. balance of payments. Some countries, including my own, were thinking that there was perhaps no urgent need for the deliberate creation of international reserves, and out of this discussion suddenly originated the expression, "Well, couldn't we do it on the basis of preparing for a contingency?" Then we said this may be the right word; we should plan for a future contingency, have "contingency planning." Maybe I involuntarily contributed a little bit, but I think the first person to use that expression was Secretary Fowler.

Chapter VII

International Reserves
and
Domestic Economic Policies

Chairman: MARTIN R. GAINSBRUGH
Position Paper: SIR ROY HARROD

CHAIRMAN GAINSBRUGH: One of the men who is most directly responsible for the idea of holding this session and for the high quality of subsequent participation is Philip Cortney. When he leaves we hope that he will feel that he has been given a generous and receptive hearing. He is a close and dear personal friend of many years. Greater love hath no man than to bell down a man as I did Philip at his last contribution. When we last left you, Philip, we had fallen from the twentieth floor to the tenth.

MR. CORTNEY: We have heard a great number of ideas, some more interesting than others, but I doubt that we have reached any consensus on why a monetary reform is necessary and why it is urgent.

Discussions regarding the lack of international gold liquidity continue to be confused with those about international liquidity (mainly credit and not money) as defined by the International Monetary Fund. Yet there is no lack of international credit liquidity; on the contrary, we are suffering a plethora of this kind of "liquidity."

The vital role of gold in our present international monetary system is being minimized or even distorted by many who are prejudiced against gold. We were also told that the advocates of return to the gold standard have no concern for full employment and economic growth! It is obvious that some of my opponents are victims of a wrong diagnosis of the causes of the Great Depression.

We were told also that gold derives its value (purchasing power) from its relationship to the dollar. Mr. Emminger has challenged the equilibrating virtue of the gold mechanism on faulty reasoning. Mr. Emminger also asserted that "the price of gold is an entirely artificial one." On this last point I am in agreement with him, except that by the word "artificial" he and I mean two different things (read my expatiation on the price of gold in my prepared paper).

The relationship between the world's monetary gold stock, the global volume of money supply, the general price level and the annual production of gold seems to baffle a majority of people, instructed or not. Hence the vital importance of the price of gold, after a considerable inflation of money and prices, concomitant with a big world war, is badly understood or not understood at all. Many people among the instructed seem to think that the President of the United States has the power and discretion, in the present circumstances, not to approve a rise in the price of gold, or that he can even lower the present price of gold.

Yet despite all the campaigning against gold and all the efforts to minimize its role in our international monetary system, no one with any authority is giving any encouragement or endorsement to plans, from the academic world, aiming at an international monetary system without gold. With all due respect to Mr. Emminger this is not due to some belief in something magic about gold, as he said in his prepared speech. The demand for gold and the confidence in gold is due to experience of people in the mismanagement of paper money by governments, and also, at times, it should be said, because many, if not most, finance ministers and central bankers have only the most rudimentary knowledge of monetary phenomena and monetary issues.

Having been convinced by our discussions that an elucidation of the gold-price issue requires a comprehensive treatment of the subject, I have decided to expatiate on the price issue in my prepared paper for this conference. I hope you will all do me the honor of reading it.

CHAIRMAN GAINSBRUGH: Philip, we won't cease trying to meet your high standards. This is the third time the Board has conducted a discussion dealing with the gold problem. We are not at all averse to trying once more, if your patience isn't exhausted, Philip, ours is not.

I do think that, judged by my own standards, and I have been with the Board for a good long while, the quality of this discussion from the time it was begun, compares favorably with anything I have experienced in the past at Board meetings or other professional discussions.

We have had deep, well-rounded presentations from men in government and in education, as well as men deeply versed in business. This has been a balanced discussion from all points of view rather than a single-centered presentation. When the proceedings are published, I am confident the judgment of the outside world will be, as in past sessions the Board has devoted to this topic, that our time here has been used very productively.

Selfishly, but I hope understandably, I have reserved for myself the privilege of being in the chair for Sir Roy Harrod's presentation. Sir Roy, what I am about to say shows how you are judged by your peers. I have asked them to give me some pertinent background material and for once I believe the barrier of our common language has been penetrated in this brief tribute to Sir Roy.

The names of Harrod and Keynes have become associated in many minds, probably because Sir Roy was chosen by Sir Geoffrey Keynes as the man best qualified to write the definitive life of his brother, the late Lord Keynes. They had a long association and mutual respect for one another. But it would be wrong to label Sir Roy as a Keynesian. He is in fact a distinguished economist in his own right.

His college at Oxford University, Christ Church, founded by Cardinal Wolsley, likes to do things in its own way. While other colleges style their professors "Fellows" of the college, Christ Church call them simply "Students." Sir Roy has for many years been a Student of Christ Church. (He, too, likes to do things in his own way.) When he was an undergraduate, a student in the ordinary sense of the word, he was reputed to have produced the shortest paper in history ever to earn a first class in Greats.

Sir Roy has been adviser to, and more important, a stern critic and castigator of successive British governments. Nevertheless, a few years ago he was honored with a knighthood. Yet, though he walks with kings, he has never lost the common touch, and he remains the tutor and encourager of many students who have risen to distinction. William Busschau is one of them.

SIR ROY HARROD: I must thank you for the very gracious way in which you have just introduced me.

What you said about my book has just reminded me that Mr. Philip Cortney was responsible for one of the most pleasant moments of my life. I gather that he has also been partly instrumental for this very pleasant weekend. He was responsible for one of the most pleasant moments of my life, because I had just brought my wife to America for the first time. I had been here myself many times before. It was pouring rain in New York, absolutely pouring. She got a ghastly cold and spent our two days in New York in bed. Then, when we got on the train to get to the conference in White Sulphur Springs, Virginia, and we were in the dining car, Philip Cortney came in, and his were pretty well the first words she had ever heard uttered by an American citizen in the United States of America. He didn't see me, but went up to a friend and said, "Have you read your Harrod?" That was my life of Keynes, just out. I am afraid that my wife got rather an inflated idea of my fame in this country.

Well, sirs, I was asked to produce a position paper, but I

was not quite certain what a position paper was. When I give lectures in the university, or papers to my classes, I, of course, have to adopt an attitude of objectivity with regard to all points of view. But when I come to a conference, I generally find it more helpful if I take up a specific position. When I was asked to write a "position" paper, that was what I thought the instruction required, but I am no longer sure. So perhaps my paper is rather too "positional" in that sense.

I was a little depressed when I wrote the paper. Since I have been here in Tarrytown I have been soothed by a number of speakers starting with Ralph Young, ending with Mr. Emminger. Of course, we have been stirred up by Philip Cortney. I have been soothed by these discussions, and don't feel quite so pugnacious as I did. Nonetheless I will stick to my position tenaciously.

The Process of Adjustment

The crucial question in the study of requirements for international liquidity is how quickly we wish to see adjustments made that correct international imbalances of payments. This takes us back to the prior question of what the causes of imbalances may be.

Taking a negative balance, we may divide causes into (1) inflation and (2) structural change. Inflation divides into demand inflation and cost inflation. In regard to adjustment when there is demand inflation, we may say right away that the more quickly remedial, i.e., deflationary, measures are adopted, the better. In the old days this was effected through the automatic working of the gold standard. If a demand inflation is left uncorrected, it is likely to gather momentum, so that the imbalance will become greater. If demand inflation were the sole cause of international imbalances, one could agree with the disciplinarians of continental Europe, who advocate an immediate dose of the deflationary medicine, whenever there is an imbalance.

There are some doctrinaire economists who appear to believe that an external imbalance is a sure sign of domestic demand inflation. I would suggest that either their economics is wrong, or they are using words in an unnatural sense. If a country has, say, 5 per cent unemployment, not regionally concentrated, if its business profits are low, and if its price level is steady, but at the same time it has an external imbalance, it would be a misuse of words to call its condition inflationary, and it would be bad economics to suggest that this combination of conditions cannot occur. Such a condition was a very frequent occurrence in the interwar period.

Cost inflation may be defined as a condition in which the demand for goods and services is well within the capacity of the country to meet, but prices are rising because wages and other rewards to factors of production are rising at a rate exceeding the increase in the productivity of the factors. The classic instance of this state of affairs was the great upsurge of wages and prices that occurred in France in 1936 when demand was gravely deficient, but there have been many other instances. In such a case demand deflation by means of fiscal and monetary policies is not a proper remedy. In such circumstances demand deflation would cause an increase of unemployment, which in itself is irrational, without necessarily curing the excessive level of wages etc., which, in the circumstances supposed, is the cause of the imbalance. If it serves wholly or in part to rectify the imbalance, this will be because, by reducing employment and incomes, it reduces the demand for foreign, as well as for domestic, goods. This is not a rational remedy.

Before discussing what would be a rational remedy, I will deal with the other type of cause of trouble, namely, structural change. This is doubtless a much abused expression. I use it as a catchall, to cover everything except inflation of either of the above kinds. An adverse balance may occur because of inventions or improvements in productive processes abroad, which enable foreign supplies to undercut domestic suppliers, assuming the costs of the latter to be unchanged, at home and/or abroad. Or there may be a change of taste on the part of the buyers at home or abroad. For instance, the British balance has recently suffered severely from a quite inordinate fashion in Britain for foreign-made goods; this has been quite a distinct change of attitude during the last ten years. Or, to cite the American case, there may be an increased inclination to invest money overseas, whether directly or by portfolio, and this will cause an over-all deficit, unless fortuitously the merchandise balance has at the same time improved sufficiently. A change of this kind may be due to an altered mental outlook, or to an improvement in the political situation, or in general prospects overseas. As with cost inflation, so with structural change, the creation of domestic unemployment does not appear to be a rational remedy. I assume that we also exclude as undesirable the imposition of tariffs or other trade restrictions in such circumstances.

This being granted, it seems that the adjustment process must be slow-working. In the case of cost inflation, if this has gone too far, devaluation may be the only remedy. But, if the cost inflation is moderate only, it would be better for the country to get a grip on its domestic situation and check the cost inflation, by guide lines. The British have now embarked on what is called an incomes policy. Although it has not had marked success at the outset, it is hoped that this policy will bear fruit in a year or two. It is too much to hope in the modern world for a reduction of wages, etc., but if, in a world of rising productivity, a given country can hold the line on the wages front, then it should be able to increase its competitiveness.

The same kind of remedy would be appropriate in the case of an adverse structural change. The country should work hard to deal with the adverse movement by ensuring that incomes rise less at home than they do abroad. It is clear that this remedy, unlike deflation or import restriction, will only produce its remedial effect slowly.

Quick Adjustments

There is one case where I think it is expedient to make an adjustment quickly, and that is where an imbalance of payments is a result of domestic demand inflation. Nothing but

harm can be done by delaying it. The answer to a demand inflation is deflation. The sooner you execute deflation the better.

I don't think that actually the size of the reserve will make
very much difference to the speed of this process of adjustment.
I would suggest that most industrial countries probably have a
sufficient sense of responsibility, so that if they see demand inflation getting underway they will make a quick adjustment, not
only for balance-of-payments reasons but also for domestic inflation reasons. The less developed countries may not do so. For
various reasons they may resort to import restrictions and so
on.

When there is no demand inflation—and I submit that in
many cases, perhaps even in most cases, an external deficit does
not result from a domestic demand inflation—then to execute
deflation would create unemployment. I think there has been
very little demand for inflation in the industrial countries since
1956, with the possible exceptions of Germany and Japan in certain periods.

Now in both of the cases, in that of cost inflation, when wages
advance more than productivity, and in that of structural
change, I would submit that it is not rational to create unemployment. That is not a sensible answer.

In the case of cost inflation, if it has gone beyond a certain
point this may be a valid reason for devaluation; but if it be
a moderate one, it would perhaps be wiser to try to hold the
line for a period to keep wages in check and to get back to
equilibrium that way. In the case of structural changes normally
I would say that you want to have a very slow process of adjustment, by such a method as guideposts which have been so
successful in this country and which we are attempting in my
country.

I was very happy and tremendously satisfied with Mr. Emminger's statement toward the end of his paper where he said if
the deficit countries have wage increases less than surplus countries that it would be all right. That is absolutely all right by me
but, of course, this must be a slow-working remedy. The central

question I want to put to those who advocate a quicker adjustment to a deficit is—what are the methods of adjustment that are quick? Assuming that you rule out the creation of unemployment which is a pretty quick working remedy, and assuming we all rule out exchange control, import restrictions and other barriers to trade, what are the quick-working remedies? I think we are entitled to know this, because this issue seems to be central in regard to the amount of reserves. The general tendency, I think in most cases, among people who do not favor more reserves is the desire for quick adjustment. Well, that may now be desirable in certain cases. But what we are entitled to ask is what are the methods of quick adjustment before assenting to the proposition that quick adjustments are normally desirable.

I think you heard the proposition or the suggestion that perhaps an adaptation of interest rates might be a quick way. That might be quick-working if the corrective to the imbalance should come through on the capital side of the external account. But that is not always so.

In certain cases what is needed is an adjustment in the capital account, and in other cases one in the merchandise account. Furthermore, if you rely on an interest rate policy you must believe—I think it was said here earlier, I am not sure—that the interest-rate policy has a very strong influence on capital movements. The relative rates of profit earnings, say, in the United States and Europe are not subject to changes in interest rate. I think that profit rates are even more important than bank rates in causing a capital movement. Furthermore a change in the interest rate may be undesirable from the domestic point of view. You may be at the point where you have no demand inflation, so that you don't want to have higher interest rates at that point. You may say we can rely on fiscal policy to maintain demand at home. Supposing you want to check the capital outflow, do we have to cause some unemployment? You say you have fiscal policy to look after the general employment question. But then I would submit this is unacceptable in domestic monetary management which is becoming all the time more skilled. We can't say that we ought to rely entirely on fiscal policy. There are questions, according to the circumstances of the country, about the right balance between investment and consumption. In certain cases the appropriate thing is to encourage investment and in other cases consumption, but in all cases we want to get the right balance. It is quite unacceptable to say the whole question of right interest rates can be left on one side to look after the external balance.

Moreover the recent levering up of the international interest rates is rather like the old days of competitive exchange depreciation. Now we have a competitive levering up of interest rates in the industrial countries, which I think harmful from the point of view of investment in those countries. And it is still worse, of course, from the point of view of the less developed countries of which we haven't heard enough over the weekend. Part of what they get from the industrial countries may be at commercial rates or at near commercial rates. The levering up of the interest rates in the industrial countries is most destructive because, as we all know, these less developed countries are going to have a very great problem in relation to the servicing of their debts and earning balance-of-payments surpluses for repaying their borrowings from the industrial countries.

My own feeling regarding these methods of quick adjustment is that we still have a vacuum. Long before I would consent to the proposition that we ought to get quicker adjustments I want that filled in. I want a more explicit account. We know that Working Party 3 is engaged in this study and seeking some agreed—Mr. Emminger gave us a phrase—"agreed rules for monetary discipline." But that also makes me uncomfortable, because, with all due respect to the great brains that may be active in Working Party 3, I doubt if anything that this Working Party 3 does will provide agreed upon rules, when the economists cannot specify what those rules should be. In a fundamental question like this, if you can't get from the academic economists any agreed rules for quick adjustment that would be effective, I don't think Working Party 3 will be able to provide us with any. I don't know whether it will. I would be rather skeptical.

I think personally that countries are likely to be too much hurried, now that we are entering the state of very narrow reserves in the world. It is perfectly true that the United States deficit has gone on over a long time, but I think the United States position has been a rather exceptional position.

Incidentally, as I said earlier, I am not one of those who sees anything greatly wrong with this succession of United States deficits. They have provided a universal stimulus to the world. They have been a benefit, in the sense they have been much better for the world than if the United States had taken any of the measures they might have had to take to correct the deficit quickly, such as cutting down aid, cutting down military expenditures overseas, cutting down imports or, worst of all, having domestic deflation.

The Need for Reserves

If it is granted that most imbalances should be eliminated slowly, then sufficient reserves are needed to tide over the period of imbalance. It is true that, if this period is too protracted, some special measures may have to be adopted, like the voluntary restraint of capital outflow recently put into operation by the United States. But I believe it will be agreed that the less reliance we have to place on measures such as this, which interfere with individual liberty, and possibly with the long run advantage of the country, the better. From this point of view the larger the reserves the better.

I believe that reserves are at present too low if countries are to avoid to the greatest possible extent using the remedies of creating unemployment or imposing import restrictions. When making a statement of this sort, one is immediately challenged with the request to supply an exact criterion for what reserves should be. It is obviously impossible to supply an acceptable criterion. The central bankers of the world are constantly telling us that they can see no shortage of reserves. I suggest that such assurances may be, consciously or unconsciously, influenced by the thought that, if they admitted that there was a shortage, this might set off a speculative crisis of unmanageable dimensions. I would add to that, that a shortage of reserves is not something that can be directly perceived even by those so well placed as central bankers. It is something that can only be argued, rather than perceived. One has to discuss the causes of maladjustment, the available and appropriate measures of readjustment and the desirability of resort to unemployment as a regular cure.

In favor of the view that there is a present shortage I would make two points. (1) World reserves are less than half what they were before the war. Of course this is not a decisive point. But no experts before the war thought they were redundant at the time, and those who met at Bretton Woods in 1944 thought that they had been insufficient. Hence the attempt to create additional liquidity via the International Monetary Fund. (2) The world has been plagued with foreign exchange crises during the last five years. Is not this rather curious, if reserves are not inadequate? Our friends in continental Europe tell us that these troubles are due to mismanagement. I would suggest that in the last decade we have had far more careful and thoughtful management of the business cycle, at least in the mature countries, than we have ever had before; and yet our predecessors, whatever other evils they may have suffered, were not plagued with perennial foreign exchange crises. I suggest that this was due to the simple fact that in the past reserves were greater than they are at present. Professor Cassel made his famous calculation that gold reserves increased by 3 per cent a year from 1850 to 1914. Since 1937 they have increased by 1.7 per cent only. Furthermore in the latter period, but not the former, there was a war causing a rise of prices which has not been reversed.

The gap has been partly filled by the dollar and sterling, but this has caused trouble, and it is generally agreed that this method of eking out reserves cannot be extended into an indefinite future.

How to Increase Reserves

I now turn to the methods for increasing reserves. I have for many years advocated raising the price of gold, more or less in proportion to the increases of other prices since 1939. I regard this as an appropriate first measure, although not the only measure, that ought to be taken. I suggest that this is a matter of plain common sense. Why is it that it should be thought proper that the prices, expressed in dollars, of all the various things that we value, food, clothing, means of transport, housing, etc., should have gone up so much, while the price of one of the most valuable things of all, the reserve asset, should have remained unchanged? One reason apparently is that a change in the price of gold cannot be discussed, because it would cause a crisis. That might be a sound reason for an embargo on discussion on some particular occasion lasting for six months or a year. But the argument that discussion would cause a crisis will go on for all time. It does not seem to point to a high degree of civilization that we cannot discuss a matter touching the welfare of the whole world very deeply, because it might cause a crisis. I myself have never observed this embargo on discussion because I should like to cause a crisis. If by a crisis we mean a soaring in the open market price of gold all over the world, of such momentum that it could not be held down by the "gold pool" or in any way whatever, I would regard such a crisis as an excellent thing—although it might grieve the heart of central bankers—doing no one any harm, and everyone much good.

I now proceed to other methods for increasing reserves, partly because it is not practically useful to go on talking about gold when no one else is willing to do so, and partly because I believe that, even if there were a once-over rise in the price of gold, some supplementary medium of reserve would also be needed.

I hold that the creation of additional reserve assets should be the responsibility of the International Monetary Fund. It is a body of ripe experience, although doubtless it has had its failures. It can draw upon the knowledge and wisdom of the central bankers of the world. I do not, however, regard it as a body likely to make adequate proposals for its own reform. Still less do I so regard the experts of the Group of Ten, or those who meet together in Working Party 3 of the OECD. They are too conservative, and look at matters from too narrow a point of view. We shall not get a reform unless a strong initiative comes from people like the President of the United States, the British Prime Minister, and others in like positions in the economically most powerful countries.

There has been much discussion as to whether the additional liquidity to be provided ought to take the form of reserve assets or credit facilities. I suggest that we need both, as indeed we now have in the International Monetary Fund. It is generally agreed that the "gold tranches" may be regarded as reserve assets, while the other drawing rights are credit facilities. To a large extent the gold tranches do not represent additional assets for the members as a collection, namely to the extent that they have arisen from the deposit of gold by members with the Fund. Furthermore, the existence of this, the major part of the gold tranches, represents a net loss of liquidity to the world, because of the repayment obligation. If a country uses its own gold, there is no repayment obligation, but if it draws upon its ordinary gold tranche, it has a repayment obligation, and of this I must speak.

Part, but only part, of what are known as the super gold tranches is a genuine net addition to reserves. If the super gold tranche of Country A is due to Country B having used part of its gold tranche, then the super gold tranche clearly represents no net addition to reserves. But if the super gold tranche is due to Country B having gone further, namely into the realm of its conditional drawing rights, then the super gold tranche of Country A is a net addition to world reserves. I add hastily that the sum total of all these super gold tranches is a most meager contribution, hardly worth taking note of.

Credit Versus Reserves

While I do not rule out additional credit facilities, I do not think that they are an adequate substitute for additional reserves. I will mention two points:

1) Credit facilities carry a repayment obligation. This may be innocuous in some circumstances, but not in all circumstances. A country which uses some of its gold reserve, or, indeed, for that matter, some of its dollar or sterling reserve, in order to tide over a period of deficit, is absolutely free to consider, at the end of the period, whether it wishes to rebuild its reserve to its previous level by having a surplus, or does not wish to do so. But if it has used a credit facility, it is under an obligation to have a surplus, in order to repay; and, as I have already said, that goes for the use of gold tranches in the International Monetary Fund also. A country may feel that it is not necessary for it to replace its reserves, or not necessary for it to do so immediately (say within five years). It may have other objectives to which it gives priority. Britain, for instance, could easily have built up a large reserve and been quite comfortable at present, had it not given priority to other objectives, such as dismantling import restrictions, making sterling convertible and undertaking heavy military expenditures overseas. I have made a calculation by which it appears that if it had operated on one part of one of these lines alone, namely, if it had maintained restrictions on finished manufactures, which are not strictly necessary to it, so as not to let them rise above the level of 1955, its present reserve would be three times as much as it is, and with that Britain would be quite comfortable.

The United States presents an even more striking example. Suppose that since 1957 we had been living in a world in which the only medium for international settlement was a credit facility. This is by no means a far-fetched idea. If the price of gold is not changed, and if the sole new medium for international settlement consists of credit facilities, in a few decades from now practically the whole of our means of settlement will consist of credit facilities, the role of gold having been reduced to negligible dimensions. And so let us bring this state of affairs forward in time and suppose that it was already obtaining in 1957. The United States would, on that hypothesis, now be under an obligation to run surpluses in the years ahead amounting to 24 billion dollars. Would this be good for the United States? And would it be good for the world as a whole? I suggest, on the contrary, that if the United States was subject to such an obligation and honorably fulfilled it, this would produce the most colossal world slump in history. And this brings out the point that the repayment obligation may be a burden, not only to the country that incurs it, but to the rest of the world, and I am sure that in these enlightened days policymakers would consider that. For instance, it may well happen that the United States will find itself in a position in which, without detriment to its domestic unemployment situation, it could run a surplus of substantial size. Would it then necessarily argue that in view of its past 24-billion-dollar deficit, it was its duty to run surpluses of commensurate magnitude in the years ahead? Would it not rather think it the better part to moderate those surpluses, for the good of the rest of the world, e.g., by extending its aid commitments, or abolishing restraints on capital outflow?

2) It appears to be in the nature of credit facilities that they should be conditional, although I believe that this was not in the mind of the British at the time of the inception of the International Monetary Fund. Credit facilities are subject to what has come to be called "multilateral surveillance." I am inclined to think that in most countries economic policymakers know a little more about what is good for their country than the agents of multilateral surveillance. I was at a meeting in Paris only a

short time ago where the United States was denounced as very wicked—and this was not by Professor Jacques Rueff—for not having taken sterner measures of domestic deflation. The comment was made in tones which implied that the audience would agree that the Americans had in fact been very culpable in this respect. While in certain periods since the war the British may have been culpable in relation to the level of demand, any student of the business cycle can now see that on the two occasions in 1957 and 1961 when they raised the bank rate to 7 per cent in consequence of multilateral surveillance, this was contrary to what correct cycle management required. And I am fairly confident that the deflationary measures adopted in consequence of multilateral surveillance in July, 1965, will likewise prove to have been contrary to sound business cycle management. I do not think that economic science has yet reached a point at which we can have much confidence in multilateral surveillance.

Notwithstanding, credit facilities may have some part to play. I suggest that they should be used as a supplementary medium of settlement to meet exceptionally hard cases and where it is considered that the repayment obligation is appropriate. But I would submit that the run-of-the-day means of settlement should consist of genuine owned reserves.

A New Reserve Unit

While the Ossola subcommittee felt itself debarred from making recommendations, and would doubtless have failed to reach agreement, even if it had been asked to do so, its report suggests that there should be no technical difficulty in creating reserve units. Indeed this merely means setting up an international printing press; but of course it must be subject to very strict control.

In regard to this I have three main points to urge:

1) The scheme must not be confined to the Group of Ten, or any other select group of countries. The creation of additional

reserve units would constitute on the occasion of creation a round of gifts. In any proper scheme such creation, and therefore such gifts, will occur regularly, say once a year, or at other suitable intervals. By a very refined management the issue might even be made to occur in appropriate amounts every day. There would normally be no repayment obligation, but only a contingent obligation on countries in net debit on the occasion of liquidation. It is not thinkable that we should have gifts of this kind confined to the rich countries only—not "thinkable," but it has been thought by some members of the Ossola subcommittee. It is argued that the less developed countries do not need, or anyhow will not choose, to add to their reserves. This has not in fact been true in recent years. But suppose that it were true. This would affect the calculation of the total amount of additional reserves needed by the world. One would, in order to make such a calculation, assume that the more developed countries will wish to add to their reserves, but not the less developed countries, and therefore that the total reserve creation should be limited by that criterion. But that has nothing to do with the initial distribution. Having decided on the total amount, one should distribute it fairly among all countries, for instance in proportion to their quotas in the International Monetary Fund. It would then be open to the less developed countries freely to decide whether they thought it expedient to add these units to their own reserve, or to spend them on much needed imports, in which case the units initially assigned to them would find their way into the coffers of the more developed countries.

It is said that the less developed countries could not put up good assets as backing for the new reserve units, since their own currencies are not internationally acceptable. But the so-called backing of the reserve units will have no role whatever to play, except in the event of liquidation. We should not be so obsessed with the liquidation problem as to violate a cardinal tenet of international justice.

2) The Ossola subcommittee did not—or so it appears from the highly technical language of the report—consider the need

for a radical reconstruction of the International Monetary Fund. In my submission it should be restructured so as to be able to operate like the central bank of a nation, namely by the transfer of deposits from the banks of one country to another in its own ledgers. This would not mean that it would be given the power, such as a national central bank has, to "create" credit. The sum total of deposits would be simply the sum total of quotas, as controlled by a four-fifths majority (weighted) of its members. Once this change was made, it would be unnecessary for the IMF to hold particular currencies in relation to its normal business. The "scarce currency" clause could be eliminated and also the General Arrangements to Borrow. As the Fund would not have to deliver currencies, it could never run short of them.

The General Arrangements to Borrow is a highly objectionable feature of the present situation. It means that a nation in the exercise of its perfectly ordinary drawing rights, as enshrined in the constitution of the Fund, may be subject to surveillance, not by the Fund, but by one or more countries independently of the Fund. The Fund is no longer master in its own house. This state of affairs should be changed at the earliest possible date.

3) I submit that the creation of new units should be governed by an automatic rule, agreed upon at the outset. I would not entrust this important matter to discretionary handling from time to time. I envisage that the new units would be held and circulate alongside existing media, namely gold, the dollar and sterling, to which other currencies could also be added. One of the few points of general agreement is that there is something unsatisfactory about the erratic nature of the increases in these other media, especially in the amounts of dollars and sterling, which depend on the vagaries of the U.S. and U.K. balances of payments. The inflow of the new medium should be made to vary in a compensatory way, offsetting variations in the accretions of gold and the reserve currencies. This could, however, be made subject to an automatic formula. The one that I have suggested is that the proportionate increase in all means of settle-

ment in year zero should be equal to the proportionate increase in the dollar value of world trade in the five preceding years, say in years minus-five to minus-one inclusive, over the dollar value of world trade in the five years minus-six to minus-two inclusive. Let this increase in all means of settlement, when translated into figures, be, in absolute amount X million dollars. Suppose that the net positive increase in gold holdings by central banks plus the net increase in reserve currency holdings or minus the net decrease be Y million dollars. Then in year zero there should be injected into the circulation X dollars minus Y worth of new units. This formula could be applied automatically every year, and I believe that it would prove very durable indeed. The distribution, as distinct from the total amount of the units, might have to be changed from time to time, as the quotas in the IMF are at present.

The Current Impasse

The above was composed before the recent meeting of the IMF in Washington. The general tenor of most speeches there seemed to support the need for a significant reform in the world monetary system. But there were dissidents. It had for long been notorious that the snail's progress of the committee successively formed to consider these matters had been due to irreconcilable points of view. Those whom I have called the dissidents have been of substantial importance in the Group of Ten, but they are of much less significance in relation to the totality of members of the IMF.

This paper is evidently not an attempt to reach some common denominator of contemporary thought, but an attempt to express my personal standpoint as clearly as I can. I shall proceed in the same vein.

I hold that the time has come when progress along lines desired by the great majority should no longer be blocked by a minority of dissidents. It is within the power of the IMF to set machinery in motion by which recommendations could be formulated representing the views of the majority; and it would be perfectly proper for it to do so. Suppose a scheme provided for the creation of reserve units and their acceptance by central banks as legal tender in discharge of net indebtedness. Such a scheme could operate and do great good, even though a minority of countries remained outside it. Indebtedness to them would have to be discharged in gold, and they on their side would, of course, have to pay in gold. The door would be left wide open for any or all of them—there might only be one—to become participants in the scheme at any time of their own choosing. I have no doubt that, after the passage of some years, they would in fact opt for participation.

I now come to a point, which, unhappily, since it is negative, may in the existing environment be the most important of all. There was much reference in the *couloirs* to political obstacles to agreement. While not underrating those, I believe that there are economic differences of even greater importance. I am not suggesting that the delegates or central bankers generally take very strong doctrinal economic positions. Nonetheless they are surely insensibly influenced by the climate of economic opinion in their own countries, and, after all, they have to be careful not to agree to proposals that would be unacceptable at home.

I come to my negative point. I would rather have no reform at all of the present system than have my country, or the U.S., or any other country, for that matter, agree to be subject to multilateral surveillance, where some of those undertaking the surveillance held one or both of the two following positions: (1) Whenever there is an external deficit, or in the great majority of cases, domestic deflation is the appropriate remedy; (2) In most instances external deficits should be corrected promptly.

I should not have my country, or any other, adhere to any scheme unless it could be stated quite explicitly at the outset that neither of the above propositions are acceptable.

CHAIRMAN GAINSBRUGH: Sir Roy Harrod's presentation is as rich, at times exotic, and at times as heady as tradition would have it.

Allan Sproul was kept by illness in his family from being with us. He was kind enough to prepare the following memorandum on his views.

ALLAN SPROUL: My own view is that gold is an anachronism in the monetary systems of the modern world. We have pretty well demonstrated this within our national boundaries. The modern world, however, is still an imperfect world and the mystique of gold must be taken into account in international monetary arrangements. As a constitutional monarch, worthy of affectionate reverence, it can be of some assistance in countering centrifugal forces which might otherwise tear the international monetary system apart.

Our long-term objective, in my opinion, should be a reduced use of gold in settlement of international balances, and the strengthening of international monetary arrangements based on confidence *cum* credit. This would be in natural accord with the evolutionary processes of both domestic and international trade and finance over many years.

Meanwhile we have to deal with the problems created in a world of sovereign nation states by the continued use and abuse of gold alongside credit instruments in the international monetary system.

Gold's primary use is its contribution to the necessary element of confidence with which no monetary system can function. In the present international monetary system the lynch pin of confidence is provided by the United States' fixed buying and selling price for gold at 35 dollars per fine ounce, which gives meaning to the term "gold dollar." If it were not for this desirable link with tradition, one would be attracted to the suggestion of Emile Despres, that the United States continue selling gold for 35 dollars an ounce, but discontinue buying it in unlimited amounts at that price, which is what keeps "gold as good as the dollar."

The abuse of gold is the by-product of tradition, fear, avarice and speculation. Tradition and fear lead some foreign central banks to maintain a high proportion of gold in their reserves, partly because of previous experiences of devaluation of reserve currencies. Fear and avarice lead some banks and others to desire a monetary equivalent which returns a good rate of interest but which carries a gold guarantee. Avarice and speculation lead private hoarders and speculators to gamble, at modest cost, on the prospects of devaluation of currencies in response to the violent winds of destruction which, periodically, attack one currency or another.

In continuing to use gold in the world's monetary system, we should improve its use and curb its abuse as best we can. First, if gold is to continue at the base of the monetary system, it should be as nearly as possible a monetary metal and not so largely a hybrid, which is at one and the same time a monetary metal and a commodity metal. The best place for gold, under present monetary arrangements, is in the reserves of the monetary authorities reposing in their vaults in beautiful idleness. It does not belong in the pockets or hoards of the people, and its use in the arts and industry is a secondary use. I have long thought, without any encouragement, that a real attempt should be made to bring all of the gold production of our world into the hands of the monetary authorities, instead of maintaining the appearance of a free market in gold and thus helping to siphon off large amounts of new production into private hands. And, incidentally, such a move would contribute modestly to broadening the base of international reserves which are now held to be in jeopardy of becoming inadequate. At least, the golden additions to reserves would be less unstable, irregular and haphazard.

Second, I would like to pursue further the idea of regularizing the gold holding policies of non-reserve currency central banks, so that a smaller percentage of gold and a larger percentage of reserve currencies and IMF drawing rights would be generally respectable and acceptable and observed. This idea, which has been put forward from time to time, never seems to get off the ground because of the presumed difficulties of the international negotiations which would be necessary to give it substance. Yet, we seem to have little hesitancy in embarking upon more glamorous negotiations for reform of the international monetary system, and little restraint in predicting their early success.

Third, the cooperative arrangements, which have been developed pretty much on an ad hoc basis between the monetary authorities of the leading financial and trading countries, should be enlarged and regularized. Established arrangements for swapping currencies and monitoring the foreign exchanges can cool off the fevers of those who promote or try to take advantage of temporary currency difficulties, outside the ordinary limits of commercial transactions, convincing them that the odds favor the "house." We can't afford to have the international monetary system used as a crap game.

Finally, I would like to mention an absurdity which sometimes enters these discussions. I think it is absurd, for example, when President de Gaulle of France says, as he did at his September press conference, that "believing it right for an international system to regulate monetary relations, we do not recognize that the currency of any particular state has any automatic and privileged value in relation to gold which is, which remains and which must remain under the circumstances, the only real standard." This idea that the "Anglo-Saxon" currencies have preempted a special role in international finance by some trick of privilege is disembodied thinking. Sterling achieved a special role in the past and the United States dollar is pre-eminent now because it is a stable currency backed by a strong economy, and because it is a currency that is used as a unit of account, a medium of exchange and a standard of deferred payment throughout much of the financial and trading world. As has been pointed out many times, if France or other European countries wish their currencies to achieve a relationship to gold similar to that of the dollar, they should transform their financial institutions, their money and capital markets and their monetary practices, and they should stand ready to sell as well as buy gold at fixed prices. Then their currencies might become important intermediary currencies as the dollar is now and, eventually, a European reserve currency might develop as the dream of a united Europe is realized.

European countries other than France, of course, have had a more genuine concern with respect to the consequences of the use of the dollar as a reserve currency in a period of persistent and substantial deficits in the balance of payments of the United States financed through the gold exchange mechanism. That, however, would get us into the whole question of international liquidity and reform of the international monetary system, which is a much larger and more complex question than the role of gold.

JOHN EXTER: After listening to Allan Sproul's statement, I wonder why in the world he ever hired me at the Federal Reserve Bank of New York. I just couldn't disagree more with some of his statements about the role of gold. As a matter of fact, the difference between us appeared while I worked for him. Even so he did not prevent me in 1955 from persuading the Treasury to remove its ban on the financing of gold transactions by commercial banks.

As far back as that I felt strongly that instead of the role of gold being subordinated in the world it ought to be made freer and more important. He and I always disagreed about the London gold market. He thought that it should never have been reopened after the war. I thought he had moved his position a bit, but I see that he hasn't.

There are many of us around this table who are troubled. Some, like Philip Cortney, are angry. I am deeply troubled. I must say I do not agree, Sir Roy, that the United States has found, or may have found, the secret of eternal life, or eternal prosperity. As a matter of fact—and here I must plump on the side of Philip Cortney—I think that if we go on with our present policies we will be faced with one of the most serious economic crises that the world has ever known.

I am also troubled that my good friend Mr. Emminger disagreed with me last night. In my few remarks then I tried to put my finger on what I felt was the heart of the problem, Federal Reserve acquisition of domestic assets.

Ralph Young said jokingly to me today, "I hope you are not going to say anything more about domestic assets." I have to say more about domestic assets because I think that is the heart of the problem.

In the case of Germany, I shall not argue with Mr. Emminger about the causal relationship. I submit to him, however, that I think he certainly would not argue that in the United States it is the balance-of-payments deficit that has caused the increase in the domestic assets of the Federal Reserve.

The first of the recent series of deficits in the U.S. balance of payments was in 1958. I was in charge of gold operations at the New York Federal Reserve in that year and sold over 2 billion dollars of gold to foreign central banks. And Robert Rouse, my colleague, bought over 2 billion dollars of government securities, domestic assets. In my mind during that year there was certainly no question about the causal relationship. It was the increase in domestic assets that was causing the outflow of gold and not vice versa.

There was no misunderstanding about that at the Federal Reserve Bank of New York, as far as I know, though there may have been a difference of opinion at the Federal Reserve Board. There were, in fact, statements from the Board from time to time that we were buying securities to offset the gold losses. This is the whole point about international adjustment, this adjustment process or mechanism that we are talking about.

We cannot have an international adjustment process, in my view, unless we tackle this problem of excessive increases in the domestic assets of central banks, whether to offset the gold losses and prevent them from contracting the reserve base, or for any other purpose.

In particular the reason this is an unstable international monetary world is that we have fixed exchange rates with free convertibility, yet two central banks, the Federal Reserve and the Bank of England, have consistently added to their domestic assets while most other central banks in the developed part of the western world have not added to theirs. As I pointed out earlier, two central banks hold virtually none at all.

With respect to Germany I would comment that it is the increase in the Bundesbank's domestic assets and the accompanying payments deficit that to my mind has contributed the most to the improvement of our balance of payments during the past few months. The Bundesbank used its dollars to pay for its payments deficit, so our liabilities to foreigners have decreased. This is one way, by the way, in which the gold exchange standard can shrink.

It is possible for central banks to go on acquiring domestic assets without bringing about the collapse of the international monetary system if they do so in unison. We have a perfect example of that in the world right now, the twelve Federal Reserve banks. Although these twelve Federal Reserve banks have been adding to their domestic assets in the past few years at a rate which I would regard as excessive, they have not experienced balance-of-payments problems among themselves. This is simply because this Federal Reserve System of ours is the most perfect gold standard system the world has ever known. Constantly, not by sudden but by gradual adjustment, day by day, each Federal Reserve bank redeems its note and deposit liabilities with gold certificates. The gold certificate ratio, the required ratio of gold certificates to notes, is today about 37 per cent. I should suspect that if I looked at the ratios of the twelve I should find some of the banks as low as 35 and other banks probably as high as 39 or 40. I regard this spread as the measurement of the imperfection of the system. It is the measure of their maximum need for gold among themselves.

To my mind this is clear evidence that we do not need more international liquidity. If the central banks of the world conducted themselves in the world as the Federal Reserve banks conduct themselves in the system, then, as Mr. Emminger's colleague, Mr. Blessing, has repeatedly pointed out, the need for international liquidity would greatly diminish. As a matter of fact, we would find ourselves with excess liquidity.

We need all this international liquidity only if some central banks persist in acquiring domestic assets much more rapidly than others.

Sir Roy Harrod pleaded for time in making this adjustment. I should prefer a world in which the adjustments were made as they are among the twelve Federal Reserve banks; immediately, but gradually, day-by-day, week-by-week. So to my mind it is a question of changing policies toward domestic assets. Mr. Bernstein says, "Why do you speak in such terms, John?" I do so because it is the only way to adjust in a fixed exchange rate system. In other words, I think our problem here in the United States, and here again I am on the side of Philip Cortney, is the problem of excessive acquisition of domestic assets by Federal Reserve banks. This is the essence of the balance-of-payments problem.

I should like to cite another reason why I am so troubled, why I think we are not on the road to eternal prosperity. It seems to me that through this Federal Reserve acquisition of domestic assets, we have produced some enormous distortions in the world economy. I do not see clearly how these distortions are going to be eliminated.

I began to call for a cessation of acquisition of domestic assets by the Federal Reserve as long ago as 1961. I no longer believe that today complete cessation is a feasible or practicable way of removing these distortions. The shock to the economy might be too sudden and severe.

The first distortion is, of course, the balance of payments. As long as we go on acquiring domestic assets at this rate that distortion is going to remain. In that case it is idle to think that we can maintain the value of gold. I personally think we should not raise the price of gold. As you can tell from the remarks I have already made, I do not think we need to add to our gold liquidity. But if we continue our present policy an increase in the price of gold is inevitable.

A second distortion is that this constant acquisition of domestic assets by the Federal Reserve has led to unrealistic business expectations. Year after year business expectations have been built upon the continuing expectation that the Federal Reserve will add more and more domestic assets to its portfolio. This is true of businessmen all over the world. It is much more difficult to change that policy now that we are adding to our domestic assets at the rate of about 4.2 billion dollars a year than it was when we were only adding, as in the first year of recovery, at the rate of 1.2 billion dollars a year.

At some point these expectations will be disappointed, as wage rates rise faster than prices and squeeze profits. Thus something in the system has got to give. With present policies it is inherently unstable.

A third distortion is in the interest rates, an enormous one. Regardless of the rate at which the Federal Reserve acquires domestic assets in the future, interest rates are going to have to go up.

The next time the discount rate goes up short-term rates will rise above long-term rates. The last time that happened in this country was early 1928. They went considerably above long-term rates in 1928 and 1929. I was not aware of the fact at that time, but I have read about it. I think they may go considerably above long-term rates again.

MR. BERNSTEIN: What about 1959, John?

MR. EXTER: In 1959 they just hit long-term rates and dropped back. I have one more comment. I just want to point out that the problem of such institutions as the savings-and-loan associations that borrow short and lend long will become acute, for many of them have for decades been conducting their businesses in the expectation that they could always borrow short at rates below those at which they lent and invested long. That expectation is now about to be disappointed.

CHAIRMAN GAINSBRUGH: John, you have again demonstrated that no matter how much time a chairman may give to an economist, he will use it all—and more—effectively.

Henry Wallich, will you take on the burden of replying to Philip Cortney's comments relative particularly to the academic profession?

MR. WALLICH: First, I would say that I admire a man who being in the minority position doesn't easily give in but plugs on and tries to convince the people who resist convincing. And I likewise would like to add that I have admired over the years the way in which Mr. Cortney has pursued this singleminded objective.

As for his criticism of the academic profession I find myself in a minority in my own profession. I don't believe in flexible rates as most of my colleagues do. I believe in the value of stability and most of my colleagues do not. I have great sympathy, therefore, with someone who is in a minority position.

I am perfectly willing to agree that people sometimes go overboard. Active minds easily get bored with the status quo. Almost any ill that we know not of is nicer to fly to than the one which we have.

Nevertheless, having said this, I find the directions in which Mr. Cortney wants to go very difficult to follow. He complains about the overexpansion of domestic credit in recent years. He then goes on to propose an increase in the price of gold which will vastly increase monetary reserves. If it has any effect at all, it will have a more inflationary effect than the credit expansion he objects to.

As far as recent credit expansion itself is concerned, while it does give one pause, one has to realize that it took place in a context of extraordinary stable prices; that the money supply taken by itself has risen less than the GNP in money prices; and I think probably less than the GNP in real terms, so that we probably have had an increase in income velocity.

This doesn't sound very inflationary. It is true that money plus time deposits has expanded more rapidly than GNP. Conceivably this may come back to haunt us some day. Mr. Cortney seems to take for granted that international stability, as he conceives of it—and I don't concede to him that his means would attain it—has automatic and total priority over all the domestic objectives. I would say we have a problem of balancing the need for international stability and the need for domestic, and these two things are not easily reconcilable. They are more nearly reconcilable in the long run than in the short.

In this country we have had tremendous pressure to give priority to domestic stability by which I mean full employment and rapid growth rather than price stability, and inadequate recognition of the need for international stability. Our balance-of-payments deficit has helped us a little to recognize the importance of the international side. But when I see this complete lack of concern in our group about full employment—I don't believe I heard the word "employment" spoken in this room more than once or twice—it seems to me that we are by-passing a major concern in this country. You can't just shrug it off. And growth is another major concern. Until it is proved to us that international stability, rationally pursued, clearly promotes domestic employment and growth, we have ahead of us the problem of reconciling these competing, not to say conflicting, objectives. In this session I am sorry to say this in a sense has not been dealt with.

MR. HABERLER: I have several things to say about Sir Roy's paper. I don't want to be misunderstood or endorse what has been said on the other side. I am not trying to travel on both sides of the road.

I largely agree with Sir Roy's theoretical analysis, but his practical proposals seem to me highly inflationary. It seems to me that Sir Roy still dwells in the 1930's and not in the 1960's.

He says we have a scarcity of liquidity. Let me look at the argument which he uses. World reserves are half of what they were before the war. Of course, if you compare the present situation with what it was immediately preceding the war, I think you get an entirely wrong picture. After the Great Depression, world reserves relative to trade volume reached an enormous level owing to the fact that world commodity prices in terms of gold had been disastrously reduced by prolonged deflation, that the price of gold in terms of all national currencies had been sharply raised by successive currency depreciations and the volume of world trade had contracted to a fraction of its predepression level by a veritable explosion of protectionist measures. This surely was not an equilibrium situation by which to gauge liquidity requirements.

I fully agree with Sir Roy that from an idealistic standpoint it is a nice idea to have large reserves in every country all the time so that balance of payments can be slowly and therefore relatively painlessly adjusted rather than quickly and hence painfully. But I would pay some attention to the admonition contained in the last report of the BIS. If you give the countries all the time they want, the chances are that they will delay adjustment. That has been very forcefully expressed in the last BIS report:

> The main impediments to prompt and effective action [to adjust the balance of payments] are not economic but political. In case after case one has seen deficit countries delay action and play around with half-measures while reserves were drawn down and liquid resources were borrowed from abroad—to avoid political difficulties. But, as the means of financing became scarce and a crisis developed, the doubts were somehow resolved and the policy measures that were impossible and could not work became possible and did work." (BIS 35th Annual Report, 1965, p. 27.)

Sir Roy continues, "The world has been plagued by foreign exchange crises during the last five years." Of course there have been a few, but I don't think that that is a sign of international scarcity of liquidity. Without any scarcity of liquidity you can have any number of crises of any intensity you like. As the BIS report points out, liquidity crises often are necessary to force governments to adjust their balances of payments.

Only if it could be shown that the balance-of-payments difficulties of the United Kingdom or the United States were due to to the fact that some other countries wanted to add to their reserves and adopted deflationary policies for that purpose, or restricted trade in order to attract reserves, could you regard the balance-of-payments crises as a symptom of international scarcity of liquidity. I suggest there has been nothing of that sort. I don't know of a single country in the whole world which has really pursued deflationary policies in the postwar period.

Sir Roy wants President Johnson and the British Prime Minister to take the initiative to determine the pace at which international reserves should be created. The Group of Ten he finds too conservative. I can only say, especially in view of the very balanced paper by Mr. Emminger last night, that I prefer to have him in charge rather than Mr. Harold Wilson or President Johnson!

Finally, let me make a comment on the present British situation. I fully agree with Lord Robbins who, in a remarkable speech in the House of Lords last summer (August 4, 1965), said that a country which operates "at 98.8 per cent of capacity" should apply a little dose of contraction before thinking of currency depreciation or something like that. "Too often, since the war, the adoption of policies to curb undue expansion has been delayed on the pretext that depression was just around the corner—as if you should delay operating the fire hose for fear of rainy weather next winter." That clearly contradicts the view of those who regard the British difficulties as a symptom of a scarcity of international liquidity and look for measures of increasing international liquidity as a cure.

I believe that Lord Robbins' diagnosis and therapy proposals for the British difficulties prove him to be the more faithful Keynesian than Sir Roy Harrod. The same goes for Mr. Bernstein who yesterday wisely remarked that at 4 per cent unemployment the rate of growth may well be higher than 2 or 1.5 per cent. If Keynes were alive, I am sure he would agree with Lord Robbins and Mr. Bernstein.

CHAIRMAN GAINSBRUGH: Mr. Bernstein cannot be with us for the closing summary, so we will grant him a minute or two for a last word before Sir Roy.

MR. BERNSTEIN: I am an old Harrodian, and what I am going to say is going to support most of what Sir Roy says. I am just going to fill the gaps that he left.

I started on this question of the responsibility of surplus and deficit countries in 1943, Lord Keynes having appeared at the U.S. Treasury with the proposal that the responsibility for correcting balance-of-payments maladjustments should be assumed by the surplus countries. Well, the U.S. Treasury was not prepared, quite properly, to accept such a responsibility in the postwar reconstruction period. It would impose on us the fish-oil theory of international economics. If Norway had a deficit because of massive reconstruction, then it would be the responsibility of the United States to inflate until the demand for fish oil in this country was enough to balance Norway's payments.

I believe in fact the surplus countries have a responsibility, but so do the deficit countries. This responsibility is not divided between them on the basis of whether they are surplus or deficit countries. Actually it is divided, as I once wrote, according to the size of the country and its role in the international payments.

If the Philippines has an excessive expansion of credit, then for every three pesos they expand there will be a dollar deficit. If the United States expands by 100 million dollars there will not be a 100 million dollar deficit. But more important, and this is the point that I think our friend Mr. Emminger can use in reply to Sir Roy, if the Philippines had a deficit and we had a corresponding surplus it would take one day's minor adjustment in the open market operations of the Federal Reserve to absorb that surplus in the U.S. monetary system. When the United States has a large and persistent deficit, then even Germany would find it difficult to undertake open market operations on the scale necessary to offset the flow of funds from the United States corresponding to the German surplus. There is that difference. The United States can make the world monetary environment. Other countries cannot.

I don't believe in deflation to adjust balance-of-payments

deficits. What I do want is something else. I want an ounce of prevention. I am not worried, by the way, about cyclical fluctuations in the balance of payments which are perfectly normal. We have lived through them. The British have lived through them. They have been measured by the National Bureau of Economic Research.[1]

What I am troubled about is this concept, if we give countries too much time to adjust then they can wait for costs to rise by 6, 8 and 10 per cent. Why can't we start working on incipient inflation when we see it appearing, say, when a country has a 3 per cent rise in manufacturing costs; that is to say when wage rates have arisen relative to productivity by that amount? We don't need three years to see that that adjustment is going to have to be made. Let's start that now.

That is the point I want to make. In my opinion we are going to find that the adjustment process is nowhere near as difficult as we have all been assuming. We have been generalizing from a series of distortions in the postwar period, which are only now coming to an end, as if it were a calamity to bring about the restoration of international payments. It may be a little harder today to adjust than in the classical period. The process of adjustment probably worked better in the old days, not because of so much more flexibility in the economy but because of a little earlier attention to the balance-of-payments problem. I should add that adjustment is somewhat more difficult today because of insistence on permanent full employment.

SIR ROY HARROD: I think the deflation that is now required of the United Kingdom is untimely and will be shown to be untimely in relation to the business cycle when we study this present phase five years hence.

I don't know if anyone here was in the room at another meeting organized by The National Industrial Conference Board in New York a few days ago, when John Stevens, the Economic Minister at the British Embassy in Washington stood up and did his stuff, and did it very well. I was also on the platform. I didn't

[1] See reference page 67.

quarrel with him for the moment, but he was rather paradoxical. He was saying about the U.K. that unemployment is up, automobile sales are down, housing starts are down, and general level of consumption is down, the index of production is stagnant, all splendid things, but quite the opposite of the sort of things we read on the front page of the letter of the First National City Bank of New York as the achievement of America. This was put as something very fine, as evidence that the deflation policy adopted in Britain was beginning to bite. But it is rather an extraordinary thing that these lugubrious phenomena should be hailed by the British representative as a sign that Britain was doing the right thing.

MR. SPIELER: Perhaps I should declare my interest right away and say that for twenty years I served as an executive and a member of the management of the Union Corporation, a company which is deeply involved in producing gold.

I appreciate the depth of thought that pervades any contribution by my distinguished countryman, Sir Roy Harrod, but I am sorry to say that I find myself in disagreement with him on one or two points. For example, in the present world economic situation I do not consider that further "growth" is the first priority. I am of course in favor of growth.

But growth can only continue if it comes from strength. If the United States continues to pursue further growth before strengthening its international payments position then I believe the danger of a sharp and contagious recession will be increased.

Unlike Sir Roy, I seriously doubt that the United States has discovered the elixir of eternal prosperity. I am a little concerned that the elixir may be laced with hootch and the feeling of intoxication may give way to an almighty hangover.

This question of creeping inflation is one that obviously is of concern to all those who are interested in producing gold. It has been agreed by almost everyone who spoke here that gold will, as far ahead as we can see, continue to occupy a critical place in our international monetary system. Even Mr. Triffin, who has for long advocated a man-made system, agrees that "for a generation or two" gold will certainly occupy a central position in our international monetary affairs. And if this is so, we have to bear in mind that gold will not be produced in sufficient quantity if there is a fixed price on the one hand and a continual rise in the cost of production on the other. Gradually gold mines will die out, or they will be killed off by the rise in costs and there won't be new mines to take their places or new sources of gold for international monetary reserves. The incentive to spend large sums of money on the hazardous and costly business of geological and geophysical exploration is crumbling steadily. It follows that whether you and I believe that an increase in the gold price would be good or bad, one thing is almost certain, namely, that a continuation of the present trend of world prices and costs will, in the absence of an increase of the gold price, lead to a significant reduction in gold output in the western world during our lifetime. This is the almost inevitable consequence of the maintenance of the status quo.

Two crucial points have occupied us during this very interesting discussion. First, the U.S. balance of payments, and second, the effect on the international monetary scene of whatever action is taken to cure the U.S. deficit.

The U.S. is in a difficult, and potentially dangerous, situation with its balance of payments. It must be recognized that the imbalance results partly from the assumption by the U.S. of heavy obligations in defense of the western world. There is a danger—I would not call it a crisis because that is a word to reserve for a very special peak of danger—in the present trend if the United States doesn't allow itself to use the main weapons for handling a situation like this, namely, some further restraint on credit creation, and some further use of the interest rate mechanism. The danger is that of a sudden sharp recession because of the confidence factor. None of us can predict what will be the reaction of people to a continued deficit and further heavy gold losses in the future. Here is an element of vulnerability which I know concerns those who are involved in United States monetary affairs. A large amount of dollars are held by private individuals and not central bankers; these individuals are not amenable to the newly established forms of international monetary cooperation. Accordingly I am fully in agreement with those who believe that the first step in order to preserve the present system from serious upheaval is for the United States to take early and effective action to balance its external accounts. I believe if the United States achieves a balance, and I think it will, there is another danger.

Assuming that the U.S. takes such action, then we may come up against the second problem mentioned earlier, namely, the effect of the United States' action on the rest of the world. In this connection I am not really troubled by the fear that the contraction of the supply of dollars will have a critically damaging effect on the supply of world liquidity. I find it difficult to be convinced by the argument that the total amount of liquid reserves—that is, gold plus dollars plus other reserve currencies plus IMF credits—must rise in proportion to the value of world trade. Although the volume of world trade is one of the factors affecting the adequacy of international liquidity, such adequacy also depends upon may factors, such as the size of fluctuations in the main trading nations' external accounts, the attitude of such nations to the question of what constitutes a "safe" reserve (this attitude can change in a short period), the distribution of the total of world monetary reserves between the different nations, and the extent of international monetary cooperation. More important than its effect on the world stock of liquid reserves is the impact of the elimination of the United States deficit on the background climate of world industrial activity and trade. If, by allowing the situation to drift further, the U.S. were compelled to take some sharper restrictive action, this could generate an atmosphere of contraction in the main trading nations that would be unconducive to new capital investment both at home and abroad. This could lead to a more general setback in business activity and could cause widespread underemployment of labor and capital resources until such time as contracyclical action could take effect.

At this stage I think the time will have arrived when we should look carefully at the possibility of taking out and dusting off a mechanism which was built into the Articles of the International Monetary Fund by the founding fathers when they provided for a universal revaluation of all currencies in terms of gold.

What was the idea that was in their minds when this device was inserted into the IMF charter? I think that one of the contingencies they had in mind was that there might come a time when the world monetary system would have to wipe the slate clean and start afresh without the distortions that have grown up as a result of the wartime and immediate postwar inflation.

I won't burden you again with the arguments in favor of such action. They have been fully aired by Philip Cortney, Donald McLaughlin, William Busschau and others here. But I think it may be worthwhile to pick up and examine some of the arguments commonly advanced against an increase in the gold price in terms of all currencies—I refuse to call it a devaluation of the dollar because it certainly wasn't envisaged in that way in the Articles of the International Monetary Fund.

One of the arguments against an adjustment in the gold price is that it would be an arbitrary and irrational way of dealing with the problem. There may be truth in this—but we must bear in mind that man is often irrational and arbitrary—and he is the person we have to deal with. When we talk of the "confidence factor" we are often recognizing that man does not always behave with cool rationality. The schemes that have been carefully produced by Mr. Roosa, Mr. Bernstein, Mr. Triffin and others, all contain an element of arbitrariness.

Another argument advanced against an increase is that it would help South Africa; and those who advance this point disagree with the policy being pursued by the South African Government. I don't ask you to agree or disagree with the policy of the government of South Africa. But everyone who knows something about Africa will recognize the stability of South Africa and that the standard of living of the people—their conditions of housing, nourishment, health and education—have improved immensely. The Bantu, although he may in one sense feel that he does not wield as much political influence as the extreme progressives would ask for him, is the aristocrat in the whole of the continent of Africa in terms of his standard of living. And people from other countries pour into the Republic of South Africa to take advantage of that standard of living there. I think therefore that we have to consider this particular objection in terms of the sum total of human welfare that has been created in South Africa and can in the future be created.

Another objection advanced is that it would help Soviet Russia. I know that there are many here who disagree with trading with Russia, but personally I would commend to you in the United States of America and others the idea of shipping your surplus manufactured goods (perhaps even shipping your excess supplies of "living bras" to Russian ladies and canned TV shows to Russian homes) in return for good Soviet gold. That is not a bad import to take in return for your excess exports to Soviet Russia!

Without doubt the most compelling objection that I have heard is that any such adjustment of all currency values in terms of gold (even though undertaken in terms of Article IV of the IMF Charter) would be a breach of faith by the United States Government and monetary authorities. Some highly respected international bankers have expressed the view that foreigners who have chosen, for their own convenience, to keep their money in the U.S. in interest-earning dollar deposits cannot reasonably expect such deposits to be gold-guaranteed—unless a guarantee was specifically given at the time of the deposit. Be that as it may, it has to be recognized that the United States Government and Federal Reserve Board officials feel strongly that even an acquiescence by the U.S. to a universal adjustment of all par values would be breaking an implied commitment to preserve the gold value of foreign-owned dollars.

The problem would be somewhat reduced if the composition of the main trading countries' reserve assets were to become less disparate—that is, if most of such countries were to move toward keeping approximately the same proportion of their international reserves in the form of gold.

I won't pretend that I can put forward a glib solution to this, but is it, in the circumstances we are talking about, beyond our ingenuity to work out an equitable solution to this problem so as to enable the U.S. Government and people to feel that they have kept faith with everybody else? I think we should possibly apply our minds to that point.

One possible approach to a solution of the "inequity" objection is to consider what contribution to world economic welfare could be made by those countries whose gold stocks were revalued. For example, France and others might make a long-term loan to the United Kingdom to enable excessive sterling balances to be funded; the U.S. and others might agree to make large loans to the International Finance Corporation for use in constructive capital and educational projects in underdeveloped countries. One could imagine a whole series of ways in which the benefits of a gold revaluation could be shared out equitably.

We should bear in mind that in the situation I have described, what the world economy needs more than anything else is, first, to eliminate the potential instability in the present system, and then from a firm base to harness the wealth and skills of the rich nations to assist the underdeveloped and poor countries to help themselves—even if occasionally they behave like stupid children, which they have done recently. Perhaps it is worth bearing in mind, as an example, that the population of India today is 480 million people and that in the year 2000 it will probably be 1,000 million people.

In the circumstances of instability and incipient contraction that I described earlier, a revaluation of gold in terms of Article IV of the IMF Charter would at least give more elbow room for a resumption of aid and constructive lending to the underdeveloped countries, and it would enable the United States to permit access once more to its capital markets. A really substantial revaluation would almost certainly ensure that gold from past hoarding and current output would flow freely into monetary reserves and in this way strengthen the whole international economic system.

Perhaps one final word, as it may be my only opportunity. I would like to thank Philip Cortney, Donald McLaughlin and all those who contributed to bringing us together. I found it a most stimulating and interesting meeting.

SIR ROY HARROD: I think I will confine my remarks to certain specific points rather than deal with the speeches which would involve going into very wide economic philosophy.

My first point comes from the speech of Mr. Bernstein. He referred to the gap in relation to surplus and deficit countries. I had a note about surplus countries but under pressure it slipped out of my view.

You will recall Mr. Bernstein made the remark about the fish oil. Well, I think that the surplus countries do feel responsibility for adjusting, but there are similar arguments in the case of the surplus countries about the possible desirability of going a bit slowly.

To take one point, sometimes people say surplus countries should let prices rise a bit. But I feel, just as one is entitled to respect the view of a deficit country which does not want to create unemployment, one must have some respect for the view of the surplus country which objects to inflation as such.

I can't altogether accept asking the surplus countries to get their balances of payments straight, and to play their part, if that means that we want them to have a bit of inflation.

Then you come to other methods, the usual methods cited. If they, the surplus countries, have import restrictions or barriers for balance-of-payments reasons, obviously they should be removed.

I come back to the point I didn't perhaps emphasize sufficiently. Not only may it be undesirable to adopt quick measures to be rid of deficits. There is also the problem that the deficits may be transitory. I mean some of these adjustments may involve a painful process of taking people away from their jobs and putting them on other jobs. But supposing their deficits are going to be transitory. Similarly in surplus countries, you can't be quite sure that the surplus you have established will go on forever unless you take some measure of adjustment. It may come an end in the ordinary course of events. The surplus countries are invited to expedite their capital exports, but have got to be confident that the surplus will last longer. They do not want to start exporting capital, if this cannot be followed up by a "continuing program."

I think that on the side of the surplus countries also there are reasons why they should play their part, along with the deficit countries, with a certain amount of slowness. A certain amount of slowness is desirable, rather than to rush as soon as a surplus appears.

The next point: Mr. Bernstein chided me about offset operations. I am making a point which is quite familiar. Surely it is possible to find some method for offsetting. The British have their special deposits, as well as open market operations. The Australians long ago devised a similar method. Surplus would not be so vast as to be incapable of being dealt with by offsetting methods. They may not be open market operations of the American type.

Finally, Mr. Bernstein's third point was, let us work on cost inflation when we see it. I entirely agree with that. He is perfectly right. To the extent we work on cost inflation as soon as we see it appear, we will of course expedite the adjustment process. All the same, again there is a question of time.

A good many months have passed since we British started with the Statement of Intent, and we haven't yet had a big result.[2] I hope we shall get results out of it. This working on cost inflation when we see it appearing, if it is going to be done on a voluntary basis by getting agreement, not only requires

[2] An agreed statement by Mr. Brown, as Secretary of State for Economic Affairs, U.K. and representatives of employers and trade unions, for cooperation in holding the distribution of incomes within the limit allowed by productivity, and in other matters. Published in the week before Christmas, 1963.

time for diagnosing the situation but also time for carrying out the policy.

Going into the arguments made by Mr. Exter, I don't accept his analysis, I am afraid. There may be occasions when there may be a remote relation between assets acquired by the central bank and deficits.

In the British case—I suppose one ought to always carry all statistics in one's head and I haven't got recent statistics—I worked these out about two or three years ago. For quite a substantial period of six years, the money supply on the checking account side rose less than the volume of the national income, less, that is, than the national income at constant prices. And yet in spite of that, within that period, deficits arose. I would submit that the matter is rather more complicated.

Finally, Mr. Spieler talked about growth. Growth to me is the number one priority, an absolute must. Some people think this is a new objective that has come up on our horizon. It isn't really new at all. Growth simply means economic welfare measured through time. There are, of course, problems in measuring economic welfare which have to be taken into account. The word "growth" does not imply a new objective. It has been introduced as a matter of methodology. In fact, it is the concept of economic welfare dynamized. The objective is not to have the greatest, the maximum possible, economic welfare this year. Some of the older economics rather look at the matter from the static point of view, and say, given all possible situations this year, we choose this one. But now we want to emphasize a somewhat different point of view; we want to look at the matter through time. Growth is merely looking at economic welfare through time. To maximize economic welfare is the objective of economic science. Therefore I say growth is the number one objective.

I want stable prices. Long-run balance-of-payments equilibrium is not an "objective"; it is a necessity. It is like keeping our promises or paying our debts. It is a question of how you do it, and of how quickly it ought to be done.

I am convinced that inflation is hostile to growth. But if you have, year after year, time after time, to sacrifice growth in order to get price stability, what is the sense? It really makes no sense. So while I am much in favor of price stability, and I believe that inflation is the enemy of growth, growth remains the number one objective; growth is simply economic welfare considered through time.

CHAIRMAN GAINSBRUGH: I know I speak on behalf of all here in first expressing our appreciation to Philip Cortney for his challenging contribution to this conference and then to you, Sir Roy, for your excellent paper.

Before surrendering the chair to our trustee Richard Chapman for the closing session, I want to thank you all for allowing us to invade your free weekend. I know we have imposed on you, but this is a privilege that we reserve for our friends.

I want to ask your indulgence, too, for the necessarily arbitrary allocation of time throughout this conference. It is difficult to maximize such valuable resources as we have had at our command throughout this symposium. Allocation of resources has been a problem of all economies in the past. Judging from the difficulties all our chairmen have had thus far in allotting time, it is equally difficult here. We thank you all for accepting the chairmen's guidance.

Chapter VIII

Conclusion

Chairman: RICHARD P. CHAPMAN
Conference Summary: JOHN B. CONDLIFFE

CHAIRMAN CHAPMAN: Our "summer-upper," John Condliffe, has been sitting here very patiently for nearly two days now. We owe him the full chance to present his ideas. I have heard occasionally some grunts that made me believe it is going to be something more than a summing up, that he will also present some ideas quite of his own.

For over twenty years he has been a resident of the San Francisco area, more recently as Professor of Economics at Berkeley, and now with the Stanford Research Institute. In between these assignments he has found time for many other activities—with the Economic Intelligence Service of the League of Nations Secretariat; the Carnegie Endowment for International Peace; and consultant to the Board of Economic Welfare; consultant to the Ford Foundation and consultant to various foreign governments.

MR. CONDLIFFE: I have listened carefully to all the speakers, read all the prepared papers and diligently taken notes of all the discussions. All except one. I was not able to stay through the arguments of my fellow economists at the rump session on flexible exchange rates. I am told they thoroughly enjoyed themselves. My feeling about flexible exchange is that we already have enough troubles with President de Gaulle and Professor Rueff.

I cannot believe that a country which is in balance-of-payments surplus would suffer in silence while a deficit country allowed its currency to depreciate because its balance of payments was out of equilibrium. It would surely resort to counter-measures.

After the speakers at this session I don't need to recapitulate all the ideas, good and not so good, that have been aired. But I can make one statement with which I am sure everyone will agree. We have not reached a consensus. I am more impressed by this fact since I came here by way of Washington, where "never is heard a discouraging word" and, in official circles at least, consensus is not only desirable but essential for survival. As our discussions went on I felt more and more at home. There is no more consensus here than there is at the University of California.

It would be presumptuous for any *rapporteur* to allocate credit, or discredit, to the ideas expressed by such a distinguished gathering of dissenters. I am not going to traverse all the arguments and I shall not try to pin them on individual participants. I beg the indulgence of those I do mention from admiration or affection. If I don't mention others it is for lack of time, not interest. In this caucus race all have won and all must have prizes.

I was deeply impressed by the tone, as much as by the content of the contribution made by Mr. Sachs to the first evening session. And perhaps you will allow me to start from there. If I seem to expand this point I plead Mr. Widenmann as my excuse.

We are not concerned here with the construction of an ideal international monetary system—a hypothetical model. What we must wrestle with is the interaction of national monetary systems managed by governments in a real world of conflicting national interests interpreted by powerful and obstinate men—a world which includes President de Gaulle and Mao Tse-tung.

To some extent these national monetary systems are influenced by the consultation and collaboration of their representatives in the International Monetary Fund. One of the crucial questions to be faced is whether the influence of these consultative discussions and cooperative international activities can be strengthened and whether operative means can be found whereby national governments may be discouraged from following dangerous policies and rewarded for good international behavior.

I do not want to be parochial, but I should perhaps mention that most of the people in the world do not live in the Atlantic Community of rich, developed nations on which our discussions have been centered. It is true that the financial and monetary strength of the world is largely concentrated in the Atlantic Community. Japan is the only non-Atlantic member of the Ten. The outer world contains some countries such as Australia and South Africa which feel strong enough to speak up for themselves. If they are cast into the outer darkness they will certainly wail and gnash their teeth.

All of the people in this outer world are struggling to develop themselves. In doing so they must either choose between our ways of freedom and authoritarian planning, or try to straddle these roads to development. No small part of the strain on the United States balance of payments, and also on the British, has come from our efforts to help and protect them. Insistently they cry for more help, and unless we can devise more effective ways of helping them, they may try to turn the IMF from a monetary into a credit union.

There is another aspect of this real world that should not be ignored. The new technology of our generation is creating a revolution in methods of production that is transforming the patterns of world trade to the disadvantage of the less developed countries. Even more important, it is transforming the ways in which productive and trading activity is organized. The greatest invention of the Industrial Revolution was not the steam engine but the joint-stock limited liability company. The new technology of our time brings us new sources of energy and new products and processes. But even more important, it is transforming the management processes of business enterprise, and of government, including monetary and fiscal management.

This results largely from the new means of communication and of data collection and processing. The area of effective management constantly widens and this widening changes the character of the managerial process. It widens in time as well as space. One of the new tools which has a very direct bearing on monetary policy is statistical forecasting. As Mr. Hoadley said, forecasting has taken on a new dimension since in some degree it not only anticipates but prepares the future. Forecasting is a dangerous tool. But its practitioners become more sophisticated. I was born too soon to become adept; but as I have watched its application to private business even more than to government, I have come to have a wholesome respect for my younger colleagues. There is less and less need to improvise hasty action against unforeseen emergencies.

Countercyclical action, for example, can be launched early enough to be effective. But I agree with Mr. Exter that if it is always action to expand, never to contract, it will eventually come to a sticky end.

Business enterprise is ahead of government in at least one respect that is important for our discussions. It already operates effectively across national boundaries and will do so more and more. Indeed, the most recent strains on the international monetary system, and on the U.S. balance of payments, were directly caused by capital movements arising from the spread of international enterprise. The measures taken to restrict such movements run the risk of slowing down the spread of technology and international enterprise. I agree emphatically with Mr. Haberler that the real danger of the new monetary techniques is that decisions tend to pass from business to government and to be made on political rather than economic grounds.

Mr. Chairman, I have taken this time to set the scene because money, after all, is only an instrument. Alfred Marshall once wrote to one of his pupils that "the only important thing to know about money is that it isn't important." What he meant, I think, was that money is not an end in itself, but a means to assure the smooth functioning of the economy.

William Busschau quoted John Law: ". . . confidence is nothing but the expectation of being paid." This seems to me a true saying; but John Law, of all people, might have been surprised to find this interpreted as "payment in gold." Any national currency will retain the confidence of its users, abroad as well as at home, as long, and only as long, as it serves them as an efficient means to get the goods and services they demand.

We live in a managed world. The question is who shall manage it and by what means, and for what ends? One of the most important aspects of management is monetary policy. When I first went to work I was paid in golden sovereigns. Now my secretary mails a piece of paper and some figures go into a bank account. Soon, I am told by my electronic colleagues, all Mrs. Machlup's dresses will be charged to a computer which will indicate to the salesman how many she can buy within the projected family budget. We have ceased to use gold in our personal transactions, and soon we shall not use much silver or even paper.

So far, those who determine the amount of credit in our national economy—not just the Treasury and Federal Reserve officials, and their experts, but commercial bankers and manufacturers and tradesmen and consumers—have managed to keep us well supplied with purchasing power without creating an intolerable measure of either demand or cost inflation. I do not mean to be disrespectful to the Secretary of the Treasury, or the Chairman of the Federal Reserve Board, but after all they are only chauffeurs with one foot on the gas pedal and the other ready to put on the brake. I leave you to speculate whose feet go on what. The motor that drives this economy is private enterprise—the cooperative and competitive activity of the community. Official policy, as Mr. Dillon told us, cannot move effectively unless public opinion is ready to support it.

If I may continue this irreverent metaphor, the chauffeur is always tempted and urged to go faster than he should. If he runs through a red light or exceeds the speed limit, the cop who pulls him up is the balance of payments, even before inflation becomes apparent in domestic prices. Adam Smith once said there is a great deal of ruin in a nation. There is certainly a great deal of inflation, and it can arise in different ways and through different channels.

I remind you that there was not much movement of commodity prices before the stock market setback in 1962 or even in 1929. We worry about the international monetary system and the balance of payments not because we expect a runaway inflation at home, but because those who deal in foreign exchange, citizens as well as foreigners, may lose confidence in the dollar or in sterling.

It seems to me that three key words kept cropping up in our discussion—confidence, adjustment and gold. I did not detect any disagreement on the necessity to maintain confidence in the dollar, and to restore confidence in sterling. Nor was there any disagreement that the only effective way to restore confidence was to bring the balance of payments into equilibrium. There were overtones, not always harmonic, in the frequent references to confidence. Some of us have the feeling that credit has been so stretched, at home and abroad, that some accident, somewhere, could touch off a break in confidence that could snowball and spread from one country to another.

Others, and I should guess a majority, believe that we now have the knowledge and the means to prevent such a disaster. Those who lived through the depression of the 1930's are perhaps a little more fearful than those whose working life came after it; but I have one comforting thought of my own on this point. I do not believe that the American banking system will collapse again as it did in 1933 for lack of effective and prompt government action. Europe was over the worst by mid-1932 and Australia before that. It was the American banking collapse that prolonged the misery.

Having said that I must add that I count myself among those

who are pessimistic about the chances of getting the politicians to keep the national inflations running in parallel so as to confine the disequilibria in international balances within manageable limits.

The knowledge and the means to act effectively and in time are immensely strengthened by the existence of the International Monetary Fund and the network of consultative cooperation that is centered on it. I once sent Per Jacobsson a motto for the BIS, taken from Rupert Brooke's poem on Fish: ". . . and sure the reverent eye must see a purpose in liquidity." In reply I got back the shortest note I ever had from him—and what he told me was that the Bank already had a motto, taken from the letters of the Abbe Sieyès who was asked how he fared in the French Revolution, to which he replied, *"J'ai vécu,"* I survived.

Mr. Schweitzer has said much the same thing. The first reason for using the IMF is that it exists and, so far, it works. We have seen it cope with speculative attacks on important currencies far greater than those which caused repeated devaluations in the 1930's. And at the same time trade has been enlarged and enormous capital movements have been facilitated. No mechanism is perfect and no doubt the IMF could be improved. I once heard Arthur Burns say that the test of a good economist was what he could do with fragmentary and imperfect data. The test of a good money manager is what he can do with the mechanisms available.

We are evolving a new breed of money managers, highly trained, to most of us convincing and to others at least plausible, knowledgeable about their opposite numbers and skillful in negotiation. After all, the art of central banking is very new. I am not going to pour any more well-deserved compliments on Mr. Emminger. I should just like to say that there are hundreds of economists in this country who would have envied him if they had heard Jack Viner bestow that accolade last night.

Mr. Emminger told us that the primary difficulty of monetary management was in reconciling national monetary needs with external stability. I once used Strindberg's description of marriage as "a system of antagonistic cooperation" to describe this dilemma. My publisher deleted this and told me to stick to economics which I knew something about.

I have not used the word "adjustment," which I don't like. It sounds to me too chiropractic. What goes on in the international aspects of monetary policy is cooperative consultation and negotiation. The mechanics after all are not so important—it is trained and experienced men who will make the system work, if it works at all.

Can it work? The technicians are confident that it can. There are many critics who are sure it cannot. But even its critics, who don't believe it can work, have said let them try it. It is indeed a great and bold experiment in international cooperation. It may founder, but if it does it will not be for technical or mechanical reasons.

I do not have time to canvass all the ingenious devices suggested for improving the machinery and creating new reserves as and when they may become needed. I have a feeling that it would be almost as hard to compress Bernstein into a paragraph as to suppress Triffin. I am not going to try to do either.

The technicians, I am sure, will be able to develop workable practices, not by formula, but by operative procedures adapted to changing circumstances.

We all remember how Per Jacobsson galvanized the IMF— just in time. If the system founders, as it may, it will be on the rock of nationalism, of failure to achieve essential cooperation from important nations, and by the failure of governments to control inflation. The problem is not technical. It is not even economic. It is political. This was beautifully illustrated by the illuminating discussion of the way in which a happy phrase, "contingency planning," recently opened the doors to negotiation.

Where does gold fit into this picture? I approach this last key word with some trepidation. Keynes consulted his psychiatrist friends to find out why the very mention of gold aroused such strong emotional reactions. Since he wrote "The Treatise On Money," the tables have been turned. Nowadays it isn't the central bankers but their critics who seem to be emotionally attached to gold. However, a wise old friend of mine used always to say, when you are in a difficult situation, it is always better to act natural than to act smart. I am going to follow his advice.

For the life of me I cannot see what there is to get excited about. Gold has had a long history as a monetary metal. It has many qualities, which once I knew by heart from Jevons's listing, that make it admirably fitted for certain monetary uses. It will continue to be used as reserve currency and a means of international payments. There will be a continuing monetary demand for all the gold that can be produced.

Donald McLaughlin, who ought to know, tells us it will be in increasing demand for a variety of industrial uses. This alone may force an increase in its price. I suspect that its price *will* go up in terms of credit standards of value, but not in the near future. I don't myself believe that an agreed revaluation of currencies in terms of gold, suitably timed, would be as disastrous as some of us fear. We have heard a good many opinions that it was a mistake not to carry out such a revaluation in the 1920's or following Bretton Woods.

But neither do I believe that such a revaluation would solve the perplexing problems of international monetary cooperation, though it might be a convenient way of adding to international monetary reserves. Even Professor Rueff admits that a restored gold standard would have to be managed by international cooperation. In any case this is not an operative question at the moment.

In face of the resolute opposition of those who manage our monetary systems, and of public opinion in the United States, those who would like to see a rise in the price of gold will, as Donald McLaughlin said, just have to wait and see. They may be in a position later on to say that they warned us. Indeed some of their past warnings are now coming true. My own feeling about this is like Sir Roy Harrod's, that a rise in the gold price is more likely to come by breakdown than by agreement.

Mr. Chairman, when I try to conclude this very sketchy sum-

mary of what has been said here about the international monetary system and its strengths and weaknesses, its imperfections
and deficiencies and dangers, as well as its promise, I am reminded of Touchstone's remark about Audrey—"an ill-favored
thing; but mine own." It's the only international monetary system
we have and, even if it creaks a bit, it hasn't worked so badly.
There is an old saying that the best is the enemy of the good. I
am not enough of a theorist, and I don't believe many of us
here are, to want to scrap what we have for something that, like
the White Knight's pudding, never has been cooked and never
will be cooked, but was a wonderful pudding to invent.

CHAIRMAN CHAPMAN: I should explain that Bruce Palmer, the
President of the Conference Board, wishes he could be with us
throughout these meetings, but he is committed elsewhere.

Speaking personally and sincerely, I thank each of you individually for coming and most especially our friends from abroad.
I am, of course, the only non-pro here, representing the great
unwashed. These other commercial bankers are moonlighting
bankers because they are really economists. I am not. Most of
you heretofore have been just distinguished names to me. I
consider it a privilege now to know all of you highly intelligent
and attractive people. We have all had as much of a day in court
as time would permit. Nothing has been solved, I agree, and
perhaps it is disappointing to some that there is not a more tan-
gible air of accomplishment. But in the adult world this must
frequently be the case. I for one regard this as time well spent.

I'd like to close with a quotation that Alexander Sachs has
kindly submitted to me, and I think it applies to our proceedings
here. It is from Chapter XII, First Corinthians, "Now there are
diversities of gifts, but the same Spirit."

Thank you all very much for coming.